Index of Recurrent Elements
in
James Joyce's
Ulysses

By William M. Schutte

Southern Illinois University Press
Carbondale and Edwardsville

Library of Congress Cataloging in Publication Data

Schutte, William M.
   Index of recurrent elements in James Joyce's Ulysses.

   1. Joyce, James, 1882–1941. Ulysses. 2. Joyce,
James, 1882–1941—Dictionaries, indexes, etc. I. Title.
PR6019.09U49   1982   823'.912   81-18374
ISBN 0-8093-1067-8   AACR2

PREFACE

This book is the result of a project begun a dozen years ago to provide students of Joyce with a tool designed, like all good tools, to save time and effort. It is intended both for individuals who, having read Ulysses once, would like to explore the complicated web of allusions which form so significant an element of the text and for more experienced Joyce scholars who wish to locate quickly all the allusions to a particular element.

The Index of Recurrent Elements is organized by page and line number of the 1961 Random House edition, so that as they begin their exploration, the first group may place it beside the text -- perhaps with Weldon Thornton's Allusions in Ulysses or Don Gifford and Robert Seidman's Notes for Joyce on the other side. When they run across the name "Bob Doran" at 74.01 in Ulysses, they will find listed in the Index all of the Doran references in the book. Almost a hundred pages further on in Ulysses, at 167.29, Doran is again referred to. Here, as for all subsequent mentions of the character, the Index refers them back to 74.01. Thus, wherever in the book a recurrent element turns up, they may immediately discover where all references to it are to be found.

More seasoned students of Joyce will also find the Index useful: through the alphabetical index at the end they will be able to locate easily any recurrent element in which they have a particular interest. No longer will they have to hunt through almost eight hundred pages to find each reference to it.

In a very much shortened form this work appeared between 1975 and 1979 in the James Joyce Quarterly. There only the primary entry for each recurrent element was listed, and the Index was keyed to both the Random House 1934 and 1961 editions. However, since it is clear that most students now use the 1961 edition for their own work and since to index both editions would make the book far too large, the 1934 references have been dropped. Those who still use that edition -- my correspondence suggests that they may still be numerous -- and those using British editions may wish to use a conversion table such as the ones provided by Clive Hart and Leo Knuth in their Topographical Guide to James Joyce's ULYSSES (Colchester, 1975) and by Shari and Bernard Benstock in their James Joyce Directory (Urbana, 1980).

In putting together this Index, I have been faced constantly with decisions about what should be included. Obviously, for example, one will wish to include references not only to Throwaway, the horse that won the Gold Cup at Ascot on 16 June 1904, but also to the throwaway that Bloom is handed at the opening of "Lestrygonians" and the newspaper which Bloom is about to throw away in "Lotus Eaters." But should one include every mention of Bloom or

Stephen, references to whom are certainly recurrent elements in the text? Or
again, is reference to two different works of Daniel Defoe to be considered
recurrence? Given Bloom's interest in Alexander Keyes' advertisement and
Stephen's concern about the Martello Tower key, should every reference to any
key be cited, or only those which seem to have a direct bearing on the themes
of Ulysses? And what should one do with a recurrence which a scholar study-
ing a limited aspect of the novel "discovers," but which to other scholars
may not appear to be a recurrence at all?

    No answers to these questions will satisfy every student of Joyce. But
decisions have had to be made, and I have made them. In doing so, I have been
guided by the conviction that the primary function of a work of this sort is
to be useful. I have also kept in mind the availability of the works of
Thornton, of Gifford and Seidman, and of Miles Hanley, whose Word Index to
James Joyce's ULYSSES has served several generations of Joyce scholars.

    With these factors in mind, I have adopted the following guidelines:

    1. Each reference to a recurrent element is recorded by page and line
number of the 1961 Random House-Modern Library edition, except where there is
repeated recurrence in any one section of the text. Then only the first in-
stance in that section is given, followed by the signs +, ++, or # to indicate
the extent of recurrence. (See the "Explanation of Symbols," which follows.)
Elements which recur only within a brief segment of the text are not usually
listed, nor are those whose recurrence is confined to one episode unless, as
with the dog in "Circe" which keeps changing its shape or Richard Best's
"don't you know," they seem to have special significance.

    2. Individuals who reappear or are referred to more than once in the
text are considered recurrent elements, and each appearance or reference to
them has been recorded, subject to the limitations indicated above. I have
made exceptions for Bloom, Molly, Boylan, Stephen, and Simon, who are so ubiq-
uitous that listing every reference to them would serve little purpose. Recurrent thoughts, physical characteristics, idiosyncrasies, and concerns of
each of these five characters and motifs associated with them have, however,
been fully recorded.

    3. A second reference to an author or to any of his works has been con-
sidered a recurrence. Thus there is an initial entry for Oscar Wilde (6.37)
which lists all references to him or to his works and groups them in an appropriate way. Two exceptions to this rule are the Bible and Shakespeare. Here
there are so many allusions and possible allusions that to list them would re-
quire many pages of indigestible entries for each. I have been encouraged to
handle this pair in a different way by the ready availability of detailed in-
formation in the Thornton Allusions and the Gifford and Seidman Notes, and, in
the case of Shakespeare, in my own Joyce and Shakespeare: A Study in the Meaning of "Ulysses." Only recurrent individual elements in the Bible and in
Shakespeare's life and works have been recorded. Thus all references to Elijah are to be found, and so are repetitions of the phrase "List! List! O
list!"

    4. Recurrent place names have been recorded when they seem likely to be
in any way significant, but I have avoided listing them simply because they
are repeated. (Poulaphouca and Mecklenburg Street are included; the Liffey

and London are not.) To track down the last two one need only turn to the
Hanley Word Index.

5. The repetition of an unusual word or phrase in Ulysses is likely to
be of some significance; hence most have been included. However, I have not
listed such words or phrases if it seems clear to me that no importance can
be attached to their repetition. The word stopgap, for example, occurs at
170.20 and stopgaps at 405.27, but I see little possibility that any thematic
relationship between the two uses of the word will ever be discovered. Therefore, listing the two occurrences would only cause confusion. For an even
more obvious case, see Magdalen (7.26 and 443.10).

6. Where two recurrent elements are so closely related as to form vir-
tually a single reference, they are so recorded. See Zinfandel and Lord Howard de Walden (174.02); sundering and reconciliation (38.12).

7. A few examples of recurrence may not readily be identified as such.
Where they are explained in Thornton or in Gifford and Seidman or in both, I
have placed appropriate identifying symbols after the entry.

*   *   *

A great many individuals have contributed most generously to the prepara-
tion of this volume, some by suggesting emendations and others by giving aid
and support in other ways.

Some of the scholars who used the preliminary version in the James Joyce
Quarterly have suggested additions, deletions, or corrections. I should like
here to express my appreciation to the following individuals for their contri-
butions: D. B. Boyd, Tom Garst, Fritz Senn, Robert Spoo, Erwin R. Steinberg,
Takashi Suzuki, David G. Wright and particularly Victory Pomeranz and Patrick
A. McCarthy, both of whom made numerous suggestions. I owe a very special
debt to Willem H. Bücking of The Hague, The Netherlands, who went through my
work with great thoroughness and contributed hundreds of useful emendations.
Without his suggestions this book would be far less accurate and complete than
it is.

Over the past few years Lawrence University's Faculty Development Fund
has made it possible for me to draw on the talents of a number of very effi-
cient and dedicated assistants. Much of the original version of the Index was
typed by three extremely accurate and competent students: Valerie Kuehn, Karen
Campbell, and Jeanne Greninger. In the final stages of this project, Robert
Spoo has been an invaluable collaborator, entering the entire text in the Lawrence computer and keeping a wary eye out for errors and inconsistencies. My
colleague Ben R. Schneider has given me the benefit of his many years' expe-
rience in computer indexing. President Richard Warch and Deans Thomas Head-
rick, Mojmir Povolny, and Michael Hittle have given strong support. To them,
and to James Evans and Lawrence Walker of Lawrence's Computer Center, I should
like to express my appreciation for all that they have done.

Finally, I should like to record my gratitude to Richard M. Kain and
James Snead for sharing with me their lists of recurrent elements in Ulysses;

to Thomas R. Staley, editor of the <u>James Joyce Quarterly</u>, for his willingness to publish the preliminary version of this work and for his continued encouragement; to John Van Voorhis and Charlotte Stewart, who saw that version through the press; and to my wife, Anne, who quite sensibly tried to stay out of this project so she could get her own work done, but who with all good humor allowed herself to be pressed into service in more than one emergency.

W. M. S.

Appleton, WI
August, 1981

CONTENTS

EXPLANATION OF SYMBOLS

+ following a page reference indicates additional recurrence within ten lines.

++ indicates frequent additional recurrence in the section of text immediately following.

\# indicates frequent additional recurrence in the remainder of an episode (or section of "Wandering Rocks").

( ) surrounding a page reference indicates that either significant recurrence seems doubtful or the relationship between the current entry and the one in parentheses seems tangential.

** precedes and follows a secondary entry.

(T) See Weldon Thornton, _Allusions in "Ulysses": An Annotated List_ (Chapel Hill: University of North Carolina Press, 1968; paperback reprint New York: Simon and Schuster, 1973).

(G) See Don Gifford with Robert J. Seidman, _Notes for Joyce: An Annotation of James Joyce's "Ulysses"_ (New York: E. P. Dutton, 1974).

TELEMACHUS

BUCK MULLIGAN
    3.01#   26.14   36.02   39.41   45.23++   88.15++   134.10
   185.05   192.26   194.15   197.19#   248.13#   253.22   259.41
   307.03   388.28   389.33   397.11+   401.31#   493.01++ 509.11
   580.04++ 599.14+ 620.12+ 664.41+ (197.28)
His castoff boots
    31.01   37.11+   48.19   49.17+   50.26   147.04   188.28
   210.27+ (620.34) (773.12)
Sex specialist
   402.01   493.01

A yellow DRESSINGGOWN ungirdled was SUSTAINED gently behind him
    3.02   599.28

INTROIBO AD ALTARE DEI
    3.05   433.09   599.21+

Come up, KINCH
    3.08#   38.04   199.27   214.27#   425.32   556.14   580.18
  Toothless Kinch
   22.28   50.36   (579.29)

Come up, . . . you fearful JESUIT (Stephen as Jesuit)
    3.08   4.09   8.31   16.27   199.27   216.22   425.32

The tower (MARTELLO TOWER)
    3.10#   44.16+   393.23   427.09   580.04   599.11+ (347.10)
  See also 164.34

FACE . . . EQUINE in its length
    3.16   39.41   (414.27)

HAIR, GRAINED AND HUED LIKE PALE OAK
    3.17   5.04   8.05   (176.24)   (215.42)   (554.33)

BLOOD AND OUNS
    3.23   599.25+   658.19

ONE MOMENT
    3.24   37.28

A LOW WHISTLE OF CALL
    3.26+   439.10

CHRYSOSTOMOS
    3.28   6.24   494.31   (42.32)   See also 8.06

A PRELATE, PATRON OF ARTS in the middle ages
    3.34   82.18

The MOCKERY of it
  Associated with Stephen
    3.37   6.06   8.32   21.13+   45.31   203.15   211.23
    394.41   502.30   505.09   570.09   580.18   See also 25.09
  Brood of mockers
    21.07   197.28   See also 28.16
  Associated with Bloom
    64.23   129.33   376.03   407.16   440.12   542.15   564.06
  Other references
    45.31   55.32   134.32   199.11+   416.08   528.26   576.08

YOUR ABSURD NAME
    3.37   210.32   See also 208.11

An ancient Greek (GREEK CULTURE)
    3.38+   5.07+   7.13   133.17++ 201.05+   249.08   504.12

Stephen Dedalus followed him WEARILY
    3.41   28.32   49.39+   197.08   281.20   354.07   420.31
    577.05+ 737.13 (150.03) (240.40) See also 18.05

The JEJUNE JESUIT
    4.09   424.24   431.02+

YES, MY LOVE
    4.12   (202.18)   (429.12)

How long is HAINES going to stay in this tower?
    4.13#   25.07   186.22   192.27   198.17   199.31   215.13
    215.32   248.14# 253.22   393.33   412.07+ 599.16+ 620.13

A ponderous SAXON (SASSENACH)
    4.17   9.14   133.22   185.08   324.05   324.42   329.41+
  See also   23.12

Because he comes from OXFORD
     4.19+   7.08++   217.39   310.14++   393.21   463.08   518.18
     See also   475.21

Raving all night about a black PANTHER
  Black panther
     4.23+   412.23++   608.23
  Step of a pard
    218.01   586.07
  Other references
    44.24   47.02   521.21

You saved men from DROWNING
  Saving from drowning
    4.28   45.30++   243.27+   621.03
  Man who drowned (Sandycove)
    21.31   45.35   75.34
  Found drowned
    50.05   122.10   659.31
  General Slocum disaster
    182.29   221.20   239.22   647.22   (762.05)
  Dodd's son
    94.26   152.33   497.28   506.12   See also 93.41
  Drowning grief
    98.39   606.08
  Other references
    114.30   328.34   359.16   492.04   705.01   762.05   764.43
    779.11   See also 25.25

I'm not a HERO
    4.29   95.04   232.34++ 242.26   264.39+   296.09   296.35
    308.39   309.33   320.01   325.25   421.14   457.15   492.02
    640.37   658.26

Lend us a loan of your NOSERAG (Stephen's)
    4.37+   16.41   50.39   210.29

BARD
  Stephen as
    5.01   6.26   15.40   214.27   262.31
  Bullockbefriending
    36.03   132.18   193.02   415.06
  Shakespeare as
    198.22   204.20
  Drinking
    15.31   215.01
  Other references
    185.07   312.05

A new ART COLOUR for our Irish poets
    5.01   424.38

SNOTGREEN
    5.02+   37.04   See also 424.38

Your mother (MAY DEDALUS)
```
    5.16++     27.39+      41.41       42.15       46.04      105.04+      134.10
   151.36+    190.13+     207.05      234.14      415.15      422.25      579.25++
   608.26++   663.04      670.15      680.08      682.14      695.26      774.24++
   778.39
```

NIETZSCHE, FRIEDRICH (hyperborean) (T) (G)
  The Antichrist
```
      5.20
```
  Thus Spake Zarathustra
```
     22.27       23.08       50.37      393.20      424.08      425.09
```

A lovely MUMMER . . . the loveliest MUMMER of them all
```
    5.26      199.26      216.16      216.30      425.31
```

PAIN . . . fretted his heart (WELTSCHMERZ)
```
    5.31       49.15       81.15       97.09      (17.39)    (171.07)    (207.41)
   See also    17.39
```

Silently, in a dream she had come to him (STEPHEN'S DREAM OF HIS MOTHER)
```
    5.32       10.15       38.11      579.25++     See also 115.04
```

An ODOUR OF WAX AND ROSEWOOD
```
    5.34       10.16       27.41      (98.36)
```

A faint ODOUR OF WETTED ASHES
```
    5.35       10.18       27.41       38.12      393.41      580.24      582.02
```

```
       ** As a great sweet mother                    5.37        5.06    **
```

Ah, poor DOGSBODY
```
    6.02        6.29       46.30      580.18      599.30+
   See also     8.20       44.33      507.30
```

```
       ** The mockery of it                          6.06        3.37    **
```

In THE SHIP (pub)
```
    6.19       23.13       38.25      199.26+     696.09
```

He's up in Dottyville (RICHMOND ASYLUM)
```
    6.20      534.08
```

```
       ** White glittering teeth                     6.24        3.28    **
```

```
       ** You dreadful bard                          6.26        5.01    **
```

BURNS, ROBERT (As he and others see me)
  "To a Louse"
```
      6.28      169.22      376.02
```
  "Comin' thro' the Rye"
```
    157.11
```
  "Address to the Unco Guid"
```
    206.36
```
  "John Anderson My Jo"
```
    215.28
```

"For A' That and A' That"
     401.30
"A Highland Lad My Love Was Born"
     425.35
"Willie Brewed a Peck o' Maut"
     425.35   426.11   427.01   427.39
"The Jolly Beggars"
     425.35
"Ken Ye Ought o' Captain Grose?"
     425.42
"Tam o' Shanter"
     598.32

        ** This dogsbody   6.29   6.02   **

        ** The aunt   6.32   5.16   **

THE LORD'S PRAYER (Lead him not into temptation -- 6.33)
     Our Father who art in heaven
          187.30   227.03
     Thy will be done
          90.21
     On earth as it is in heaven
          61.05
     Give us this day our daily bread
          57.13   356.28   614.25   647.15
     Forgive us our trespasses
          498.10
     Lead us not into temptation
          6.33   104.12
     General
          224.19

And her name is URSULA
          6.34   339.40

WILDE, OSCAR (The rage of Caliban at not seeing his face)
     The Picture of Dorian Gray
          6.37+   (649.38) (T)
     "The Decay of Lying"
          6.40+   10.39   16.09+
     "Requiescat"
          39.09
     The Portrait of Mr. W. H.
          198.29+
     "The Ballad of Reading Gaol"
          (114.42)
     Lady Windermere's Fan
          (143.24)
     "De Profundis"
          (196.24) (G)
     "The Sphinx"
          (560.06)
     Wilde's love that dare not speak its name
          49.23   202.19   207.38

Personal reference
       6.38   18.09   198.38+   214.04   (646.02)

The rage of CALIBAN
       6.37   205.07   492.20

The cracked lookingglass of a SERVANT
       6.41+   11.22   14.06   16.09+   20.27   133.12   187.34
      189.15   214.34   393.30   (567.15)   (474.06)   See also   25.09

Buck Mulligan . . . LINKED his ARM in Stephen's
       7.01   7.14   660.31

          ** The oxy chap   7.08   4.19   **

Selling JALAP
       7.11   393.33

To ZULUS
       7.11   334.07

          ** Hellenize it   7.13   3.38   **

CRANLY's arm
       7.14   32.22   184.23   184.39   187.34   211.22

          ** His arm   7.14   7.01   **

PRODIGAL SON (to think of your having to beg from these swine)
       7.15   391.02   399.09   517.33+   581.09

Why don't you TRUST me more?
       7.16   158.02   357.31   365.31   381.24   620.32   770.41

I'll bring down SEYMOUR
       7.18   22.10+

A ragging (OXFORD RAG)
       7.19+   463.08

MASKED
   Matthew Arnold
       7.30   518.19
   Lyster
      193.09   208.37
   Other references
       31.25   80.39   379.36   444.01   458.31   489.27   577.04
      See also   37.01

ARNOLD, MATTHEW (masked with Matthew Arnold's face)
       7.30   518.19
   "Shelley"
      184.11
   "Shakespeare"
      194.05

"Westminster Abbey" (T)
   (34.27)   (46.30)
The Study of Celtic Literature
   (133.32)
"Stanzas from the Grand Chartreuse"
   (242.14)

The dancing motes of GRASSHALMS
      7.32   519.14

TO OURSELVES (T) (G)
      7.33   (163.38)

OMPHALOS
      7.33   17.37   38.03   402.31   (38.01)

The blunt cape of BRAY HEAD
      7.39   343.15   764.37

      ** His fair uncombed hair   8.05   3.17 **

SILVER points of anxiety (MERCURY) -- associated with Mulligan
      8.06   19.21   456.06   494.31   (19.38)
   Mercurial Malachi
      17.06   580.10   See also   3.28

You were MAKING TEA
      8.14   12.33   55.14

Whose mother is BEASTLY DEAD
      8.20++   134.10   390.11   580.09   (441.18)
      See also   6.02   44.33

I see them pop off every day in the MATER (MISERICORDIAE HOSPITAL)
      8.27   80.36   97.22+   163.06   388.20   386.28   392.28
      397.24   403.11   406.13   425.16   705.02

RICHMOND (Hospital)
      8.27   427.20

      ** The cursed jesuit strain   8.31   3.08 **

      ** A mockery   8.32   3.37 **

Some HIRED MUTE from Lalouette's
      8.36   101.21

I am not thinking of the OFFENCE to my mother
      8.42+   39.42   218.04   580.28

LOYOLA, ST. IGNATIUS (Chuck Loyola, Kinch)
      9.14   188.25   339.10

      ** The Sassenach   9.14   4.17 **

YEATS, W. B. (And no more turn aside and brood)
  The Countess Cathleen
    "Who Goes with Fergus"
        9.22++   49.16   581.03   608.26++
      See also   9.33   609.11
    "Clauber of ten forests"
    207.02
  In the Seven Woods
      13.01   424.36
      See also   13.01
  "The Tables of the Law"
      39.37   (143.15)
  "The Adoration of the Magi"
      48.26
  "The Rose of Battle"
      133.32
  "A Cradle Song"
      184.30
  Cathleen Ni Houlihan
      184.40+   323.40   330.07   400.10   595.15
      See also   14.02   14.03
  The Secret Rose
      189.15
  "The Song of Wandering Aengus"
      214.33   217.31   249.02   (83.27)
      See also   200.14   218.05
  "Baile and Aillinn"
      216.04
  Preface to Cuchulain of Muirthemne ("The most beautiful book. . . .")
      216.27   424.38   (391.18) (T)
  "To the Rose upon the Rood of Time"
      391.20
  Other references
      192.25   198.15(G)   216.23   509.29

A CLOUD began to cover the sun slowly
        9.32   50.23   61.07   667.08

A bowl of BITTER WATERS
        9.33   46.04   (393.38+)   See also   9.22

The pantomime of TURKO THE TERRIBLE
      10.02+   57.22   596.21

        ** In a dream . . . she had come to him   10.15   5.32   **

        ** An odour of wax and rosewood   10.16   5.34   **

Bent over him with mute SECRET WORDS
      10.17   49.05   581.05

        ** A faint odour of wetted ashes   10.18   5.35   **

The GHOSTCANDLE to light her agony
      10.20   48.01   190.13

Her hoarse loud breath rattling in HORROR
    10.22   46.03   61.21   412.05+   580.27   638.12   (662.29)

LILIATA RUTILANTIUM te confessorum turma circumdet
    10.23   23.16   190.15   580.02   704.10

GHOUL! CHEWER OF CORPSES
    10.25   472.18   581.14   581.28   See also 115.04

Heard warm RUNNING SUNLIGHT
    10.30   61.32

Come down, like a good MOSEY
    10.32   160.01   See also 40.07

       ** Your symbol of Irish art   10.39   6.38 **

The school kip (DEASY'S SCHOOL)
    11.02   15.31   24.01#   518.01+   573.19++   617.15+
    See also   32.01

Four quid (STEPHEN'S PAY)
    11.02+   15.31+   30.06++   48.11   50.36   143.33   199.02
    199.24   262.40   425.06   426.06+   426.38   452.13   518.22
    556.09++ 558.22++ 594.30   607.12   608.34   617.37++ 695.33
    711.15   711.32   See also 27.25   32.01   262.40

We'll have a glorious drunk to astonish the druidy DRUIDS
    11.06   142.13+   151.15   218.08   416.24   424.36   510.09
    666.39

O, won't we have a merry time ("ON CORONATION DAY")
    11.10+   594.21   See also 31.15

I carried the boat of incense then at CLONGOWES
    11.22   39.33   45.39+   224.11   226.13   415.01+   561.15+
    670.10   See also 80.03   135.18   560.03

I AM ANOTHER NOW and yet the same
    11.22   41.37   45.19   168.02   189.36+   194.24+   198.34
    (699.08)

       ** A servant . . . server of a servant   11.22+   6.41 **

Buck Mulligan's gowned form moved briskly . . . TO AND FRO
    11.25   18.42   142.02   193.11   194.24   217.14   257.07
    271.08   286.19   346.25   366.20   367.18   501.19   506.20
    524.16   595.14   608.01

Two shafts of soft daylight fell . . . from the high BARBICANS
    11.26   44.17   599.10

Have you the KEY?
  The Martello key
     11.35+   17.19+   20.19+   22.40+   44.22   427.09   668.17
  Bloom's key
     57.01   84.09   483.25   668.09+   697.31
  John O'Connell's keys
     107.04   107.35   473.22   474.09
  Myles Crawford's keys
     130.11   144.12
  Keylessness
     44.22   57.01   84.09   144.12   438.07   668.09+   697.30
  Keyed up
     108.13
  See also
     107.35

Stephen haled his upended VALISE to the table
     12.02   42.11   44.21

Your Paris fads (STEPHEN AND PARIS)
     12.18   25.37+   34.06+   41.14++   49.22   134.29   187.10
     188.09   207.05   210.36   243.11   569.16++   645.30   666.15
     See also   41.17   467.12   755.15

I want SANDYCOVE milk
     12.19   75.34   607.04+   619.38   657.30   667.10

          ** When I makes tea . . . I makes water   12.33   8.14   **

As old MOTHER GROGAN said
     12.33+   217.10   404.04   490.27+   492.23

          ** The weird sisters . . . the big wind   13.01   9.22   **

THE YEAR OF THE BIG WIND
     13.02   138.05   396.38

A kinswoman of MARY ANN
     13.12+   (764.33)

HISING UP HER PETTICOATS
     13.22   49.36   (224.05)

The COLLECTOR OF PREPUCES
     13.33   201.03

A WITCH on her toadstool
     13.41   595.07+   600.15+

SILK OF THE KINE (Ireland)
     14.02   595.16

POOR OLD WOMAN (Ireland)
     14.03   16.24+   330.11   595.07+   600.15+   See also   17.37

BETRAYAL (her gay betrayer)
    14.05   43.27   213.07+   330.14   362.24   491.06   504.16
  Judas
    217.25   267.22   471.14   497.27   510.24   600.26   615.33
    (214.18)   (520.22)

      ** To serve or to upbraid   14.06   6.41 **

She bows her old head to . . . her medicineman; me she slights (NOBLEST ART)
    14.19   204.28   408.42

THE FALL OF MAN -- EVE
  The serpent's prey
    14.23   34.39   38.06+   132.26   199.09   391.30+   516.18
    (360.29)
  Other references to Eve
    297.16   514.05
  Other references to the Fall
    47.35   383.35   408.06   519.23
  See also
    38.06   50.25   148.01   375.21

Is there Gaelic on you? (GAELIC LANGUAGE)
    14.30+   See also 141.07

      ** Ask nothing more of me, sweet   15.20+   5.05 **

      ** Your school kip   15.31   11.02 **

      ** Today the bards must drink   15.31   5.01 **

"THE DEATH OF NELSON" (Ireland expects. . . .)
    15.32   225.19++   248.37   445.05   624.20   630.35   747.35
  See also   95.09   148.09   219.08

I have to visit your NATIONAL LIBRARY today
    15.35   146.27   161.18   168.09   176.26   179.39   183.11++
    184.01#   376.37   696.11   729.02
  Taking slips from the counter
    48.14   213.33

Your monthly wash (STEPHEN'S BATHING HABITS)
    15.38+   673.07

      ** The unclean bard   15.40   5.01 **

AGENBITE OF INWIT
    16.07   17.03   189.27   197.30   206.26   243.27+   391.25
    (60.16)

      ** The cracked lookingglass of a servant 16.09+   6.37 **

      ** A servant   16.09+   6.41 **

Wait till you hear him on Hamlet (STEPHEN'S HAMLET THEORY)
    16.13   17.39++   28.07   184.01#   248.32+
    See also   18.10   18.12

WOULD I MAKE MONEY by it?
    16.16   214.07

You PUT YOUR HOOF IN IT now
    16.22   648.08   (23.12)

      ** From the milkwoman   16.24+   14.03 **

      ** Your gloomy jesuit jibes   16.27   3.08 **

      ** Your snotrag   16.41   4.37 **

      ** Agenbite of inwit   17.03   16.07 **

DRESS THE CHARACTER. . . . PUCE GLOVES AND GREEN BOOTS
    17.03   41.28   240.10

WHITMAN, WALT (Do I contradict myself?)
  Song of Myself
    17.05   187.37
  "Notes on British Literature"
    201.23

      ** Mercurial Malachi   17.06   8.06 **

There's your Latin quarter hat (STEPHEN'S HAT)
    17.08   41.28   47.33   50.25   88.06   192.15   210.27
    503.11   569.20   578.19   601.16   607.12++   613.02   698.03
    See also   192.15

COME OUT, KINCH. YOU HAVE EATEN ALL WE LEFT, I suppose
    17.13   214.34   (114.21+)   (180.22)   (472.15)

And going forth he met BUTTERLY
    17.16   486.31

Taking his ASHPLANT from its leaning place
    17.17   19.12   20.15   37.18   44.32   48.19   49.27
    50.28   192.16   210.27   228.26   242.21   423.04   431.10
    432.11   433.04++ 503.11   519.16   574.21   575.12   578.16+
    583.03   583.16++ 586.09   601.03   607.12++   613.02   698.03
    See also   48.19

      ** The huge key in his inner pocket   17.19+   11.35 **

      ** Ours is the omphalos   17.37   7.33 **

WHEN THE FRENCH WERE ON THE SEA ("Shan Van Vocht") (T) (G)
    17.37   330.11   600.17   See also   14.03

      ** What is your idea of Hamlet?   17.38++   16.13 **

Buck Mulligan shouted in PAIN (IN STOMACH)
    17.39   165.12   299.18   (5.31)   (171.07)   (207.41)
    See also   5.31

THOMAS AQUINAS
    17.40   47.27   205.23++   208.09   214.29   339.29   360.06+
    361.27   633.35+   637.26

And the FIFTY-FIVE REASONS (G)
    17.40   (25.17)

He pulled down neatly the peaks of his PRIMROSE WAISTCOAT
    18.02   45.23   197.24   248.38   406.18   417.39

Stephen said LISTLESSLY
    18.05   71.08   223.26+   229.24   271.22   See also   3.41

       ** We have grown out of Wilde   18.09   6.37 **

He proves by algebra that HAMLET'S GRANDSON IS SHAKESPEARE'S GRANDFATHER
    18.10   21.11   28.07   208.16   412.34   (708.04)
    See also   16.13

He himself is the GHOST OF HIS OWN FATHER (STEPHEN ON SHAKESPEARE)
    18.12+   28.07   187.39#   412.34   (123. 18)   See also   16.13

ELSINORE. <u>THAT</u> <u>BEETLES</u> <u>O'ER</u> <u>HIS</u> <u>BASE</u> <u>INTO</u> <u>THE</u> <u>SEA</u>
    18.25   37.16   44.28   197.13

"RULE BRITANNIA"
  The sea's ruler
    18.33   30.33
  Rules the waves
    325.25   630.11
  Never will be slaves
    329.15
  See also   30.35   73.02

Southward over the BAY, EMPTY save for the smokeplume of the mailboat
    18.33   30.33

THE SON striving to be ATONED WITH THE FATHER
    18.37   See also 21.09   88.19   152.39

       ** A doll's head to and fro   18.42   11.24 **

The brims of his PANAMA HAT quivering
    19.01   19.21   197.24   214.40   215.26   248.14   423.04

<u>I'm</u> <u>the</u> <u>queerest</u> <u>young</u> <u>fellow</u> (THE BALLAD OF JOKING JESUS)
    19.03
  <u>My</u> <u>father's</u> <u>a</u> <u>bird</u>
    19.04   41.18

Joseph the joiner
    19.05   19.29   391.37
Tell Tom, Dick and Harry
    19.17   659.09
See also   41.15   82.40   135.23
Bred in the bone
    19.18   372.05   650.06   655.06
See also   41.15

      ** Wine becomes water again   19.11   12.33 **

      ** At Stephen's ashplant   19.12   17.17 **

      ** Mercury's hat   19.21   8.06   19.01 **

      ** Joseph the Joiner?   19.29   19.03 **

You're not a BELIEVER, are you?
    19.23   249.12

CREATION FROM NOTHING
    19.34   37.41+

      ** A smooth silver case   19.38   (8.06) **

In which twinkled a GREEN STONE
    20.01   55.41   See also 186.35

      ** Trailing his ashplant by his side   20.15   17.17 **

      ** He wants that key   20.19+   11.35 **

DANTE ALIGHIERI (Now I eat his salt bread)
  Paradiso
    20.20   138.28   391.19   391.34
  Inferno
    37.08   113.41   138.23+   138.27   184.37   207.12   698.14+
    (192.03)
  Purgatorio
    (138.21)
  Other references
    296.42   637.25

ALL
    20.20   44.26   49.24   582.14

      ** The servant of two masters   20.27+   6.41 **

The imperial BRITISH STATE . . . ROMAN catholic and apostolic CHURCH
    20.34   589.28   See also 30.35

WE FEEL IN ENGLAND that we have treated you rather unfairly
    20.39   186.34

It seems HISTORY IS TO BLAME
    20.40   30.34   412.13   587.14
    See also   24.07   34.22   34.27

NICENE CREED (et unam sanctam catholicam et apostolicam ecclesiam)
    20.42+   38.10+   197.29+   207.22   See also 329.23+   424.32

Symbol of the apostles in the mass for pope Marcellus (PALESTRINA)
    21.03   82.19

The vigilant angel of the church militant . . . menaced her HERESIARCHS
    21.06   38.18   208.07   523.13

PHOTIUS and the brood of mockers
    21.07   26.14   197.28

       ** Brood of mockers   21.07   3.37 **

ARIUS
    21.08+   38.16+   523.13

Upon the consubstantiality of the SON with the FATHER
  Consubstantial
    21.09   38.15   38.29   89.05+   197.15   391.40   682.13
  Subsubstantial
    391.41
  Transubstantial
    391.40   682.09
  Unsubstantial
    199.25
  See also   18.37   88.19   152.39

The subtle African heresiarch SABELLIUS
    21.11   197.29   208.07+

       ** Himself his own son   21.11   18.10 **

       ** In mockery   21.13+   3.37 **

THE VOID awaits
    21.13   207.26   598.27   697.26+   699.11   734.04

WEAVE
  Weave the wind
    21.14   25.20
  Weave . . . windingsheet
    33.39   597.17   (87.21)
  Other
    26.17   194.23+   577.14

JEWS . . . OUR NATIONAL PROBLEM
    21.21   33.29+   36.10   142.25++   331.17#   643.43++

There's FIVE FATHOMS out there
    21.28   50.04   (212.09)

ABOUT ONE (o'clock)
    21.29   50.05

      ** The man that was drowned   21.31   4.28 **

Is the brother with you, Malachi? (MULLIGAN'S BROTHER)
    21.39   397.16

I got a card from BANNON

| 21.41 | 62.36 | 65.40 | 66.13+ | 66.33 | 89.20 | 285.04 |
| 372.17 | 397.14+ | 401.34# | 509.11 | 542.16 | 693.23+ | (695.16) |

MILLY BLOOM (sweet young thing down there)
  Photo job at Mullingar

21.42	62.01++	66.05++	89.20+	99.15+	155.39	156.35+
285.04+	372.16+	397.20	403.28++	425.41	427.05	542.16+
693.21+	695.16	764.23				

  Other references

66.01++	90.16	155.27	156.29	172.12	175.12	181.15
278.34	368.16	368.32	372.05++	379.31++	414.31	448.18
677.03	692.33++	720.25	721.06	723.03	736.06	742.22
746.11	754.07	758.10	766.10++	770.36	773.17	775.14
780.15						

Its GARLAND OF GREY HAIR
    22.05   23.19   40.02

      ** Seymour's back in town   22.10+   7.18 **

That red Carlisle girl, LILY
    22.15   (25.02)

SPOONING with him last night ON THE KINGSTOWN PIER
    22.17   24.40+   (67.10)

      ** The Uebermensch . . . superman   22.27   5.20 **

      ** Toothless Kinch   22.28   3.08 **

      ** Give us that key   22.40   11.35 **

HE WHO STEALETH FROM THE POOR LENDETH TO THE LORD
    23.07   390.24

      ** Zarathustra   23.08   5.20 **

HORN OF A BULL, HOOF OF A HORSE, SMILE OF A SAXON
    23.12   181.18   187.37   (16.22)   (32.01)

HALF TWELVE
    23.13   38.26

      ** The Ship   23.13   6.19 **

** <u>Liliata</u> <u>rutilantium</u>   23.16   10.23 **

** The priest's grey nimbus   23.19   22.05 **

I will not sleep here tonight (STEPHEN'S DECISION NOT TO RETURN TO THE TOWER)
      23.20   41.40   44.22   427.10+   668.16   (44.14)
      See also   455.19

USURPER
      23.24   212. 04   665.25

NESTOR

** YOU, COCHRANE (Deasy's school)   24.01#   11.02 **

What city sent for him? (PYRRHUS)
    24.01++   133.29+   See also 172.02

BLAKE, WILLIAM (Fabled by the daughters of memory)
  A Vision of the Last Judgment
    24.07   587.14
  The Marriage of Heaven and Hell
    Wings of excess
     24.09
    Time one livid final flame
     24.10   43.33+   583.04   (32.34)
    Dragon scaly folds
     26.02
  Ruin of all space, shattered glass and toppling masonry
    24.09   43.33+   391.18   583.05   (242.15)
    See also   34.22
  The human form divine
    140.13
  "Auguries of Innocence"
    33.38   597.17
  The Book of Los
    37.20
  Milton
    184.20(G)   186.17   507.11(G)
  "The Question Answered"
    199.06
  "To Nobodaddy" and "Let the Brothels of Paris Be Opened"
    205.41   395.04
  "Merlin's Prophecy"
    589.28
  Other possible references
    (38.26)   (48.07)   (210.36)   (216.14)(T) (589.08)

A CORPSESTREWN PLAIN
    24.18   32.35

      ** Kingstown pier   24.40+   22.17 **

Nor ever been innocent (INNOCENCE)
    25.01   217.20   371.38   471.28   553.15   774.38

      ** Lily   25.02   (22.15) **

      ** For Haines's chapbook   25.07   4.13 **

A JESTER at the court of his master
    25.09   215.09   216.14   217.36   580.05
    See also   3.37   6.41   338.15

Had Pyrrhus not fallen (HISTORICAL BACK KICK)
    25.14   34.25   See also 24.01

Had . . . JULIUS CAESAR not been knifed to death
    25.14   109.27   193.32   297.07   635.25   776.28   (26.15)

ARISTOTLE (the infinite possibilities they have ousted)
  Possibilities
    25.17+   25.35   193.34   194.31   213.14   217.26   423.27
    (196.13)
  Form of forms
    26.05   44.26   48.23   189.39   432.20
  Ineluctable modality
    37.01++   48.22   48.37   217.26   378.05   505.06   560.05
    697.27
  Diaphane—adiaphane
    37.04++   394.05
  Other ideas (T) (G)
    192.16   192.18   394.08   418.19+
  Personal reference
    37.05+   185.24++ 204.05+   212.01   432.26   687.27+

      ** Weave, weaver of the wind   25.20   21.14 **

      ** Tell us a ghoststory   25.22   (19.34) **

MILTON, JOHN (Weep no more)
  "Lycidas"
    25.25++   26.07   50.09   215.25   630.15   660.39   (97.09)
    (110.33)   See also 4.28
  Paradise Lost
    184.21   184.35   (38.03)   (129.22)   (241.29+) (598.13)   (619.06)
  "L'Allegro"
    208.20
  "Comus"
    (28.11)
  "On the Morning of Christ's Nativity"
    (580.15)

```
** Actuality of the possible as possible  25.35        25.17  **

** Paris                                        25.37+      12.18  **
```

With FAINTLY BEATING FEELERS
```
    25.41       56.07
```

BRIGHTNESS-DARKNESS (in my mind's darkness a sloth . . . shy of brightness)
```
    26.01+      26.16       28.16       28.31       34.04+      38.10       44.12
    48.18       48.31       84.39       241.30      301.13      345.22+     384.41
    390.03      393.41+     413.35+     583.05      (44.20)     (183.21)    (196.35)
    (343.40)    (383.01)    See also  34.03
```

Shifting her DRAGON SCALY FOLDS
```
    26.02       (598.33)        See also 24.07
```

```
    ** Form of forms                        26.05       25.17  **

    ** Through the dear might of Him         26.07+      25.25  **

    ** The scoffer's heart        26.14      3.01       21.07  **

    ** To Caesar what is Caesar's            26.15      (25.14) **

    ** From dark eyes                        26.16      26.01  **

    ** Woven on the church's looms           26.17      21.14  **
```

STEPHEN'S RIDDLE
  The cock crew . . . To go to heaven
```
    26.33++     28.02       557.16      558.02      559.10+     600.17
```
  The fox burying his grandmother under a hollybush
```
    27.08       28.03       46.08       46.41       193.20+     496.16      559.10+
    572.21      (114.42)
  See also      60.11       492.22      502.12
```

On his CHEEK, dull and BLOODLESS
```
    27.19       101.19      181.30
```

MR DEASY told me
```
    27.25#      37.23       132.09++    189.33+     199.02      518.01      573.19++
    617.16      See also  11.02        32.01
```

She had loved his WEAK WATERY BLOOD drained from her own
```
    27.37       28.26
```

Was that then real? The only true thing in life? (AMOR MATRIS)
```
    27.38       28.25       207.27      778.22
```

```
    ** His mother's prostrate body          27.39+      5.16   **
```

The fiery COLUMBANUS in holy zeal bestrode
```
    27.39       42.08       339.27
```

EDWARD VII (Albert Edward, Prince of Wales)
      31.15   32.13   73.04   102.17   132.34   151.04   165.34
      330.37+   333.33   587.14   589.27   590.15++   593.07+   594.18+
      646.09   751.28++   752.08
      See also   11.10   116.18   330.37   (297.12)

O'CONNELL, DANIEL (Since O'Connell's time)
      31.18+   93.39   104.41   108.05   135.21   143.29   599.02
      654.31+

I remember THE FAMINE
      31.19   329.38+

The ORANGE LODGES
      31.19   573.22   See also 574.01

For repeal of the UNION
      31.20+   230.19

You FENIANS forget some things
      31.22   163.36   (296.39)   See also 43.25   81.27

WILLIAM III (Glorious, pious and immortal memory)
      31.23   252.31   330.14   397.13

        ** Masked and armed   31.25   7.30 **

CROPPIES lie down
      31.26   See   91.01

We are all Irish, ALL KINGS' SONS
      31.30   45.29   294.16

PER VIAS RECTAS
      31.32   573.30

The ROCKY ROAD TO DUBLIN
      31.36   573.21

SOFT DAY, SIR JOHN. SOFT DAY, YOUR HONOUR
      31.37   574.02

I have a letter (DEASY'S LETTER)
      32.01++   38.25   48.11   132.05++   398.211++
   The dictates of common sense
      32.07   33.14
   Prompt ventilation of this important question
      32.20   (633.22)
   Foot and mouth disease
      32.41   33.11+   132.17+   135.20   144.15   153.19   293.31
      315.03+   647.23   648.11
   May I trespass on your valuable space
      33.01   (230.37)

Galway harbour scheme
    33.04   639.31
Pluterperfect imperturbability
    33.06   420.03
By a woman who was no better than she should be (HELEN OF TROY)
    33.07   34.40   132.26   148.26   201.18
Rinderpest
    33.12   399.25+
Emperor's horses at Mürzsteg, lower Austria
    33.12   132.31
Mr Henry Blackwood Price
    33.14+   (730.29)
Allimportant question
    33.15   364.27
Take the bull by the horns
    33.16   201.34   399.26   (23.12)
Thanking you for the hospitality of your columns
    33.16   48.12
Torn off section
    48.12   132.08+

     ** The princely presence   32.13   31.15 **

Lord Hastings' REPULSE . . . SHOTOVER, the duke of Beaufort's CEYLON, PRIX
   DE PARIS
    32.15   50.20   573.14

ELFIN RIDERS sat them
    32.17   573.16

The SHOUTS OF VANISHED CROWDS
    32.19   143.28+

     ** Where Cranly led me   32.22   7.14 **

     ** Time shocked rebounds   32.34   (24.07) **

     ** Uproar of battles . . . deathspew   32.35   24.18 **

SPEAR SPIKES baited with men's BLOODIED GUTS
    32.36   596.21

     ** Jews . . . signs of a nation's decay 33.29+   21.21 **

     ** The harlot's cry . . .   33.38   21.14   24.07 **

A MERCHANT . . . is ONE WHO BUYS CHEAP AND SELLS DEAR
    34.01   290.21+   633.12

They SINNED AGAINST THE LIGHT
    34.03   393.29   428.09   See also 26.01   413.40

     ** The darkness in their eyes 34.06+   26.01+ (101.36) **

They are wanderers on the earth to this day (THE WANDERING JEW)
    34.05++   61.16   217.35   338.27   385.04   388.32   418.03
    506.07   727.36   (200.14)   (498.28)   (695.01)

       ** The Paris Stock Exchange   34.06+   12.18 **

       ** Vain patience to heap and hoard   34.13   29.40 **

Time . . . would SCATTER all
    34.13   143.30

HISTORY . . . is a NIGHTMARE from which I am trying to awake
    34.22+   137.17   See also 20.40   24.07   34.27

       ** Gave you a back kick?   34.25   25.14 **

All history MOVES TOWARDS ONE GREAT GOAL, the manifestation of God
    34.27   46.30   563.17   (7.30)
    See also   20.40   24.07   34.22

A SHOUT IN THE STREET
    34.33   186.15   394.32+   505.05   574.06

       ** A woman brought sin into the world   34.39   14.23 **

       ** A woman who was no better . . . Helen 34.41   32.01 **

The runaway wife of MENELAUS
    34.41   132.27   201.18

Ten years the Greeks made war on TROY
    34.42   144.26   201.19

FAITHLESS WIFE . . . MACMURROUGH'S WIFE . . . O'ROURKE
    34.42+   132.27   323.13   324.03+

Brought the STRANGERS to our shore
    34.42   184.40   323.40+   393.22+

KITTY O'SHEA (A woman too brought Parnell low)
    35.02   650.23+   (751.24)

PARNELL, CHARLES STEWART (A woman too brought Parnell low)
    35.02   95.39   111.05   112.35+   163.42   165.12+   165.23
    298.03   334.40   483.19   492.22   599.04   640.41   648.43++
    654.06++ 660.40+   681.17   716.39   (156.08)(G) See also 165.02

I will FIGHT FOR THE RIGHT till the end
    35.04   36.01

And here WHAT WILL YOU LEARN more?
    35.14   144.31   215.12   (376.02)

Telegraph . . . THE EVENING TELEGRAPH
    35.22+   116.29   121.31   123.13++   128.28+   137.03   146.16+
    379.15   397.22   469.15   632.18++   647.08++   675.38   745.28
    773.23

IRISH HOMESTEAD
    35.22   191.29   193.02   398.06   510.23

WILLIAM FIELD (I wrote last night to Mr Field, M.P.)
    35.26   314.42   315.26+

A MEETING OF THE CATTLETRADERS' ASSOCIATION today
    35.27   293.28   314.41+

At the CITY ARMS HOTEL
    35.27   170.42   174.23   293.28   305.40+   315.13   338.16
    373.17   378.11   680.23   738.02   758.02   760.39   765.06
    772.14

Still I will HELP HIM IN HIS FIGHT
    36.02   See also 35.04   112.02

        ** Mulligan   36.02   3.01 **

        ** The bullockbefriending bard   36.03   5.01 **

PERSECUTED THE JEWS
    36.10   331.17   332.36+   488.23   688.36   716.18   771.22
    See also   21.21

        ** On gaitered feet   36.19   29.08 **

The sun FLUNG SPANGLES
    36.22   475.06

        ** Dancing coins   36.22   29.25 **

PROTEUS

[SANDYMOUNT Strand]
    37.01#   116.06   117.10   149.11+   251.18   346.04#   647.28
    657.30   704.17   705.03

        ** Ineluctable modality   37.01++   25.17 **

SIGNATURES OF ALL THINGS I am here to read
    37.02+   44.36   48.24   562.02   (381.34)

        ** Snotgreen   37.04   5.02 **

COLOURED SIGNS
    37.04++   48.27+   182.08   644.28+

        ** Diaphane . . . adiaphane   37.04+   25.17 **

        ** He adds [Aristotle]   37.05+   25.17 **

By KNOCKING HIS SCONCE against them (T) (G)
    37.06   (186.15+)   See also 48.26

        ** Maestro di color che sanno   37.08   20.20 **

Shut your eyes and see (SEEING -- NOT SEEING)
    37.10++   181.25++

        ** His boots . . . buck's castoffs   37.11+   3.01 **

        ** Crackling wrack and shells   37.12   29.37 **

NACHEINANDER . . . NEBENEINANDER (GOTTHOLD EPHRAIM LESSING)
    37.14+   49.18   559.11

IF I FELL OVER A CLIFF
        37.16   550.12+   628.16   See also   18.25

            ** That beetles o'er his base   37.16   18.25   **

            ** My ash sword   37.18   17.17   **

TAP with it
        37.18   180.31#   250.02#   257.11   281.15#

THEY DO
        37.19   81.09

            ** My two feet in his boots   37.19   37.11   **

            ** Los Demiurgos   37.20   24.07   **

            ** Wild sea money   37.22   29.37   **

            ** Dominie Deasy   37.23   27.25   **

RHYTHM begins
        37.26   42.22   432.20   (374.04)

            ** One moment   37.28   3.24   **

            ** And ever shall be . . .   37.32   29.24   **

They came down the steps from LEAHY'S TERRACE
        37.33   379.14

FRAUENZIMMER (Florence MacCabe and Anne Kearns)
        37.34   45.07   145.03++   242.07+   254.39   579.12

            ** Our mighty mother   37.35   5.06   5.13   **

Number one swung LOURDILY
        37.36   See also 145.32

Her MIDWIFE'S bag
        37.37+   190.33   202.27   242.09   384.33   394.14   397.32
        499.02

DICKENS, CHARLES (the other's GAMP poked in the beach)
    Martin Chuzzlewit
        37.37
    Pickwick Papers
        188.01
    Bleak House (T)
        220.24   235.34   253.41   575.30
    Little Dorrit (G)
        371.27
    David Copperfield
        420.42+   421.08

A Tale of Two Cities
   767.08(G)   767.30(G)
Our Mutual Friend
   (635.32)
Parody
   140.06-140.09   420.30-421.28

From THE LIBERTIES, out for the day
   37.38   246.34

BRIDE STREET
   37.39   314.12

    ** Creation from nothing   37.41+   19.34 **

Trailing NAVELCORD. . . . CORDS of all LINK BACK
   38.01+   86.39   112.30   391.31   411.11   (7.33)   (85.08)
   (318.25)

    ** Your omphalos   38.03   7.33 **

    ** Will you be as gods?   38.03   (25.25) **

    ** Kinch here   38.04   3.08 **

Put me on to EDENVILLE
   38.04   394.20

ADAM Kadmon
   38.06   47.28   137.22   297.16   779.33
   See also   34.39   148.01

    ** Heva, naked Eve   38.06   14.23 (24.07)(T) **

BELLY WITHOUT BLEMISH
   38.07   392.01

Buckler of . . . WHITEHEAPED CORN
   38.08   199.09

ORIENT AND IMMORTAL, STANDING FROM EVERLASTING TO EVERLASTING
   38.08   242.05

Womb of sin (WOMB - SIN - DEATH)
  womb of sin
   38.09+   386.07
  womb-tomb
   48.08   138.30   392.30

THE MAN WITH MY VOICE
   38.11   43.10   659.02+
   See also   76.30   89.04   201.09   211.25

    ** A ghostwoman   38.11   5.32 **

<u>H.M.S.</u> <u>Pinafore</u>
   290.14
<u>Patience</u>
   516.13
<u>Iolanthe</u>
   (319.28)

Skeweyed WALTER (GOULDING)
   38.36++   273.12

In his broad bed NUNCLE Richie
   39.02   211.17   213.11   See also   38.34

Master SHAPLAND TANDY
   39.07   44.05

        ** Wilde's <u>Requiescat</u>   39.09   6.37 **

CRISSIE . . . LUMP OF LOVE
   39.13   88.19   213.11   See also 357.03

Nothing in the house but BACKACHE pills
   39.26   88.28   272.14   283.09   447.15
   See also   125.03   272.14

THE GRANDEST NUMBER . . . IN THE WHOLE OPERA
   39.29   278.14

        ** Clongowes   39.33   11.22 **

HOUSES OF DECAY
   39.33   (45.32)

The fading prophecies of JOACHIM ABBAS
   39.37+   40.01+   243.03   See also   9.22

SWIFT, JONATHAN (a hater of his kind)
  Personal reference
     39.38+   573.11
  "Cousin Stephen, you will never be a saint" (T) (G)
     40.19   249.10
  <u>Gulliver's</u> <u>Travels</u>
     39.38   329.22
  <u>An</u> <u>Analytical</u> <u>Discourse</u> <u>upon</u> <u>Zeal</u>
     205.13 (T)
  <u>The</u> <u>Drapier's</u> <u>Letters</u>
     588.18
  Other reference (parody)
     399.31—401.28
  <u>Tale</u> <u>of</u> <u>a</u> <u>Tub</u> (T)
     (205.13) (T)
  "A Cantata"
     (486.21) (T)
  See also   39.39
            NOTE: Possible references to Swift's <u>Polite</u> <u>Conversation</u>

are not recorded here since all are commonplaces. Where they
are repeated, they are crossreferenced elsewhere. For a list
of possible references, see Thornton, p. 550.

His MANE FOAMING IN THE MOON, his EYEBALLS STARS
     39.39   573.12

          ** Oval equine faces   39.41   3.16 **

          ** Temple   39.41   31.03 **

          ** Buck Mulligan   39.41   3.01 **

          ** What offence   39.42   8.42 **

          ** Descende calve (T) (G)   40.01+   39.37 **

          ** Garland of grey hair   40.02   22.05 **

BASILISKEYED
     40.04   194.21   454.29   530.17

MOSES (Fat with the fat of kidneys of wheat)
     40.07(T)   45.07+   139.33   142.11++   149.22+   216.34   242.26
     345.12   387.20   393.25   394.15   459.25   466.16   470.27
     495.14   495.24   676.15   687.21+   729.28   (96.30)   (463.09)
     (659.26)   (729.28)   See also   10.32

Another taking HOUSEL
     40.12   385.38

The imp HYPOSTASIS tickled his brain
     40.14   689.29

          ** Cousin Stephen . . .   40.19   39.38 **

ISLE OF SAINTS
     40.19   337.39   See also   41.05

You prayed to the devil in SERPENTINE AVENUE . . . FUBSY WINDOW
     40.22   571.19

Dyed rags PINNED round a squaw
     40.24   46.06   See also   78.38

On the top of the Howth tram (BEN HOWTH)
     40.25   297.15   343.14   346.04   357.24   376.14   378.12
     (223.13)   (688.35)   See also   176.01

Books you were going to write with letters for titles (ALPHABET BOOKS)
     40.31   48.39

Those strange PAGES of one long gone
     40.38   242.37

BUNNY'S FACE. Lap, <u>LAPIN</u>
    41.19   592.14

<u>Je suis</u> SOCIALISTE
    41.23   592.17

       ** Latin quarter hat   41.28   17.08 **

       ** Dress the character   41.28   17.03 **

Your GROATSWORTH of <u>mou</u> <u>en</u> <u>civet</u>
    41.31   190.41   See also 187.27

FLESHPOTS OF EGYPT
    41.32   86.15   208.33   513.28   (266.02)   See also 257.30

       ** Other me   41.37   11.22 **

PROUDLY WALKING
    41.40   42.22

       ** After fiery Columbanus   42.08   27.39 **

FIACRE and Scotus on their creepystools (ST. FIACRE)
    42.08   327.31   339.28

       ** You dragged your valise   42.11   12.02 **

Across the slimy pier at NEWHAVEN
    42.12   210.36

Mother dying COME HOME FATHER
    42.15   (71.11)

       ** The aunt thinks   42.16   5.16 **

FRENCH, PERCY (Then here's health to Mulligan's aunt)
  "Matthew Hanigan's Aunt"
    42.18+
  "Phil the Fluter's Ball"
    319.30
  "Shlathery's Mounted Fut"
    424.31
  "The Mountains of Mourne"
    (263.07)

       ** Sudden proud rhythm   42.22   37.26   41.40 **

       ** With gold teeth   42.32   (3.28) **

WELLPLEASED PLEASERS
    42.34   191.26

       ** Kevin Egan   42.36++   41.17 **

GREEN FAIRY . . . FANG (ABSINTHE, the GREENEYED MONSTER)
       42.38   43.07   43.20   199.09   425.12   427.02+   500.19
       591.28   (55.24)

              ** Patrice his white   42.38   41.18 **

              ** Green fairy's fang   43.07   42.38 **

ARTHUR GRIFFITH
       43.08   57.35   72.41   163.42   325.04   334.38   335.39
       337 18+   599.04   748.40+   772.24
The Resurrection of Hungary
       337.33   484.24 (G)
See also   57.36   72.41   163.38

              ** Your father's voice   43.10   38.11 **

Its SPANISH TASSELS
       43.11   592.10

M. DRUMONT, famous journalist
       43.12+   50.33   592.13

Know what he called QUEEN VICTORIA?
       43.13   50.33   85.01   102.13   161.29   170.34   255.05
       300.05   330.29+   334.24   596.16   678.40   721.33   (421.12)

Old hag with yellow teeth. VIEILLE OGRESSE WITH THE DENTS JAUNES
       43.13   592.13

MAUD GONNE, beautiful woman
       43.14   72.40

THE FROEKEN . . . who RUBS MALE NAKEDNESS in the bath at Upsala
       43.16   85.07

Most LASCIVIOUS thing. . . . LASCIVIOUS people
       43.20   50.02   551.04

              ** Green eyes. . . . Fang   43.20   42.38 **

The BLUE FUSE burns deadly between hands
       43.22   579.13

Raw face bones under his PEEP OF DAY BOY'S HAT
       43.24   592.11

STEPHENS, JAMES (How the headcentre got away)
       43.25   68.27   163.36+   316.22   484.12   See also 31.18

VEIL ORANGEBLOSSOMS
       43.26   579.26

Drove out the road to MALAHIDE
    43.27   223.15   425.42   452.09   621.05
The joy bells were ringing in gay Malahide
    223.16   482.27
Lord Talbot de Malahide
    223.17   402.29   616.34

BROWNING, ROBERT (Of lost leaders)
  "The Lost Leader"
    43.27
  "Love Among the Ruins"
    108.15
  "Parting at Morning"
    191.10
  "Fra Lippo Lippi"
    (209.33) (G)
  "One Word More"
    (507.30)

      ** The betrayed   43.27   14.05 **

      ** Flame of vengeance . . . masonry   43.33+   24.07 **

OLD KILKENNY: SAINT CANICE
    44.03   339.33

He takes me, Napper Tandy, by the hand ("THE WEARIN' OF THE GREEN")
    44.05   595.17   643.18   (39.07)   (510.05)

Remembering thee, O SION (ZION)
  Sion–Zion
    44.09   437.13   487.04   See also 151.07
  Restoration of the church in Zion
    151.16   676.08   689.01

      ** Seeds of brightness   44.12   26.01 **

The KISH LIGHTSHIP
    44.13+   67.03   379.23   382.01   550.19   630.37

TURN BACK
    44.14   154.37   197.04   (23.20)   See also 51.04   61.23

      ** The tower   44.16+   3.10 **

      ** The barbicans   44.17   11.26 **

      ** In the darkness . . . they wait   44.20   (26.01) **

      ** My obelisk valise   44.21   12.02 **

      ** I will not sleep there   44.22   23.20 **

      ** He has the key   44.22   11.35 **

"She is Far from the Land"
    305.35
"Where is the Slave"
    306.22
"Though the Last Glimpse of Erin"
    363.30
"Those Evening Bells"
    363.31
"Love's Young Dream"
    365.02   529.23
"When He Who Adores Thee"
    426.01
"The Song of O'Ruark"
    653.33
Personal reference
    162.29

When MALACHI wore the collar of gold
    45.13   296.37   340.17

I MOVED AMONG THEM
    45.18   57.27

      ** That I, a changeling   45.19   11.22 **

      ** Bayed about   45.22   (29.19) **

      ** A primrose doublet   45.23++   18.02 **

PRETENDERS
    45.25   490.02   592.03   622.40

Thomas Fitzgerald (FITZGERALDS -- GERALDINES -- EARLS OF KILDARE)
  Thomas Fitzgerald
    45.26   230.16+   344.07   628.12
  Gerald Mor Fitzgerald
    231.21
  Lord Edward Fitzgerald
    241.07+   599.06
  James Fitzmaurice Fitzgerald
    328.06
  Other
    231.14+   245.10

      ** All kings' sons   45.29   31.30 **

      ** Saved men from drowning   45.30++   4.28 **

The courtiers . . . their own house (BOCCACCIO, THE DECAMERON)
    45.31   207.18

      ** Who mocked Guido   45.31   3.37 **

      ** House of . . .   45.32   (39.33) **

"Sinbad the Sailor"
   636.33   678.32   737.17+
Other
   215.04   659.28

His blued feet out of TURNEDUP TROUSERS slapped the clammy sand
   47.11   (183.12)

The ruffian and his strolling mort (CANTING LANGUAGE)
   47.13++   191.01   425.39   426.31+   598.06

Two Royal Dublins (ROYAL DUBLIN FUSILIERS)
   47.18   72.38   457.19   479.33   596.15   649.01   730.04
   749.17

BLACKPITTS. . . . FUMBALLY'S LANE
   47.19+   145.04+

In the DARKMANS clip and kiss
   47.26   (181.39)

     ** Aquinas tunbelly   47.27   17.40 **

     ** Unfallen Adam rode   47.28   38.06 **

     ** Hamlet hat   47.33   17.08 **

     ** Sands of the world (G)   47.34+ (184.10) **

     ** Sun's flaming sword   47.35   14.23 **

Trekking TO EVENING LANDS
   47.35   50.26

TIDES, MYRIADISLANDED
   47.37   49.35+   281.30+

     ** Oinopa ponton   47.38   5.07 **

Behold the handmaid of the moon (MARY, MOTHER OF CHRIST)
   47.39   88.34   207.23   259.39   346.09#   385.09   389.10
   390.09   391.24+   414.29   438.30   520.28   521.21   600.10
   681.16   See also 82.09   339.20   346.08

The handmaid of the moon (WOMAN AND MOON)
   47.39   50.01   702.01+

     ** Ghostcandled   48.01   10.20 **

OMNIS CARO AD TE VENIET
   48.01   391.23

HYDE, DOUGLAS (He comes, pale vampire . . . to her mouth's kiss)
  Stephen's Vampire Poem
     48.01   132.12+   138.16+   390.03   570.11+   608.23   (236.05)
     See also   176.19+
  Lovesongs of Connacht
     186.25   198.18   248.33   312.06   412.09
  The Story of Early Gaelic Literature (In lean unlovely English)
     186.28+   197.04

His BAT sails bloodying the sea
     48.02   441.24   576.30   See also 363.32

GLUE 'EM WELL
     48.05   441.24   576.30

        ** Womb. . . . allwombing tomb 48.08   38.09   (24.08) **

        ** Banknotes   48.11   11.02 **

        ** Old Deasy's letter   48.11   32.01 **

TEAR the blank end off
     48.12   132.08+   (70.01)   See also 61.37   79.19

        ** Slips from the library   48.14   15.35 **

        ** Darkness shining in the brightness 48.18   26.01 **

Delta of CASSIOPEIA
     48.18   210.09   700.41   728.06   See also 210.07

Me sits there with his AUGUR'S ROD
     48.19   217.31   218.05   574.21   See also 17.17

        ** Rod of ash   48.19   17.17 **

        ** In borrowed sandals   48.19   3.01 **

        ** Manshape, ineluctable   48.22   25.17 **

        ** Form of my form   48.23   25.17 **

        ** Signs on a white field   48.24   37.02 **

BERKELEY, GEORGE (The good bishop of Cloyne)
     48.26   240.12   (166.36)   See also 37.06

        ** Veil of the temple   48.26   9.22 **

        ** With coloured emblems   48.27+   37.04 **

        ** Darkness is in our souls   48.31   26.01 **

        ** Ineluctable modality   48.37   25.17 **

```
     ** Alphabet books                      48.39        40.31    **

I am LONELY here
      49.04+        81.10        192.36       193.21     256.34       257.15       275.32+
     280.10        281.41        287.04       289.13     290.09       427.25       456.28
     704.32          See also 283.32

     ** That word known to all men          49.05        10.17    **

MALLARMÉ, STÉPHANE (I am caught in this burning scene. . . .)
   "Afternoon of a Faun"
      49.12+
   Personal reference
     187.04++    558.21       570.30

     ** Among gumheavy serpentplants         49.14        46.16    **

     ** Pain is far                          49.15         5.31    **

     ** And no more turn . . .               49.16         9.22    **

     ** A buck's castoffs                    49.17         3.01    **

     ** Nebeneinander                        49.18        37.14    **

Beat the ground in TRIPUDIUM
      49.20       574.22

     ** Girl I knew in Paris                 49.22        12.18    **

     ** Wilde's love                         49.23         6.37    **

     ** All or not at all                    49.24        20.20    **

     ** My ashplant                          49.27        17.17    **

REARING HORSES
      49.31       (573.31)

It slops . . . BOUNDED IN BARRELS
      49.32+       79.36+      116.23+      117.17

It flows PURLING
      49.33       399.30

Widely FLOWING, FLOATING foampool, FLOWER unfurling
      49.33        79.38        86.40       See also  72.31       73.11       782.18

     ** The upswelling tide                  49.35+       47.37    **

He saw the writhing weeds lift LANGUIDLY
      49.36        86.42        348.31       576.29

     ** Hising up their petticoats           49.36        13.22    **
```

SWAY reluctant ARMS
     49.36   544.22   553.11   (89.22)

      ** They are weary   49.39+   3.41 **

      ** The moon . . . a naked woman   50.01   47.39 **

      ** Lascivious men   50.02   43.20 **

      ** Five fathoms out there   50.04   21.28 **

      ** At one he said   50.05   21.29 **

      ** Found drowned   50.05   4.28 **

A CORPSE rising SALTWHITE
     50.07+   114.37

      ** Silly shells   50.07   29.37 **

A PACE A PACE a porpoise
     50.08   534.25

      ** Sunk though he be . . .   50.09   26.25 **

METEMPSYCHOSIS (God becomes man becomes . . .)
  Stephen
     50.13+
  Bloom
     64.14+   64.32+   109.01   110.24   154.07   182.31   269.13
     284.41   288.18   377.30+   382.15   408.36   414.29   473.10
     490.16   653.35   686.31
  Molly
     754.01
  Featherbed mountain
     50.14   See also 234.25

      ** Dead breaths   50.14   41.03 **

      ** _Prix_ _de_ _Paris_   50.20   32.15 **

BEWARE OF IMITATIONS
     50.21   684.13

      ** Clouding over   50.23   9.32 **

      ** I thirst   50.23   41.05 **

Allbright he FALLS
     50.24   210.37   See also 207.40

Proud LIGHTNING OF THE INTELLECT
     50.25   133.22

LUCIFER, dico, qui nescit occasum
    50.25   83.25   184.22   184.35   203.14   330.42   427.14
    553.17   637.09   See also 14.23   558.27

      ** My cockle hat   50.25   17.08 **

      ** His my sandal shoon   50.26   3.01 **

      ** To evening lands   50.26   47.35 **

      ** Ashplant   50.28   17.17 **

ALL DAYS make their END
    50.29   213.17   214.37   528.29   (109.37)

TENNYSON, ALFRED (Of all the glad new year, mother)
  "The May Queen"
    50.31+
  "Flower in the Crannied Wall"
    91.20
  The Princess
    202.06
  "Merlin and Vivien"
    277.10   287.33
  "Ulysses"
    144.25(G)   176.41(G)
  "The Charge of the Light Brigade"
    484.04   588.13
  "Enoch Arden"
    624.27   (655.20)
  "Locksley Hall"
    628.15
  Personal reference
    50.31   202.06   588.11
  "To Virgil"
    (196.24)(G)
  In Memoriam
    (260.25)   (486.18)

      ** Old hag with the yellow teeth   50.33   43.13 **

      ** Monsieur Drumont   50.33   43.12 **

      ** Shells   50.35   29.37 **

      ** With that money   50.36   11.02 **

      ** Toothless Kinch   50.36   3.08 **

      ** The superman   50.37   5.20 **

      ** My handkerchief   50.39   4.37 **

Ought I GO TO A DENTIST
    50.35   563.20

FOR THE REST let look who will
     51.02   (546.18)

BEHIND. PERHAPS THERE IS SOMEONE
     51.03   217.22

Rere regardant (LOOKING BACKWARD)
     51.04   62.07   154.37   197.04   394.21
     See also   44.14   61.23

Threemaster (The ROSEVEAN)
     51.05   249.36   625.14   647.11

CROSSTREES
     51.06   197.32

CALYPSO

Mr Leopold Bloom ATE WITH RELISH the INNER ORGANS of beasts and fowls
    55.01   173.31   269.34   271.06

LIVER slices fried (Bloom's fondness for)
    55.03   164.42   269.11#   528.27

Grilled . . . KIDNEYS
  Mutton Kidneys
     55.04   56.10
  Pork kidneys
     56.11#   464.29   484.27   498.23   711.12
  Burned kidney
     65.23   151.15   269.13   728.35   754.03

BREAKFAST (MOLLY'S)
    55.07++   62.14++   677.06   728.35   779.41   (532.27)

      ** Cup of tea soon   55.14   8.14 **

Just how she stalks over my WRITING-TABLE
    55.20   542.23   729.18   779.39

GREEN FLASHING EYES
    55.24   (42.38)

      ** Said mockingly   55.32   3.37 **

      ** Green stones   55.41   20.01 **

      ** Running to lap   56.03++   41.18 **

They SHINE IN THE DARK
    56.06   (151.22+)   (301.16+)

      ** Feelers in the dark   56.07   25.41 **

No good eggs with this DROUTH (DROUGHT)
    56.09   396.29   671.11

At BUCKLEY'S
    56.10   764.24

      ** Better a pork kidney   56.11   55.04 **

At DLUGACZ'S
    56.11   58.38++   68.28   279.39   763.27
  Ferreteyed
    59.12   60.11   464.27

On quietly CREAKY BOOTS he went up the staircase
    56.16   90.27   See also 37.11   183.12   184.06

The loose BRASS QUOITS OF THE BEDSTEAD JINGLED
    56.27   63.19   469.26+   547.06   731.06   769.34   772.05+
    780.07   See also 253.42

ALL THE WAY FROM GIBRALTAR
    56.28   547.06   772.07

GIBRALTAR
    56.29   60.40   269.28   326.22   380.10   491.13   547.06
    629.33   637.15   709.07+   727.02   730.04   741.38#   (667.21)

Hard as nails at a bargain, old Tweedy (MAJOR BRIAN COOPER TWEEDY)
    56.32   57.19   72.36   269.21   319.38   377.19   409.18
    457.13   596.06   596.21++   601.18+   652.42   667.26   710.04
    730.03   730.25   738.37   741.30   746.41   748.29   752.18
    755.15   755.27   756.11   757.20+   759.26   765.28   772.07
    782.26   See also 56.34

At PLEVNA that was
    56.32   484.07   710.11   757.21

He had brains enough to make that CORNER IN STAMPS
    56.34   741.30   763.01

Over his initialled HEAVY OVERCOAT
    56.37   755.05

His lost property office secondhand WATERPROOF
    56.37   502.05   525.13

Lots of officers are IN THE SWIM too
    56.38   81.09

PLASTO'S HIGH GRADE HA[T]
    56.40   68.20+   71.29+   92.12   279.29   279.37   286.37
    455.05   493.18   (377.29)

White slip of paper (POST OFFICE CARD)
    56.41   71.31   72.22+   79.42   279.29   286.37   455.10+

      ** For the latchkey   57.01   11.35 **

POTATO I have
    57.02   183.35   425.24   435.27   437.07   438.29   466.09
   476.13+   478.10   499.03   529.03   555.23++

(ST.) GEORGE'S CHURCH
    57.09   70.10+   279.08   471.24+   482.28   577.08   666.11
   704.07+   772.28

BLACK CONDUCTS, reflects (REFRACTS is it?) the heat
    57.10   267.29   374.33   443.08   674.05

PADDY DIGNAM (But I couldn't go in that light suit)
  Funeral
    57.11   58.14   63.37   70.07+   71.14+   71.25   73.24++
    75.33   84.10   85.11   87.01#   118.20+   122.19   157.01+
   232.02   238.35   279.08   288.38   313.29   376.06   380.22
   396.28   427.26+   472.11++   647.23++   655.14   704.16   728.37
   742.34   773.23++
  Death
    64.33   68.31   70.07+   91.16   95.17+   157.08   164.19
   171.34   240.32   251.25   277.26   289.39   300.29++   354.40+
   373.08   380.35   705.03   739.15
  Face, blazing
    95.24   251.28
  Fund for his family
   161.21   246.13+   247.28#
  Bloom's five shilling contribution to the fund
   246.21   277.27   279.18   711.16
  Boots
   251.36   568.13
  Bloom's visit to Dignam's home
   313.07+   370.20   372.29   380.35+   729.06
  Insurance policy (Scottish Widows' Assurance Society)
   313.06   380.35   568.14   (723.03)   See also 280.29
  Other references
   102.39+   219.04   300.29++
  See also   313.07

      ** Our daily   57.13   6.33 **

Somewhere in THE EAST
    57.15++   60.40++   368.40   705.11
  The Far East
    71.35+
  See also   47.05   59.16   60.16

COLERIDGE, S. T. (Walk along a strand. . .)
  "Kubla Khan"
    57.18+

Biographia Literaria
    205.19
"The Rime of the Ancient Mariner"
    217.37   636.16   659.15

        ** Old Tweedy's big moustaches   57.19   56.32   **

        ** Turko the terrible   57.22   10.02   **

        ** I pass on   57.27+   45.18   **

Violet, colour of MOLLY'S NEW GARTERS
    57.30   180.17   368.34   730.17   740.19   750.41
    See also   460.28

One of these instruments what do you call them: DULCIMERS
    57.32   273.42   517.18

Kind of stuff you read: IN THE TRACK OF THE SUN
    57.33   368.40   709.16

The HEADPIECE over the FREEMAN leader (FREEMAN'S JOURNAL)
    Headpiece . . . Homerule sun rising up in the northwest
    57.35+   164.14   376.27   482.03   (120.31)
    Bloom's copy for June 16, 1904
    72.16   74.41   77.11++   80.42   85.22++   91.12+   100.33
    103.16   104.35   183.35   279.06+   286.30   676.12   711.13
    Bloom's job with
    106.31   116.27#   177.07++   200.21+   297.42   388.02   413.03
    427.05   458.19   480.27   485.34   498.26   554.25   752.12
    772.23
    Other references
    111.37   117.16   118.07   119.32   136.26   137.23   458.19
    484.09   754.43
    See also   163.38

        ** Arthur Griffith   57.35   43.08   **

IKEY touch that
    57.38   201.01   466.16

He approached LARRY O'ROURKE'S (Public House)
    57.40++   255.17   281.38   489.07   538.07   586.20   750.34+
    My bold Larry
    58.07   281.38

N. G. AS POSITION
    58.02   (98.40)

If they ran a TRAMLINE ALONG THE NORTH CIRCULAR
    58.03   98.08+   221.03   478.21   719.06

The Russians, they'd only be an eight o' clock breakfast for the Japanese
    (RUSSO-JAPANESE WAR)
    58.11   295.34   427.34   647.18

```
            ** Poor Dignam                          58.14      57.11   **

Blossom out as ADAM FINDLATERS
      58.23      781.26

Blossom out as . . . DAN TALLONS
      58.24      679.18

            ** General thirst                       58.25      41.05   **

A bob here and there, DRIBS AND DRABS
      58.27      272.21

How much would that tot to off the porter in the month? (INCOME FROM PORTER)
      58.31+      79.29+

SLIEVE BLOOM
      58.37      343.18      (118.30)

            ** Dlugacz's window                     58.38++    56.11   **

The NEXTDOOR GIRL
      59.04++    68.06       68.36     72.14     538.07     727.19
   Her crooked skirt swinging
      59.10      59.26       280.07
   Her moving hams
      59.36      72.14       727.17    (734.28+)

            ** The ferreteyed porkbutcher           59.12      56.11   **

The MODEL FARM AT KINNERETH on the lakeshore of Tiberias
      59.16      464.25      (466.10)     See also   60.16

MOSES MONTEFIORE
      59.17      719.31

BLURRED CATTLE CROPPING
      59.18      60.28       464.25

Those mornings in the cattlemarket (CUFFE, JOSEPH, CATTLE DEALER, BLOOM'S
      JOB WITH)
      59.21      97.41       294.38     315.08+    399.18     409.30     465.13
      586.20     680.27      731.32     752.20     772.19

            ** Crooked skirt swinging               59.26      59.10   **

NOW, MY MISS
      59.30      68.28

            ** Her moving hams                      59.36      59.04   **

WEAK PLEASURE within his breast
      60.01      78.24
```

A CONSTABLE OFF DUTY cuddled her in Eccles Lane
    60.02   163.23

      ** Eager fire from foxeyes   60.11   56.11 **
                                            See also 26.33

AGENDATH NETAIM: planter's company
    60.16   68.28   168.35   174.40   183.30+   279.40   382.17
    414.12+   464.20   495.27   497.13   707.09   718.16   (16.07)
    See also   59.16

BLEIBTREUSTRASSE 34, Berlin, W. 15
    60.26   174.41   464.31   718.16   (214.09)

      ** Cattle, blurred in silver heat   60.28   59.18 **

OLIVES
    60.29   675.11   779.29

I have a few left from ANDREWS
    60.30   526.30

Wonder is poor CITRON still alive in Saint Kevin's parade
    60.33+   122.35   156.02   497.17+   544.20   586.40   754.10

And Mastiansky with the old cither (MASTIANSKY FAMILY)
  Julius Mastiansky
    60.33   108.28   497.17+   586.40   667.28   731.26
  O. Mastiansky
    544.21
  Mrs. Mastiansky
    749.36

      ** Hold, cool waxen fruit   60.35   (47.07) **

They fetched high prices too MOISEL told me
    60.38   162.02   544.20   705.01

Arbutus place: PLEASANTS STREET: pleasant old times
    60.38   538.10

      ** All that way (the East)   60.40++   57.15 **

      ** Gibraltar   60.40   56.29 **

WHATDOYOUCALLHIM
    61.02   273.41   301.01   586.22   761.05   See also 121.31

      ** On earth. . . . (Lord's Prayer)   61.05   6.33 **

      ** A cloud . . . cover the sun   61.07   9.32 **

BARREN LAND, BARE WASTE
    61.09++   414.13   (381.41)

The CITIES OF THE PLAIN: Sodom, Gomorrah, Edom
      61.12   492.16   540.29

A DEAD SEA in a dead land . . . the grey sunken cunt of the world
      61.13+   72.03+   414.19+   544.25   727.10

A bent HAG crossed from Cassidy's clutching a noggin bottle
      61.15   375.30   538.07

        ** Oldest people (WANDERING JEW)   61.16   34.05 **

        ** Horror seared his flesh   61.21   10.22 **

COLD OILS SLID ALONG HIS VEINS, chilling his blood
      61.22   67.18   70.05

Age crusting him with a salt cloak (LOT'S WIFE)
      61.23   154.37   See also 44.14   51.02

Those SANDOW'S EXERCISES
      61.25+   435.25   681.23   709.18   721.33+
   On the hands down
      61.26   531.06

YES, YES
      61.31   449.28   738.01#

        ** Sunlight came running   61.32   10.30 **

RUNNING . . . SWIFTLY, IN SLIM SANDALS . . . GIRL WITH GOLDEN HAIR
      61.32   66.38   542.17   576.04   See also 348.14
   See also   10.30   348.14

He stopped and GATHERED (THE LETTERS)
      61.35   68.23

BOYLAN'S LETTER
   Mrs Marion
      61.37   63.28   67.13   75.14   269.07+   369.42   439.17
      440.09   441.02
   Torn envelope
      63.24   67.08   75.17   (48.13)   (70.01)   (72.30)
   Other references
      758.09++

        ** Mullingar. Milly   62.01#   21.42 **

        ** His backward eye   62.07   51.04 **

        ** Hurry up (Molly's breakfast)   62.14++   55.07 **

Tossed SOILED LINEN
      62.17++   547.05

Say they won't eat pork.   KOSHER
      62.30   171.42   446.24

The CHIPPED EGGCUP
      62.33   675.10

NEW TAM (MILLY'S)
      62.35   66.04   404.36

MR COGHLAN
      62.35   66.06

LOUGH OWEL PICNIC
      62.35   65.40   66.08

        ** Young student (Bannon)   62.36   21.41 **

Blazes BOYLAN'S SEASIDE GIRLS
      62.36   66.15+   67.06+   109.05   180.21   274.13+   281.22+
      285.20   371.32   372.32   414.38   542.18   577.14

His own MOUSTACHECUP, sham crown Derby
      62.37   675.07   677.01   694.31   780.15

SILLY MILLY's birthday gift
      62.38   66.15   113.31   694.10

LOVER, SAMUEL (O, Milly Bloom, you are my darling. . .)
  "O Thady Brady"
      63.01
  "The Bowld Sojer"
      297.13   588.24
  "The Low-Backed Car"
      311.07   665.19+
  "Handy Andy"
      530.04
  "The Girl I Left Behind Me" (G)
      (191.01)
  "The Birth of St. Patrick" (G)
      (307.39)

Poor old PROFESSOR GOODWIN . . . a courteous old chap
  Courtesy
      63.05   747.25
  Hat
      63.07   155.30
  Concerts
      156.10++   268.14+   745.19   747.22+   (642.32)
  Other references
      284.32   575.01+   731.26   775.21

Her cream (MOLLY'S CREAM)
      63.13   65.08   177.19+   675.21   677.05   780.17

        ** Set the brasses jingling   63.19   56.27 **

** Torn envelope   63.24   61.37   **

** Bold hand. Marion   63.28   61.37   **

He's BRINGING THE PROGRAMME
    63.29   92.11

MOZART, W. A.
  Don Giovanni
    "La ci darem la mano"
     63.31   64.04   77.15+   93.25   120.35   197.05   441.08+
     445.23+   517.16++   536.25   622.16+   780.18
    "Don Giovanni, a cenar teco"
     179.35++   496.25
    Other references
     196.29   223.38   282.11+   467.10   561.21+   661.27
    "Twelfth Mass"
     82.17   661.09
  The Magic Flute
    282.39

With J. C. DOYLE
    63.31   93.07

LOVE'S OLD SWEET SONG
    63.31   75.18+   274.06   364.40   445.07   491.02   518.11
    706.26   754.40   762.25   763.09   763.22

** (Dignam's) funeral   63.37   57.11   **

He took up a leg of (MOLLY'S) soiled DRAWERS from the bed
    63.40   375.02   730.17   746.03++   750.19   768.34   780.20++

It MUST HAVE FELL DOWN
    64.03   653.37

** Voglio e non verrei   64.04   63.31   **

Wonder if she pronounces that right (MOLLY'S PRONUNCIATION)
  The problem
    64.04   120.34   441.12   622.16
  The solution
    658.41   695.12   696.04   774.28   779.23

THE ORANGE-KEYED CHAMBERPOT
    64.07   547.14   653.38   730.33   769.41++   771.29   779.06

To search the text with the HAIRPIN (MOLLY'S)
    64.12   156.29   774.01   759.07

```
        ** Met him what?                      64.14++    50.13  **

FROM THE GREEK
      64.20      744.36

O, ROCKS!
      64.22      154.09+     284.41      473.12     (737.25+)

The same YOUNG EYES
      64.24      367.10+     382.17      542.19

DOYLE, LUKE
   Charades at Dolphin's Barn
      64.24      158.31      377.16     705.08     747.06     747.15     771.10
   Matrimonial gift
      707.25+
   See also      280.17
```

<u>RUBY, THE PRIDE OF THE RING</u>
```
      64.25+       91.12     454.14++    535.16     539.12     653.35     751.41
      (445.23)   (482.25)
```

```
Trapeze at HENGLER'S (CIRCUS)
      64.30      624.11      696.20

        ** Dignam's soul                      64.33      57.11  **

Get another of PAUL DE KOCK's
      64.39      269.13      282.36     465.31     538.06     765.11+

Must get that CAPEL STREET (LIBRARY) book renewed (STARK-MUNRO LETTERS)
      64.42      229.10      652.20     708.30     711.20      See also 300.28

        ** The sluggish cream                 65.08      63.13  **
```

The <u>BATH OF THE NYMPH</u> over the bed
```
      65.11+      341.31+     544.33++    727.34     753.23+

Given away with the Easter number of PHOTO BITS
      65.12      546.02      755.01

        ** A smell of burn                    65.23      55.04  **

Stubbing his toes against the BROKEN COMMODE
      65.27      547.11      730.27     769.42

        ** Young student (Bannon)             65.40      21.41  **

        ** Picnic (at Lough Owel)             65.40      62.35  **

Dearest PAPLI
      66.01       89.20      380.02     427.05     542.21     544.09     720.27
      721.07
```

      ** My new tam   66.04   62.35 **

      ** The photo business   66.05   21.42 **

      ** Mr Coghlan   66.06   62.35 **

All the BEEF TO THE HEELS were in
    66.08   168.14   372.21   397.20   See also 166.07

      ** Lough Owel . . . picnic   66.08   62.35 **

      ** Young student . . . Bannon   66.13+   21.41 **

      ** Those seaside girls   66.15+   62.36 **

      ** Silly Milly   66.15   62.36 **

To knock up MRS THORNTON
    66.23   162.05   494.21

BLOOM, RUDY (she knew from the first poor little Rudy wouldn't live)
  As defective child
    66.25+   96.04+   774.35
  Would be eleven now
    66.26   609.20   774.34
  Other references
    87.20   89.03   111.13   151.29   168.04   285.05+   338.06
    390.31   414.01   609.20++   701.08   736.11

      ** Young student (Bannon)   66.33   21.41 **

      ** Slim legs running   66.38   61.32 **

DESTINY (FATE, KISMET)
  Destiny
    66.39   249.19   373.28   390.33   482.25   580.29   692.03
  Fate
    275.19+   289.26   348.33   381.09   528.10   562.11   626.32
    654.07
  Kismet
    289.26   452.13   468.26   (376.07)
  Other
    168.32   (67.18)

On the <u>ERIN'S KING</u>
    67.03   152.32   379.28   550.19   630.38   (654.20)   (271.19)
    See also   271.19

      ** The Kish   67.03   44.13 **

Not a bit FUNKY. Her pale BLUE SCARF loose in the wind
    67.04   379.32   542.18

      ** All dimpled cheeks and curls   67.06+   62.36 **

That bee or bluebottle here Whitmonday (BLOOM'S BEE STING)
    68.18   97.28   163.06   378.21   386.30   425.14   710.38+
    764.35   (515.35)

      ** My hat   68.20+   56.40 **

      ** Picking up the letters   68.23   61.35 **

DRAGO'S shopbell ringing
    68.23   180.41   275.13

Queer, I WAS JUST THINKING that moment (COINCIDENCE)
    68.24   92.20   165.05   165.30   180.41   263.42   275.03+
    427.05   450.16   624.13   637.28   646.39   662.12   675.35+
    685.09+   685.16

(BOYLAN'S) brown BRILLIANTINED HAIR over his collar
    68.24   180.41

      ** James Stephens   68.27   43.25 **

O'BRIEN (G)
    68.27   (93.11)   (716.37)

      ** That fellow Dlugacz   68.28   56.11 **

      ** Agenda what is it?   68.28   60.16 **

      ** Now, my miss   68.28   59.30 **

ENTHUSIAST
    68.29   164.10+   288.24+

BLOOM'S DEFECATION
    68.30++   728.36   See also 70.01

      ** For (Dignam's) funeral   68.31   57.11 **

      ** The king . . counting house   68.35   68.07 **

      ** Nobody. (Next door girl)   68.36   59.04 **

      ** Our prize titbit   68.39++   67.39 **

THREE POUNDS THIRTEEN AND SIX
    69.02   69.17   108.35

Bring on PILES again
    69.08   376.31

      ** Three pounds thirteen and six   69.17   69.02 **

I'm SWELLED AFTER that CABBAGE
    69.24   103.40

Morning after the BAZAAR DANCE. . . . That was the first night (she saw Boylan)
       69.27   92.32   167.19+   368.35   374.31   530.06

When May's band played PONCHIELLI'S DANCE OF THE HOURS
       69.28+   374.31   576.04++   (138.26+)

Her FANsticks clicking
       69.30   527.04++   541.03   (763.15)

POETICAL IDEA pink, then golden, then grey, then black
       69.39   113.26   166.11   280.23   352.21   See also 166.08

        ** He tore away half   70.01   (48.12)   (61.37) **

        ** The prize story   70.01   67.39 **

WIPED HIMSELF with it
       70.01   458.19   459.23+   See also 68.30

        ** Lightened and cooled in limb   70.05   61.22 **

        ** What time is (Dignam's) funeral   70.07+   57.11 **

        ** Bells of George's Church   70.10+   57.09 **

The OVERTONE following through the air. . . . Poor Dignam!
       70.14   474.05

LOTUS EATERS

SIR JOHN ROGERSON'S QUAY
     71.01   240.14

Could have given that ADDRESS too. (for receiving answers to advertisements)
     71.03   See   72.30

          ** Listlessly holding her caskhoop   71.08   18.05   **

          ** Come home to ma, da   71.11   (42.15)   **

          ** At eleven (Dignam's funeral)   71.14+   57.11   **

Daresay CORNY KELLEHER bagged that job
     71.15   89.24+   90.05   98.18   100.41#   163.18   221.28
     224.33#   301.42+   320.29   321.41   324.17   339.20   579.11
     585.28+   603.25#   614.41   647.34+

With my TOORALOOM TOORALOOM tay
     71.17+   106.08   491.07   604.23   608.08+

          ** Get some from Tom Kernan   71.24   67.24   **

TOM KERNAN
     71.24   90.01   90.39+   99.28#   161.21   172.11   238.03
     239.13#   252.12   257.17   276.34#   470.01   483.28+   647.39
     704.19   726.34   729.32   773.26+   See also   91.04   91.07

          ** Funeral (Dignam's)   71.25   57.11   **

          ** His high grade ha   71.29+   56.40   **

          ** Card behind the headband   71.31   56.41   **

          ** Snaky lianas   71.36   46.16   **

Those CINGHALESE lobbing around in the sun
       71.37   374.38

In DOLCE FAR NIENTE
       71.38   660.14

Flowers of idleness (BYRON)
       71.40   (124.01)

Hothouse in BOTANIC GARDENS
       71.41   108.29

Sensitive plants (SHELLEY)
       71.42   (184.10)

            ** The dead sea   72.03   61.13 **

Because the WEIGHT of the water. . . . the VOLUME is equal of the weight?
   (ARCHIMEDES' LAW)
       72.05+   181.27   282.30+   672.04   See also 213.28

VANCE in high school. . . . teaching
       72.08   376.23

THIRTYTWO FEET PER SECOND, per second. LAW OF FALLING BODIES (ISAAC NEWTON)
       72.10++   152.29   486.24   528.17   550.11   (282.31)

            ** How did she walk   72.14   59.04 **

            ** The folded Freeman   72.16   57.36 **

TOO LATE BOX
       72.21   528.15

            ** He handed the card   72.22+   56.41 **

While the (WESTLAND ROW) POSTMISTRESS searched a pigeonhole
       72.24   586.28

He . . . glanced rapidly at the typed envelope (of MARTHA'S LETTER)
   Envelope (later torn)
       72.30   73.09+   79.19   81.35   91.27   586.08
       See also   48.12   61.37
   Letter
       72.34   77.10   77.32++   91.27+   182.11   279.13   368.08+
       380.23   414.31   721.11++   722.22   735.11   See also   71.03
   I do wish I could punish you for that
       77.36+   83.02   280.06   368.18   (535.14)
   I called you naughty boy
       77.36++   160.12   168.07   275.06   279.22+   288.17   377.16
       381.37   382.14
   I do not like that other world
       77.36   115.06+   160.13   279.24   381.36   581.16

Please tell me what is the real meaning of that word
    77.37   160.14   381.36
Are you not happy in your home
    77.38   263.34   277.33   377.15
I often think of the beautiful name you have
    78.01   275.04   285.23   See also 72.31
When will we meet
    78.01   274.13
Write me a long letter
    78.04   279.21
Do not deny my request
    78.07   81.23
Before my patience are exhausted
    78.07   91.29   279.25
Then I will tell you all
    78.08   83.01   168.32   279.23   372.34
I have such a bad headache today
    78.09   79.01   368.08
Do tell me what kind of perfume does your wife use. I want to know
    78.12++   79.03   85.04   123.10   160.14   274.15   275.24
    280.07   382.16   See also 350.13   374.29

HENRY FLOWER, Esq.
    72.31   77.32++   79.23   86.40   91.20+   263.33   279.12++
    285.23   288.17   290.19   327.27   373.36   455.19++   492.31
    498.24   517.15++   522.13++   536.26   544.09   627.16   714.32+
    721.11   722.22   735.12   (670.01)
Don Miguel (Poldo) de la Flora
    759.35   778.07
See also   49.33   72.30   73.11   782.18

      ** Old Tweedy's regiment   72.36   56.32 **

      ** Royal Dublin Fusiliers   72.38   47.18 **

That must be WHY THE WOMEN GO AFTER THEM. UNIFORM
    72.39   456.01

      ** Maude Gonne   72.40   43.14 **

      ** Griffith   72.41   43.08 **

Griffith's paper (THE UNITED IRISHMAN)
    72.41   334.06   See also 43.08

Overseas or halfseasover (BRITISH) EMPIRE
    73.02   133.24+   329.18+   334.20   409.11   594.29   641.13+
    See also 18.33   20.34   30.35

      ** Never see him (Edward VII)   73.04   31.15 **

A mason, yes (FREEMASONRY)
    73.05   105.22   177.28+   182.34   300.13   445.03   456.18+
    498.27   501.10(G)   526.11   585.06   590.21+   596.24   599.01
    609.13+   748.35   772.24

Curse your noisy PUGNOSE (TRAMCAR DRIVER'S)
       74.29   160.37   368.19   435.17   436.02   538.19   586.30

               ** Paradise and the peri   74.30   45.12 **

Well, what are you GAPING AT?
       74.33   604.12   748.19

               ** The newspaper baton   74.41   57.36 **

What is home without/ PLUMTREE'S POTTED MEAT?
       75.02   446.25
   Under the obituaries
       154.40   171.32+   684.05+
   Boylan's gift
       227.13   675.12   731.15   741.32
   See also   145.03++

My missus has just got an ENGAGEMENT (M'COY'S WIFE)
       75.05   76.10+   234.08   234.20

               ** Valise tack again   75.07   67.24 **

A swagger affair in the ULSTER HALL, BELFAST
       75.11   76.16   382.09   747.38   749.20   See also   75.23

WHO'S GETTING IT UP?
       75.12   172.26++

               ** Mrs Marion Bloom   75.14   31.37 **

Not UP yet (MOLLY)
       75.14   93.24

               ** Queen was in her bedroom   75.14   68.07 **

Blackened court cards laid along her thigh by sevens (MOLLY'S CARDS)
       75.16   774.41+   776.10   778.08

               ** Torn strip of envelope   75.17   61.37 **

               ** Love's/ Old/ Sweet/ Song/   75.18+   63.31 **

It's a kind of a tour, don't you see? (MOLLY-BOYLAN TOUR)
       75.23+   92.37+   172.24   319.21+   733.01   747.37+   763.10+
       (627.02+)   (658.40+)   See also   75.11

               ** My name at the funeral   75.33   67.24 **

               ** The funeral (Dignam's)   75.33   57.11 **

               ** Drowning case   75.34   4.28 **

               ** At Sandycove   75.34   12.19 **

** Into the newspaper   77.11++   57.36   **

** Voglio e non. . . .   77.15+   63.31   **

A wise tabby, a blinking SPHINX
    77.25   560.06

MOHAMMED cut a piece out of his mantel (sic.) not to wake her
    77.26   297.08   387.09

When I went to that old DAME'S SCHOOL. . . . MRS ELLIS'S
    77.28   682.28   712.13

** A yellow flower   77.30++   73.11   **

** Dear Henry (Martha's letter)   77.32++   72.31   **

** The flower   78.14   73.11   **

** Weak joy   78.24   60.01   **

Could MEET one Sunday AFTER THE ROSARY
    78.27   81.23   263.36   (80.23)

THANK YOU
    78.27   263.27   See also 130.24

Those two SLUTS that night IN THE COOMBE
    78.37   79.08   167.31   552.27

O, MARY LOST THE PIN OF HER DRAWERS
    78.38++   81.18   279.23+   368.38   553.02   See also   40.24

** Such a bad headache   79.01   72.30   **

** What perfume does   79.03   72.30   **

MARTHA, MARY. I saw that PICTURE somewhere (sisters of Lazarus)
    79.06++   117.29   368.41   535.31

** Sluts in the Coombe   79.08   78.37   **

Like the HOLE IN THE WALL AT ASHTOWN
    79.15   672.16

The TROTTING MATCHES
    79.16   768.03

** Envelope, tore it . . . into shreds   79.19   72.30   **

** Henry Flower   79.23   72.31   **

LORD IVEAGH once cashed a sevenfigure checque for a million
    79.24   283.25   299.32

LORD ARDILAUN has to change his shirt four times a day
    79.27+   299.32

      ** Twopence a pint   79.29+   58.31 **

      ** Barrels bumped   79.36+   49.32 **

      ** Flowing . . . flowers . . . froth   79.38   49.33 **

      ** Took the card   79.42   56.41 **

      ** Work M'Coy for a pass   80.02   67.24 **

      ** Pass to Mullingar   80.02   67.22 **

Sermon by the very reverend JOHN CONMEE S. J.
    80.03   80.13+   190.01   219.01#   225.01   226.13   242.33
    246.10   415.01   416.11+   561.22+   579.08   690.04
    See also   11.22   135.18

Saint PETER CLAVER AND THE AFRICAN MISSION
    80.04   81.29   223.02+

Prefer an ounce of opium (OPIUM-POPPIES)
    80.06   84.27   108.28   473.25   485.16   (80.35)

GLADSTONE, W.E. (Prayers for the conversion of)
    80.07   434.01   716.41   721.03

In the (NATIONAL) MUSEUM
  Buddha
    80.10   192.03   297.17   508.02   771.35   (185.38)
  Goddessses
    176.25+   183.14   201.04+   380.22   490.15   637.29   653.11
    729.34   753.14   (727.03)
  Bloom's attempt to see anal hole
    176.38   201.11   259.41   285.34   551.02
  Other references
    198.20   729.01
  See also   176.26

Clever idea SAINT PATRICK   the shamrock
    80.12   169.26   198.28   200.12   307.40   323.09   332.22
    333.41   704.18   773.28

MARTIN CUNNINGHAM knows him
    80.13   87.01#   121.11   219.06   246.01#   288.12   303.16
    313.05+   333.16   336.14#   339.18   469.30   568.26+   626.33
    647.37   704.18   773.28
  Twirling his beard
    90.01+   90.37   94.10   246.09   247.25

His face like Shakespeare's
    96.27   568.26   See also 117.23

     ** Work him about . . . Molly   80.14   67.24 **

That FATHER FARLEY who looked a fool but wasn't
    80.15   490.22+

BLUB LIPS (NIGGERLIPS)
    80.19   222.42   254.38   371.23   443.27

     ** Lap it up like milk   80.20   41.18 **

     ** To be next some girl   80.23   (78.27) **

Who is my neighbour? (THE GOOD SAMARITAN)
    80.24   393.19   467.16   613.03   See also 122.29   333.24

In their CRIMSON HALTERS
    80.26   81.01   81.25   456.11   See also 184.02

THE PRIEST WENT ALONG BY THEM . . . holding the thing in his hands
    80.28++   154.23

Corpus. Body (CORPUS IN PARADISUM; CORPUS MEUM)
    80.34   104.25   277.27   599.26

Good idea THE LATIN. STUPEFIES THEM FIRST
    80.35   103.35   284.06   (80.06)

Why the CANNIBALS cotton to it
    80.37   171.35   646.25

     ** Their blind masks   80.39   7.30 **

     ** Newspaper (Freeman)   80.42   57.36 **

     ** Their crimson halters   81.02   80.26 **

     ** In the same swim   81.09   56.38 **

     ** They do   81.09   37.19 **

     ** Not so lonely   81.10   49.04 **

LOURDES cure
    81.12   145.32   552.21

WATERS OF OBLIVION
    81.12   412.34   724.37

The KNOCK APPARITION
    81.12   552.21

     ** Lulls all pain   81.15   5.31 **

WAKE THIS TIME NEXT YEAR
    81.15   (377.23)

      ** Lost the pin of his   81.18   78.38   **

I. N. R. I.?. . . . IRON NAILS RAN IN
    81.20+   151.24

I. H. S. . . . I HAVE SINNED. . . . I HAVE SUFFERED
    81.20   154.23   498.16   544.11   551.16

      ** Meet . . . after the rosary   81.23   78.27   **

      ** Do not deny my request   81.23   72.30   **

      ** The light behind her   81.24   38.35   **

      ** Ribbon around her neck   81.25   80.26   **

THE INVINCIBLES (PHOENIX PARK MURDERS--JAMES CAREY)
    81.27   136.04++   138.01+   163.19   304.30   305.11   621.37
    629.09++   641.41++   See also 31.22   136.12   170.41

      ** Peter Claver   81.29   80.04   **

      ** The flower (Martha's)   81.34   73.11   **

      ** Tear up that envelope   81.35   72.30   **

CHALICE . . . TOSSED OFF THE DREGS SMARTLY
    81.37   267.07   (599.13++)

GUINNESS'S PORTER
    81.39   117.17   131.20   145.34   152.15+   240.35   276.27
    295.38   299.31+   332.16   382.01   425.20   492.07   532.28
    534.08

      ** Cantrell and Cochrane's   81.41   76.21   **

OLD GLYNN
    82.06   288.29   499.06

(ST. FRANCIS XAVIER CHURCH) in Gardiner street
    82.08   219.03   222.01   661.20

The STABAT MATER of Rossini. . . . Quis est homo!
    82.09+   282.22   661.16   748.33

FATHER BERNARD VAUGHAN's sermon first
    82.10   219.29++

Christ or PILATE
    82.10   131.24   219.14

MERCADANTE: SEVEN LAST WORDS
      82.16   282.22   290.34   342.24   661.08

        ** Mozart's twelfth mass   82.17   63.31 **

        ** Those old popes   82.18   3.34 **

        ** Palestrina for example (T)   82.19   21.03 **

Having EUNUCHS in their choir. . . . strong BASSES
      82.22+   270.39+   283.39

O GOD, OUR REFUGE AND OUR STRENGTH
      82.37(G)   426.28++

        ** Joseph   82.40   41.15 **

        ** I will tell you all   83.01   72.30 **

PENANCE. Punish me, please (BLOOM'S VIEW)
      83.02   379.26

        ** Punish me, please   83.02   77.36 **

WALLS HAVE EARS
      83.06   443.06

He HAD HIS ANSWER PAT for everything
      83.17   398.17

BLESSED MICHAEL, ARCHANGEL, DEFEND US. . . . SNARES OF THE DEVIL
      83.22+(G) 427.06+

        ** Thrust Satan down   83.25   50.25 **

        ** Spirits who wander   83.27   (9.22) **

Better be SHOVING ALONG
      83.30   285.13   (607.14)

BROTHER BUZZ
      83.30   495.05   498.06

A car of PRESCOTT'S DYEWORKS
      83.42   180.14   372.08   775.33

Better get that LOTION made up
      84.03++   168.26   183.39   281.24   286.36   375.28   440.16
      750.43

Sweny's in Lincoln place (F. W. SWENY AND CO.)
      84.04   440.25+   676.08   751.02

HAMILTON LONG'S (chemists)
      84.05   551.11

Founded in the year of THE FLOOD
    84.06   395.17+   757.13

HUGUENOT churchyard near there
    84.06   168.20   175.31   188.21   259.39   326.18   514.06
    772.12

       ** Forgot that latchkey   84.09   11.35 **

       ** The funeral affair   84.10   57.11 **

AQ. DIST. FOL. LAUR. TE. VIRID
    84.20   (488.12)

Overdose of LAUDANUM
    84.26   412.21

LOVEPHILTRES
    84.26   521.20

       ** Paragoric poppysyrup   84.27   80.06 **

Then ORANGEFLOWER water
    84.36   85.05   440.16   521.20

And WHITE WAX also
    84.38   358.33   440.16   521.20   (348.18+)

DARKNESS OF HER EYES. . . . SPANISH
    84.40   275.26   277.30   See also 26.01   285.38   373.23

Looking at me, the SHEET UP TO HER EYES
    84.40   (281.27)

       ** Old queen's sons   85.01   43.13 **

       ** What perfume does your?   85.04   72.30 **

PEAU D'ESPAGNE
    85.04   762.17

       ** Tha orangeflower   85.05   84.36 **

Time to get a bath (BLOOM'S BATH)
    85.06#   89.38   91.28   101.22   380.22   676.14   711.14
    728.37
  Do it in the bath
    85.09   368.17

       ** Massage. . . . Nicer if a girl   85.07   43.16 **

       ** In your navel   85.08   (38.01) **

       ** Funeral be rather glum   85.11   57.11 **

Mr Bloom raised a CAKE (OF SOAP) to his nostrils
       85.17#   87.26   100.30+   123.01+   183.39   286.35   375.27+
       437.07   440.21+   498.28   613.23   672.42+

          ** The newspaper baton   85.22++   57.35   **

          ** Bantam Lyon's voice   85.24++   74.02   **

WHAT'S THE BEST NEWS?
       85.25   225.12   243.38

That FRENCH HORSE. . . . MAXIMUM THE SECOND
       85.34+   573.14   648.30

Ascot. GOLD CUP
       85.40+   128.03   173.27   178.41   325.29++   345.09   379.16
       604.09   647.20   648.18+   675.36   717.28+   764.38
       See also   125.10

I was just going to THROW IT AWAY
       85.42   676.13   See also 151.07

I'll risk it, he said (TIP ON THROWAWAY)
       86.07   179.10+   335.18   534.11   See also 325.31+

          ** Towards Conway's Corner   86.08   74.03   **

SCUT
       86.08   341.12

          ** Fleshpots of Egypt   86.15   41.32   **

CYCLIST doubled up
       86.19   155.18   237.16   254.19   358.16   376.16   579.15

"JOHNNY I HARDLY KNEW YE" (doubled up like a cod in a pot)
       86.19   271.38   579.15

There's HORNBLOWER standing at the porter's lodge
       86.23+   254.26   497.09+   578.21   586.10   773.18

          ** Take a turn in there on the nod   86.24   67.24   **

The KILDARE STREET CLUB
       86.29   240.06   244.41   452.20

DONNYBROOK FAIR more in their line
       86.30   496.22

WALLACE, W.V. (In the stream of life we trace. . . .)
   Maritana (Opera)
     "In Happy Moments Day by Day"
       86.32   153.30   155.42   417.23   (164.17++) (394.14+)

"There is a Flower that Bloometh"
  358.18   461.28   517.28   759.37
"Farewell, My Gallant Captain"
  651.26
"O Maritana! Wildwood Flower"
  774.17+
Other references
  626.20+
  See also   778.05
"The winds that waft my sighs to thee"
  778.05

     ** His navel   86.39   38.01 **

     ** Floating . . . flower   86.40   49.33   72.31 **

     ** Languid   86.42   49.36 **

HADES

  ** Dignam's funeral   87.01#   57.11 **

  ** Martin Cunningham   87.01#   80.13 **

Mr Power (JACK POWER)
    87.03#   162.36   238.34   246.11#   336.16#   470.01   647.37
    704.18   773.35+

Thanking her stars she was PASSED OVER
    87.16   (122.15)

Slop about in SLIPPERSLAPPERS
    87.18   475.19   586.16

Molly and MRS FLEMING making the bed
    87.20   89.39   93.24   675.26   764.28   768.18   768.36

  ** Molly and Mrs Fleming making the bed 87.20   66.25 **

  ** Our windingsheet   87.21   21.14 **

  ** That soap   87.26   85.17 **

RATTLED ROLLING over the cobbled causeway
    87.36   See   96.12

  ** Ringsend   87.39   41.09 **

IRISHTOWN
    87.40   147.06   242.08   372.39   651.43   656.13

  ** A wide hat   88.06   17.08 **

  ** That Mulligan cad   88.15++   3.01 **

VIRGIL
  The Aeneid
    His fidus Achates
      88.15   614.22
    Other references
      111.29   144.25   315.01   617.35   (99.09)
  Eclogues
    149.24
  Georgics
    390.04
  Personal reference
    149.20

      ** His aunt Sally   88.17   38.28   **

      ** Drunken little cost-drawer   88.18   38.34   **

      ** Crissie . . lump of dung   88.19   39.13   **

The WISE CHILD THAT KNOWS HER OWN FATHER
    88.19   273.08   413.27   (623.16)
    See also   18.37   21.09   152.39

GOULDING, COLLIS AND WARD he calls the firm
    88.23   232.11   252.22   266.10   269.35   287.33   289.19
    See also   38.34
  Collis and Ward
    240.42   299.16   446.30

Waltzing in Stamer street with IGNATIUS GALLAHER
    88.25   135.29++

The LANDLADY'S TWO HATS PINNED ON HIS HEAD
    88.26   446.29

      ** That backache of his   88.28   39.26   **

He's IN WITH A LOWDOWN CROWD
    88.31   262.35

A contaminated BLOODY . . . RUFFIAN
    88.32   302.35

      ** His blessed mother   88.34   47.39   **

      ** Or his aunt   88.35   5.16   **

      ** If little Rudy had lived   89.03   66.25   **

      ** His voice in the house   89.04   38.11   **

Walking beside Molly in an ETON SUIT
    89.05   609.21

** Me in his eyes. . . . from me   89.05+   21.09   **

That morning in RAYMOND TERRACE
        89.07   772.10

THE TWO DOGS at it by the wall
        89.08   375.09   749.36   778.29   See also   44.33

        ** Milly . . . Mullingar   89.18+   21.42   **

        ** Dearest Papli   89.20   66.01   **

        ** Young student   89.20   21.41   **

Their four TRUNKS SWAYING
        89.22   90.36   (49.36)

DO YOU FOLLOW ME?
        89.27   604.10   604.24   606.18

        ** Glad I took that bath   89.38   85.06   **

        ** Mrs Fleming   89.39   87.20   **

        ** Did Tom Kernan turn up?   90.01   71.24   **

        ** Martin Cunningham   90.01   80.13   **

He's behind with NED LAMBERT
        90.03#   123.15#   225.23   230.04#   339.21   240.20   241.02
        276.39+   320.03#   470.01   647.40   704.19

He's behind with . . . (JOE) HYNES
        90.04#   118.20++   180.13   292.06++   317.11#   339.21   375.30
        381.15   472.01+   486.32   488.20+   586.24   647.26   647.41
        704.20   739.02   See also 119.22

        ** And Corny Kelleher himself?   90.05   71.15   **

        ** M'Coy   90.07   67.24   **

        ** Milly never got it   90.16   21.42   **

Poor old ATHOS! Be good to Athos, Leopold
        90.20+   528.23   723.39+   See also   44.33   76.26

        ** My last wish   90.20   76.26   **

        ** Thy will be done   90.21   6.33   **

        ** My boots were creaking   90.27   56.16   **

        ** Their trunks swayed   90.36   89.22   **

        ** Twirled . . . his beard   90.37   80.13   **

```
        ** I tore up the envelope?              91.27        72.30   **

        ** Read it in the bath                  91.28+       85.06   **

        ** My patience are exhausted            91.29        72.30   **

        ** The hazard. . . . An hour ago        91.30        76.41   **

ANTIENT CONCERT ROOMS
     91.40      259.25

Past the QUEEN'S THEATRE
     92.04      167.36       343.32

Hoardings.  EUGENE STRATTON
     92.05      222.41       254.37       443.18

        ** Mrs Bandman Palmer                   92.05        76.23   **

        ** See Leah tonight                     92.06        76.23   **

I SAID I
     92.06      735.19       739.01       740.13     See also  92.09

BOUCICAULT, DION (or The Lily of Killarney)
  The Lily of Killarney
     92.06      295.15       297.14       297.18     311.10    354.40      380.20
     426.02      426.19       642.08       747.36
  The Shaughran
     163.19
  Arah-Na-Pogue
     297.13
  The Colleen Bawn
     297.14      311.10       426.19       642.08
  Personal reference
     167.36

BENEDICT, SIR JULIUS
  The Lily of Killarney
     92.06      295.15       297.14       297.18     311.10    354.40      380.20
     426.02      426.19       642.08       747.36
  The Colleen Bawn
     297.14      311.10       426.19       642.08
  The Bride of Venice
     285.20

ELSTER GRIMES OPERA COMPANY
     92.07+     627.18

The GAIETY (THEATRE)
     92.09      284.26       636.35       664.25     678.30    729.37      731.31
     735.18      740.14       767.13       769.12
     See also    76.23        92.06        271.13

        ** Work a pass                          92.09        67.24   **
```

    ** Coming in the afternoon   92.11   63.29 **

    ** Plasto's   92.12   56.40 **

SIR PHILIP CRAMPTON'S memorial FOUNTAIN bust
    92.12   170.36

    ** That moment I was thinking   92.20   68.24 **

From the door of the RED BANK (RESTAURANT)
    92.21   175.03   See also 175.02

PASSED
    92.22   99.38   100.10

FASCINATION (sexual)
    92.25   163.42   165.17   361.15   477.16   537.01   540.28
    722.32

INSTINCT
    92.26   174.40   360.30   378.02   516.31   693.36   694.14
    See also   350.07

    ** Night of the dance dressing   92.32   69.27 **

Shift stuck between the cheeks behind (MOLLY'S SHIFT)
    92.33   226.02   289.33   375.03   747.37   763.37   780.20

    ** Concert tour   92.37+   75.23 **

    ** Down to the county Clare   92.42   76.26 **

    ** J. C. Doyle   93.07   63.31 **

And MADAME
    93.09   93.24+

SMITH O'BRIEN. . . . Must be his deathday
    93.11+   599.03

Four BOOTLACES for a penny
    93.17   538.06

    ** Tweedy, crown solicitor   93.19   (56.32) **

That silk hat. . . . Relics of old decency ("THE HAT MY FATHER WORE")
    93.20   378.28

Terrible COMEDOWN, poor wretch
    93.21   268.36   274.24   283.22   543.22

Kicked about like SNUFF AT A WAKE
    93.22   378.28

O'CALLAGHAN on his last legs
     93.22+   645.36

       ** And Madame   93.24+   93.09 **

       ** Twenty past eleven. Up   93.24   75.14 **

       ** Mrs Fleming is in to clean   93.24   87.20 **

       ** Voglio e non vorrei (Mozart)   93.25   63.31 **

A THRUST. A THROSTLE. There is a word throstle that expressed that
     93.28   256.24   272.34   276.32

Not pleasant for (POWER'S) WIFE
     93.34   773.36

Yes, it was CROFTON met him
     93.36   (336.16)

Barmaid in JURY'S (HOTEL)
     93.38   332.22

Or the MOIRA, was it? (pub)
     93.38   518.24

       ** The hugecloaked Liberator's form   93.39   31.18 **

REUBEN J. DODD
     93.41++   152.23   183.01   244.04++   252.23   267.20+   322.21
     474.22   497.27+   506.07+   (313.11)   See also   4.28
    Barabbas
     94.27   245.35
    One and eightpence too much
     95.07   288.11   452.33   539.34
    See also   4.28

The corner of ELVERY'S ELEPHANT HOUSE
     94.01   272.05

As the carriage passed (SIR JOHN) GRAY'S STATUE
     94.08   150.06   276.18

       ** He caressed his beard   94.10   80.13 **

He determined to send him to the ISLE OF MAN
     94.21   94.33   120.32   (541.04)

That confirmed bloody HOBBLEDEHOY, is it?
     94.23   548.26

       ** He tried to drown   94.26+   4.28 **

       ** Drown Barabbas!   94.27   93.41 **

They used to drive a STAKE of wood THROUGH HIS HEART in the grave
       96.29   111.18

          ** Broken (heart)   96.30   95.22 **

          ** Found . . . clutching rushes   96.31   (40.07) **

And that awful drunkard of a wife of his (MARTIN CUNNINGHAM'S WIFE)
       96.33+   568.29

SHOULDER TO THE WHEEL (Sisyphus)
       96.36   (587.30)

THE GEISHA (JONES, SIDNEY). And they call me the jewel of Asia/ of
   Asia/ the geisha
       96.40   215.31   327.11   410.33   509.23++   569.03

          ** Rattle his bones   97.01+   96.12 **

          ** That afternoon at the inquest   97.02+   76.26 **

          ** The letter. For my son   97.08   76.26 **

          ** No more pain   97.09   5.31 **

          ** Wake no more   97.09   (25.25) **

THE GORDON BENNETT (AUTOMOBILE RACE)
       97.15   98.27   99.33   427.33   536.26   647.19

          ** A rollicking rattling song   97.19   96.12 **

HAS ANYBODY HERE SEEN KELLY? . . . He's as bad as old Antonio
       97.20+   112.14   624.28   632.10   See also 631.27

HANDEL, G. F. (Dead March from Saul)
   Saul
       97.21   555.02
   The Messiah
       183.07   479.28   499.05   599.32+
   Joshua and Judas Maccabeus
       264.39+

          ** The Mater Misericordiae   97.22   8.27 **

Where old MRS RIORDAN died
       97.25+   174.22   305.41+   490.25   586.21   680.20++   738.05++

Nice young student that was (DIXON)
       97.28   163.06   386.26++   493.28   509.10

          ** Bite the bee gave me   97.28   68.18 **

He's gone over to the lying-in hospital (NATIONAL MATERNITY HOSPITAL)
    97.29   159.01   163.07   373.12   380.21   383.01#   518.25
    696.12   757.37

HUNNH! the drover's voice cried. . . . HUNNH!
    97.38   414.16   415.21

SPRINGERS
    97.40   294.38   399.17

            ** Cuffe sold them   97.41   59.21 **

For Liverpool probably (LIVERPOOL CATTLE TRADE)
    97.41   382.07   399.15

DICKY MEAT
    98.04   114.23

Off the train at CLONSILLA
    98.05   99.22

            ** Tramline . . . to the quays   98.08+   58.03 **

Municipal FUNERAL TRAMS
    98.13   489.24

Like they have in MILAN
    98.13   682.11   724.25

            ** Poor lookout for Corny   98.18   71.15 **

            ** Gordon Bennett Cup   98.27   97.15 **

            ** With wax   98.35   (5.34) **

            ** Drowning their grief   98.39   4.28 **

            ** Tiptop position for a pub   98.40   (58.02) **

Man stood on his dropping barge between clumps of turf (BARGEMAN)
    99.09++   221.35   396.30   (88.15)

            ** Carrion dogs   99.15   44.33 **

            ** Mullingar . . . to see Milly   99.15+   67.22 **

            ** To see Milly   99.15+   21.42 **

WREN had one the other day (AUCTIONEER)
    99.17   543.05   710.15

            ** Clonsilla   99.22   98.05 **

They drove on past BRIAN BOROIMHE (Brian Boru)
    99.25   296.36   678.28   679.05

    ** Better ask Tom Kernan   99.28#   71.24 **

    ** Last lap   99.33   97.15 **

Silent SHAPES . . . WHITE . . . HOLDING OUT CALM HANDS
    99.34   100.23   (108.24)

    ** Passed   99.38   92.22 **

That is where Childs was murdered . . . SAYMOUR BUSHE (CHILDS MURDER CASE)
    100.02+   139.24++   410.27   412.14   412.33+   456.22   465.05
    690.06

MURDERED HIS BROTHER.
    100.05   208.35   412.33

BETTER FOR NINETYNINE GUILTY TO ESCAPE. . . .
    100.08   456.25

MURDERER'S GROUND
    100.10   412.38

    ** It passed darkly   100.10   92.22 **

    ** She mightn't like me to come   100.18   67.22 **

GLASNEVIN CEMETERY
    100.22#   125.17   240.31   598.22   647.29   704.17   723.14

    ** White shapes . . . Vain gestures   100.23   99.34 **

    ** Change that soap now   100.30+   85.17 **

    ** Replacing the newspaper   100.33   57.35 **

    ** Mr. Kernan   100.40++   71.24 **

    ** Corny Kelleher stood   100.41#   71.15 **

He handed one (wreath) to the boy (MASTER PATRICK DIGNAM)
    101.02   101.24   101.40   102.35++   104.33   110.29   112.23
    219.04   234.01   246.01+   250.20#   254.28+   302.06+   355.01
    379.17   568.15   647.35   704.21

Then MOUNT JEROME for the Protestants
    101.12   105.26   108.26   598.23

    ** Fish's face, bloodless   101.19   27.19 **

    ** The mutes shouldered the coffin   101.21   8.36 **

    ** Stepping out of that bath   101.23   85.06 **

    ** The boy   101.24   101.02 **

Who is that beside them? Ah, the brother-in-law (BERNARD CORRIGAN)
      101.25   102.37   104.33   112.24+   250.26   251.25+   647.36
      704.20

            ** Father poisoned. . . . Anniversary   101.31+   76.26   **

A face with DARK thinking EYES (BLOOM'S)
      101.36   217.36   259.37++   413.18   463.28   (34.03)
      See also   26.01   260.19

            ** The youngster   101.40   101.02   **

Martin is trying to get the youngster (Dignam's) into ARTANE
      101.41   219.03   496.26+

There are MORE WOMEN THAN MEN IN THE WORLD
      102.10   580.24

I hope you'll follow him soon. For Hindu widows only (SUTTEE)
      102.11   544.31

            ** The old queen   102.13   43.13   **

ALBERT (of Saxe-Coburg-Gotha)
      102.13+   161.31   330.28

            ** Her son   102.17   31.15   **

            ** Martin . . . to get the whip   102.32+   57.09   **

            ** The eldest boy   102.35++   101.02   **

            ** With the wife's brother   102.37   101.25   **

JOHN HENRY MENTON is behind
      102.38++   115.12++   121.18   158.16   240.41   245.17   247.40
      253.28   299.15   455.16   470.02   473.14   498.25   586.18
      647.36   655.11   704.20   731.26   739.03
  His oyster eyes
      106.33   115.39   160.05   253.29   739.08   See also 165.02
  Bloom shows up at bowls
      106.23   115.16   (422.11)

            ** I often told poor Paddy   102.39+   57.11   **

            ** Both unconscious   103.06   (76.26)   **

CORNY KELLEHER, laying a WREATH at each fore corner
      103.13   104.32   606.26

            ** His unfolded newspaper   103.16   57.36   **

KNELT HIS RIGHT KNEE UPON IT
      103.17   529.17

Balancing with the other a little book against his TOAD'S BELLY
    103.23   473.23

Who'll read the book? I, said the rook ("WHO KILLED COCK ROBIN?")
    103.24   471.13

The priest (FATHER COFFEY)
    103.25++   284.08   473.23+
  His croak
    103.26   277.28   473.27   (283.22)   (507.19)

DOMINE-NAMINE
    103.27   257.04   284.03   284.08   289.39   473.27   (285.15)

BURST sideways like a sheep in clover
    103.30+   292.34   398.28   408.28

With a belly on him like a POISONED PUP
    103.31   277.28

      ** Prayed over in Latin   103.35   80.35 **

CRAPE WEEPERS
    103.36   603.25

      ** Swelled after cabbage   103.40   69.24 **

Must be an infernal lot of bad gas round the place (GRAVE GAS)
    103.41+   108.08

      ** Et ne nos inducas   104.12   6.33 **

      ** In paradisum   104.25   80.34 **

      ** Corny Kelleher gave one wreath   104.32   103.13 **

      ** To the boy   104.33   101.02 **

      ** To the brother-in-law   104.33   101.25 **

      ** Folding the paper again   104.35   57.36 **

      ** The O'Connell circle   104.41   31.18+ **

      ** How many broken hearts   105.02   95.22 **

      ** Her grave   105.04+   5.16 **

      ** Mason, I think   105.22   73.05 **

      ** Mount Jerome   105.26   100.01 **

      ** I am the resurrection   105.31+   96.14 **

That TOUCHES a man's INMOST HEART
      105.31+   310.08

            ** Broken heart   105.36   95.22   **

DAMN THE THING ELSE
      105.39   107.32

COME FORTH. . . ! And he came fifth
      105.42   516.05

            ** With your tooraloom tooraloom   106.08   71.18   **

At MAT DILLON'S in Roundtown
   Menton dances with Molly
      106.19   .
   Bloom bowls with Menton and sees Stephen
      106.23   115.14+   422.05++   680.06   774.40   775.14
   Dillon's lilactree
      115.19   275.24   422.09   680.06   714.18
   Bloom and Molly at
      275.17+   376.41+   542.11
   Dillon's gift clock
      694.16   707.22
   Other references
      377.17   667.27   731.28   758.15+
   See also   115.19

            ** Evening . . . at bowls   106.23   102.38   106.19   **

Yes, he was . . . in WISDOM HELY'S (STATIONERY STORE)
      106.26   114.09   155.01   155.20   263.33   364.10   465.13
      586.19   720.37+   731.32   753.21   772.19   See also 154.25

            ** Some canvassing for ads   106.31   57.35   **

            ** John Henry Menton's large eyes   106.33   102.38   **

JOHN O'CONNELL. . . . He never forgets a friend
      106.37++   473.21++

            ** Puzzling two keys   107.04   11.35   **

            ** Damn the thing else   107.32   105.39   **

Keys: like KEYES'S AD
      107.35+   116.27++   119.37++   129.17+   146.21+   161.18   180.12
      183.08   260.40   323.33+   372.08   380.22   381.15   474.09
      483.25   489.19   586.20   647.39   683.33   728.38   729.31
      775.33   See also   11.35

She disturbed me writing (BLOOM'S LETTER TO MARTHA, to which hers is a reply)
      107.38   739.13

THE SHADOWS OF THE TOMBS WHEN CHURCHYARDS YAWN
     108.04+   445.21

          ** Daniel O 'Connell   108.05   31.18   **

          ** Gas of graves   108.08   103.41   **

Whores in TURKISH graveyards
     108.13   281.26   439.09   644.11   730.19
     See also   85.06   381.12

          ** Love among the tombstones   108.15   43.27   **

ROMEO
     108.15   196.25   333.25

          ** In the midst of death   108.16   96.14   **

          ** With his hand pointing   108.24   (99.34)   **

          ** Mount Jerome   108.26   100.01   **

          ** Poppies . . . produce best opium   108.28   80.06   **

          ** Mastiansky told me   108.28   60.33   **

          ** The Botanic Gardens   108.29   71.41   **

Those JEWS they said KILLED THE CHRISTIAN BOY
     108.31   544.03   690.17++   695.16

          ** Three pounds thirteen and six   108.35   67.39   **

          ** Cells . . . changing about   109.01   50.13   **

          ** Simply swirling   109.04   62.36   **

Peter (ST. PETER)
     109.10   390.12   391.36   393.33   401.04   401.29   562.03

GRAVEDIGGERS IN HAMLET
     109.14   213.04

NEW LEASE ON LIFE
     109.19   627.41

          ** We come to bury Caesar   109.27   25.14   **

Now who is that lankylooking galoot over there in the MACINTOSH?
     109.29   110.10   112.07+   254.35   290.05   333.33   376.07
     427.17+   485.08+   511.24   647.47+   729.23

DEFOE, DANIEL (Say Robinson Crusoe was true to life)
     Robinson Crusoe
     109.36+   153.16   495.17

Moll Flanders
 756.25+
Parody
 398.10-399.31

Every Friday buries a THURSDAY
 109.37   (50.29)   (567.25)

IRISHMAN'S HOUSE IS HIS CASTLE
 110.07   347.12

    ** The chap in the macintosh   110.10   109.29 **

When we lived in LOMBARD STREET WEST (Bloom's home)
 110.15   155.19   166.39   168.03   289.33   372.15   374.17
 667.30   745.23   747.22   772.11   781.23

Must get that grey suit of mine turned by MESIAS
 110.17   279.35   476.05   497.21+   732.32

    ** All suddenly somebody else   110.24   50.13 **

    ** Poor papa went away   110.26   76.26 **

    ** The boy by the gravehead   110.29   101.02 **

    ** Feel no more   110.33   (25.32) **

DONIZETTI, GAETANO (Last act of Lucia)
  Lucia di Lammermoor
   111.02   (297.09)
  La Figlia del Regimento
   269.20

FOSTER, STEPHEN (Shall I never more behold thee?)
  "Gentle Annie"
    111.02
  "Uncle Ned"
    213.12
  Other possible references
    (161.33)   (330.35) (G)

    ** Even Parnell   111.05   35.02 **

Mamma poor mamma (ELLEN HIGGINS)
 111.13   435.27   438.17++   548.26   555.16   682.11   721.10
 (485.12)

    ** And little Rudy   111.13   66.25 **

BY JINGO, that would be awful!
 111.16   535.07

    ** To pierce the heart   111.18   96.29 **

** The dismal fields   111.29   88.15   **

** Put down M'Coy's name too   111.36+   67.24   **

** On the *Freeman* once   111.37   57.36   **

LEAVE HIM UNDER AN OBLIGATION
    112.02   115.40

** Macintosh   112.07+   109.29   **

** Anybody here seen? Kay ee double ell   112.14   97.20   **

** The boy propped his wreath   112.23   101.02   **

** The brother-in-law   112.24+   101.25   **

** His navelcord   112.30   38.01   **

** By the chief's grave   112.35+   35.02   **

** Old Ireland's hearts   113.05   (95.22) **

** I'll be at his grave   113.09   76.26   **

Who KICKED THE BUCKET
    113.14   164.23   580.19

I travelled for CORK LINO
    113.16   253.02   355.08

** Eulogy in a country churchyard   113.18   46.39   **

WORDSWORTH, WILLIAM (Whose is it Wordsworth. . . ?)
    113.19   206.40
  "Matthew"
    207.01
  "The Two April Mornings"
    207.03
  "Grace Darling"
    (376.15)

THOMAS CAMPBELL
    113.19   165.31

Old DR MURREN's (grave)
    113.20   162.08

Better VALUE FOR THE MONEY
    113.25   772.01   See also 265.16

** Flowers are more poetical   113.26   69.39   **

Like stuffed. Like the WEDDING PRESENT ALDERMAN HOOPER gave us
    113.29   694.16   707.26+   731.33

```
        ** Silly-Milly                        113.31      62.38  **

The SACRED HEART that is
  Statue
      113.34+      125.16
  Other references
      438.30       469.15      582.18+    590.16

APOLLO that was
      113.39       419.04

FAITHFUL DEPARTED
      113.41       344.38

        ** How many? (Dante)                  113.41      20.20  **

AS YOU ARE NOW, SO ONCE WERE WE
      113.42       535.22

        ** Wisdom Hely's                       114.09     106.26  **

An OBESE GREY RAT toddled along the side of the crypt
      114.13+      118.25      277.27     284.08     474.16     (412.37)

An OLD STAGER
      114.14       638.13

ROBERT EMMET was buried here by torchlight
      114.18       240.27      305.35     306.24++   655.24
  Last words
      257.23+      290.34++    543.21     550.24+

PICK THE BONES CLEAN
      114.21+      472.15+    (17.13)    (180.22)

        ** Corpse is meat gone bad             114.23      98.04  **

I read in that VOYAGES IN CHINA
      114.24       708.35

        ** Ashes to ashes                      114.28      96.14  **

        ** Drowning . . . the pleasantest      114.30       4.28  **

        ** Saltwhite . . . mush of corpse      114.37      50.07  **

Last time I was here was MRS SINICO's funeral
      114.41       695.21      711.08

        ** Poor papa too                       114.41      76.26  **

        ** The love that kills                 114.42(T)   (6.37) **

        ** Scraping up the earth               114.42     (26.33) **
```

My GHOST will haunt you after death
      115.04   123.18   188.06++   412.22++
      See also   5.32   10.25   18.12   165.02

       ** That other world   115.06+   72.30   **

PLENTY TO SEE AND HEAR AND FEEL YET
      115.06+   242.17

       ** Menton. John Henry   115.12++   102.38 **

       ** Mat Dillon's long ago   115.14   106.19 **

       ** Evening on the bowling green   115.16   102.38 **

Molly and FLOEY DILLON linked
      115.19   377.18   422.15   743.10   758.13+   770.19

Excuse me, sir. . . . YOUR HAT IS A LITTLE CRUSHED
      115.22+   121.18+   655.12

       ** Oyster eyes   115.39   102.38 **

       ** Get the pull over him   115.40   112.02 **

AEOLUS

    ** Nelson's Pillar   116.03   95.09 **

Blackrock, Kingstown . . . Harold's Cross (TRAMCAR ROUTES)
     116.04+   149.09

CLONSKEA
     116.04   586.37

RATHMINES
     116.06   146.19   148.01   149.09+

    ** Sandymount Green   116.06   37.01 **

    ** Ringsend   116.06   41.09 **

His Majesty's vermillion mailcars . . . ROYAL INITIALS, E. R.
     116.18   485.02   See also   31.15

    ** Rolled barrels dullthudding   116.23   49.32 **

    ** There it is (The Freeman)   116.27#   57.35 **

RED MURRAY
     116.27++   586.25

    ** Alexander Keyes   116.27++   107.35 **

    ** The Telegraph office   116.29   35.32 **

The DOOR OF RUTTLEDGE'S OFFICE CREAKED again
     116.30   117.25   121.25   282.10

DAVY STEPHENS
     116.30   469.12+

Of course, if he wants a PAR (PARAGRAPH)
   117.05   121.01   146.24   147.08   260.40   375.32

WILLIAM BRAYDEN, ESQUIRE
   117.09+   586.25

      ** Sandymount   117.10   37.01 **

      ** <u>Freeman</u> . . . <u>National</u> <u>Press</u>   117.16   57.36 **

      ** Dullthudding . . . barrels 117.17   49.32   81.39 **

STEERED BY AN UMBRELLA (RAPIER)
   117.18   117.29   522.24

Don't you think his FACE IS LIKE OUR SAVIOUR?
   117.23+   517.21   (118.09)   See also 80.13

      ** The door of Ruttledge's office   117.25   116.30 **

      ** Mary, Martha   117.29   79.06 **

      ** Steered by an umbrella sword   117.29   117.18 **

MARIO the tenor
   117.30+   517.23

In MARTHA (opera by F. von Flotow)
   117.35+   288.17   289.01   290.19   661.27+
"The Last Rose of Summer"
   256.34   257.15   288.05++ 289.12   290.29   (755.14)
"<u>M'appari</u>" ("When first I saw that form endearing")
   117.36+   256.26+ 271.25++ 273.30++ 277.23   289.01   290.08
   380.33   414.31   456.13   522.15   661.31

      ** <u>Freeman</u>!   118.07   57.36 **

      ** One of our saviours also   118.09 (117.23) **

NANNETTI's reading closet
   118.16   118.28++ 146.26   156.04   180.12   246.15   260.38
   314.39+   315.26+ 381.13   550.22   586.19   684.09   (550.06)

      ** Hynes here too   118.20++   90.04 **

      ** Account of the funeral   118.20+   57.11 **

RULE THE WORLD today
   118.23   (288.13)

His machineries are pegging away too (BODY AS MACHINE)
   118.23   176.37

      ** That old grey rat   118.25   114.13 **

```
        ** The foreman's spare body          118.28++   118.16  **

IRELAND MY COUNTRY
        118.30      124.23      331.31      335.35    337.24      (58.37)    (457.29)
        See also    119.11      357.33      591.12

The stale news in the OFFICIAL GAZETTE
        118.33     (342.37++)

Phil Blake's PAT AND BULL STORY
        119.05      447.21

Dear Mr Editor. . . . I'D LIKE THAT PART
        119.07      487.15      488.10

MORE IRISH THAN THE IRISH
        119.11      623.21         See also 118.30

LONG JOHN (FANNING) is backing him
        119.20      244.09      245.14      247.04#    252.32      267.21      282.04
        289.38      299.17+     314.36      375.17     471.10+

If you want to DRAW THE CASHIER
        119.27      297.34

        ** Towards the Freeman's              119.32      57.36  **

Three bob I lent him. . . . (BLOOM'S LOAN TO HYNES)
        119.33      180.13      323.32      375.30    472.02      486.32
        See also    90.04

In MEAGHER'S (Pub)
        119.33      375.31

        ** This ad . . . Keyes                119.37++   107.35  **

        ** Innuendo of home rule             120.31     (57.35)  **

        ** Isle of Man                       120.32      94.21  **

        ** Ask him how to pronounce          120.34      64.04  **

        ** That voglio                       120.35      63.31  **

A Kilkenny paper (KILKENNY PEOPLE)
        120.38      146.26      179.38      200.22+

        ** Just a little par                 121.01     117.05  **

        ** Martin Cunningham                 121.11      80.13  **

GAUGING [AU] THE SYMMETRY OF A PEELED PEAR UNDER A CEMETERY WALL
        121.15      278.20      500.17      653.29
```

** I could have said   121.18   115.22+   **

** When he clapped on his topper   121.18   102.38   **

GOOD AS NEW
    121.20   653.31

** That door too . . . creaking   121.25   116.30   **

Where's the ARCHBISHOP'S LETTER
    121.30   647.19   648.11

** In the <u>Telegraph</u>   121.31   35.22   **

WHERE'S WHAT'S HIS NAME
    121.31   156.04   See also 61.02

MONKS, sir? (THE DAYFATHER)
    121.33++   647.38

** Found drowned   122.10   4.28   **

Nearing the END OF HIS TETHER now
    122.11   639.17   665.05

AND IT WAS THE FEAST OF THE PASSOVER . . . Pessach
    122.15+   378.38   723.30   (87.16)

** mangiD kcirtaP   122.19   57.11   **

** Poor papa   122.19   76.26   **

With his HAGADAH book
    122.20+   378.37   382.18   487.08   723.28

READING BACKWARDS
    122.20   609.20

NEXT YEAR
    122.21   382.18

In JERUSALEM
    122.21   332.40   335.37   477.14   504.31++   508.14+   726.36
    (484.23)

Into the HOUSE OF BONDAGE
    122.23   143.11   330.05   378.38   697.34   (212.26)

<u>SHEMA</u> <u>ISRAEL</u> <u>ADONAI</u> <u>ELOHENU</u>
    122.23   544.26

<u>ALLELUIA</u>
    122.23   124.17   (431.15)

Justice it means (BLOOM ON JUSTICE)
        122.29   182.28   332.41   716.05   728.08

EVERYBODY EATING EVERYONE ELSE
        122.29   170.26   619.05   See also 333.24

TWENTYEIGHT. TWENTYEIGHT DOUBLE FOUR
        122.35   127.31

        ** Same as Citron's house   122.35   60.33   **

        ** THAT SOAP   123.01+   85.17   **

In Thom's next door when I was there (BLOOM'S JOB AT THOM'S)
        123.05   155.20   342.40   377.40   550.13   708.16   772.19

        ** What perfume does your wife   123.10   72.30   **

        ** Evening Telegraph office   123.13++   35.22   **

        ** Ned Lambert it is   123.15#   90.03   **

        ** ERIN, GREEN GEM   123.17   (45.12) **

        ** The ghost walks   123.18   115.04   (18.12) **

PROFESSOR MACHUGH murmured softly
        123.18#   263.02   462.27+
    Ponderous pundit
        134.05   263.01

Heartburn on your ARSE. . . . OVERARSING
        123.23++   244.17   342.09   370.30   401.17   430.26   458.19
        459.26   470.10   640.07   751.38
    Kiss my arse
        146.32   147.10   205.27   734.38

        ** Or again, note. . . .   123.25++   91.08   **

        ** And Xenophon looked   124.01   5.08   **

BYRON, LORD (And Xenophon looked upon Marathon)
    Don Juan
        124.01+   625.26   734.28   (675.35)
    Childe Harold's Pilgrimage
        376.28
    "Maid of Athens"
        519.01
    "Bride of Abydos"
        659.14
    "Hours of Idleness"
        (71.40)
    "Fare thee well"
        (522.21)

Other references
    495.14   743.11   743.40   775.11

Old Chatterton, the VICE-CHANCELLOR
    124.11   585.07

        ** Alleluia   124.17   122.23   **

A recently discovered fragment of CICERO's
    124.20   394.04   622.41

        ** Whose land?   124.23   118.30   **

        ** His speech last night?   124.27++   91.08   **

Excuse me, J. J. O'MOLLOY said
    124.32#   225.23   230.07#   319.42#   463.04++   488.05

That HECTIC FLUSH spells finis for a man
    125.03   277.03   285.10   464.35   See also 272.14
    See also   277.03

OR AGAIN IF WE BUT CLIMB THE SERRIED MOUNTAIN PEAKS
    125.05   125.26

Is the editor to be seen? (MYLES CRAWFORD)
    125.07#   263.02   323.33   381.15   397.22   458.12+   470.02
    648.13
    His scarlet beaked face
    126.22   127.10   136.39   146.07   458.13+

LENEHAN
    125.10#   174.01   174.18   230.01   232.23#   252.38   261.41++
    307.03   324.27#   387.42#   470.02   490.10+   491.15+ 509.10
    564.01++   586.24   617.02   648.27   731.30   750.03+
    His riddle
    130.34   131.28   132.03   134.16+   426.17   455.26   491.13
    See also   130.28
    His yachting cap
    147.02   235.12   564.14
    Puts Lyons off Throwaway
    335.17   426.21
    His version of Gold Cup race
    415.21++   648.27
    See also   338.04

        ** The statue in Glasnevin   125.16   113.34   **

        ** In Glasnevin   125.17   100.22   **

Believe he does some literary work for the Express (DAILY EXPRESS)
    125.17   161.01   192.23

With GABRIEL CONROY
    125.18   377.40

Myles Crawford began on the Independent (IRISH INDEPENDENT)
     125.19   270.25   298.03+

AESOP'S FABLES (Hot and cold in the same breath)
  "The Man and the Satyr"
     125.21   535.12
  "The Dog in the Manger"
     161.15
  "The Wolf and the Crane"
     262.19
  "The Wolf in Sheep's Clothing"
     338.26
  "The Crow and the Pitcher"
     378.02
  "The Fox and the Grapes"
     553.22
  "The Dog and his Shadow"
     642.34
  "The Ass and the Wolf"
     651.38

          ** Or again if we but climb   125.26   125.05   **

HIS NATIVE DORIC
     126.01   282.41

WHAT WETHERUP SAID
     126.14+   660.09

          ** A scarlet beaked face   126.22   125.07   **

The SHAM SQUIRE
     126.26   241.11   296.40   485.12

          ** Crowed . . . scarlet face   127.10   125.07   **

O, HARP EOLIAN (HARP)
     127.13   167.35+   271.18+   421.37   522.25   704.25
     See also   45.12

Seeing the COAST CLEAR
     127.18   660.11   See also   41.04

Is that CANADA SWINDLE CASE on today?
     127.28   322.03+   647.19

          ** Twentyeight   127.31   122.35   **

Lenehan came out with SPORT's tissues
     128.02   229.38   388.02   398.15

Who wants a DEAD CERT. . . ?
     128.03   426.21

```
        ** For the Gold cup                        128.03      85.40  **

SCEPTRE with O. MADDEN up
    128.03       174.02       233.12+    265.34    325.33+    397.25      415.20++
    416.20       573.14       648.22

Screams of NEWSBOYS
    128.06++     143.25       144.28+    146.04++   469.13
  Mocking Bloom
    129.27+      376.01       505.24+    See also 586.09++

        ** Evening Telegraph here                   128.28+     35.22  **

Which auction rooms? (DILLON'S AUCTION ROOMS)
    128.30       129.18       151.33     237.06++    539.32      See also 226.31

WE ARE THE BOYS OF WEXFORD/Who fought with heart and hand
    129.13       285.02       451.17+    (163.13)

        ** This ad of Keyes's                       129.17+    107.35  **

        ** Around there in Dillon's                 129.18     128.30  **

        ** The world is before you                  129.22     (25.25) **

        ** The young scamps after him               129.27     128.06  **

        ** A mocking kite                           129.33      3.37   **

HUE AND CRY
    129.34       193.21       586.17     587.04

PADDY HOOPER is there
    130.07       137.26

        ** Jingling his keys                        130.11     11.35   **

THANKY VOUS
    130.24       140.25       263.37     (473.27)    See also  78.27

BALFE, M. W. ('Twas rank and fame that tempted thee)
  The Rose of Castille
    130.28       134.19       256.08     256.13+     257.15     264.28+      276.39+
    286.14       290.29       297.03     See also 125.10
  The Siege of Rochelle
    234.28       354.37
  The Bohemian Girl
    273.24
  Other
    162.34

What was their civilization? . . . CLOACAE: sewers
    131.12+      133.24       See also  38.18

        ** Let us construct a watercloset           131.18     38.18   **
```

** First chapter of Guinness's   131.20   81.39   **

** Pontius Pilate is its prophet   131.24   82.10   **

** First my riddle   131.28   125.10   **

Mr O'MADDEN BURKE . . . came in from the hallway
    131.30#   230.17   263.04   490.04

** What opera resembles   132.03   125.10   **

** The typed sheets   132.05++   32.01   **

** Bit torn off   132.08+   48.13   **

** Mr Garrett Deasy   132.09++   27.25   **

** On swift sail flaming . . . mouth   132.12+   48.01   **

** Foot and mouth?   132.17+   32.01   **

** Bullockbefriending bard   132.18   5.01   **

Knew HIS WIFE TOO. THE BLOODIEST OLD TARTAR GOD EVER MADE
    132.22+   573.26

** A woman brought sin   132.26   14.23   **

** For Helen, the runaway wife   132.26   32.01   **

** Of Menelaus   132.27   34.41   **

** O'Rourke, prince of Breffni   132.27   34.42   **

A WIDOWER . . . a GRASS one
    132.29   624.36

** Emperor's horses. Habsburg   132.31   32.01   **

** The king (Edward VII)   132.34   31.15   **

** Wild geese   132.35   41.17   **

** We serve them   133.12   6.41   **

** But the Greek!   133.17++   3.38   **

KYRIE ELEISON!
    133.18+   393.01

** The Saxon know not   133.22   4.17   **

** Radiance of the intellect   133.22   50.25   **

** The closetmaker   133.24   38.18   **

** The cloacamaker   133.24+   131.12   **

** Pyrrhus   133.29+   24.01   **

** They went forth to battle   133.32   9.22   **

** Ponderous pundit MacHugh   134.05   123.18   **

** Mulligan says   134.10   3.01   **

** Whose mother is beastly dead   134.10   8.20   **

** But my riddle! What opera. . . .   134.16   125.10   **

** The Rose of Castille   134.19   130.28   **

See the WHEEZE?
    134.19   268.38   297.35

** Paris, past and present   134.29   12.18   **

** In quiet mockery   134.32   3.37   **

BULWER-LYTTON, EDWARD (In the lexicon of youth . . .)
  Richelieu
    135.16
  Eugene Aram
    756.22

SEE IT IN YOUR EYE. . . . SCHEMER (FATHER DOLAN'S PANDYING STEPHEN)
    135.18   190.01   561.11++   See also 11.22   80.03
    See also   11.22   190.01

** Foot and mouth disease!   135.20   32.01   **

** Meeting in Borris-in-Ossory   135.21   31.18   **

Father Son and HOLY GHOST
    135.23   197.29   389.24   595.20   See also 19.03

** THE GREAT GALLAHER   135.29++   88.25   **

We'll PARALYSE EUROPE
    135.31   458.19

Doing billiardmarking at THE CLARENCE (HOTEL)
    135.33   260.41

** Murder in the Phoenix park   136.04+   81.27   **

JOE BRADY and the rest of them
    136.12   138.07   304.30

Where SKIN-THE-GOAT drove the car
    136.12+   137.05   138.07   621.37#

That CABMAN'S SHELTER . . . down there at Butt Bridge
    136.15   613.09+   621.33#   675.38   729.13

      ** Holohan told me   136.16   73.29 **

And poor GUMLEY is down there too
    136.18+   322.22   616.04   618.36+   639.07   660.37

Inspiration of GENIUS
    136.26   190.21   192.24   195.01   195.39   411.29   415.11
    646.29   673.19   (408.18)   (635.19)

      ** Weekly Freeman   136.26   57.36 **

      ** Like a cock's wattles   136.39   125.07 **

      ** Evening Telegraph here   137.03   35.22 **

      ** Skin-the-goat   137.05   136.11 **

BURKE'S publichouse
    137.11   423.01   423.11   424.30   518.25

      ** Nightmare from which. . . .   137.17   34.22 **

DICK ADAMS (G)
    137.18   642.27

      ** Madam, I'm Adam   137.22   38.06 **

      ** The Old Woman of Prince's street   137.23   57.36 **

There was weeping and GNASHING OF TEETH over that
    137.24   148.27   257.06   286.27   371.16

      ** Paddy Hooper   137.26   130.07 **

TAY PAY who took him on to the Star (T. P. O'CONNOR)
    137.27   330.23

He was ALL THEIR DADDIES
    137.29   423.30   (145.10)

The brother-in-law of CHRIS CALLINAN
    137.31   234.26++   488.16+   586.23   731.30

      ** Talking about the invincibles   138.01+   81.27 **

The RECORDER (SIR FREDERICK FALKINER)
    138.02   182.34+   322.15++   344.23   470.24++

LADY DUDLEY was walking home through the park
     138.03   161.26   252.03#   526.06   579.17

          ** That cyclone last year   138.05   13.02   **

          ** Joe Brady   138.07   136.12 **

          ** Skin-the-goat   138.07   136.11 **

Like (JAMES) WHITESIDE
     138.11   139.08

Like ISAAC BUTT
     138.11   599.04

          ** That mouth for her kiss   138.16+   48.01   **

          ** Dressed the same . . . two by two(G)   138.21   (20.20) **

          ** La tua pace   138.23+   20.20   **

HE SAW THEM THREE BY THREE, APPROACHING GIRLS . . . ENTWINING
     138.26+   (69.28+)

          ** Per l'aer perso   138.27   20.20   **

          ** Quella pacifica oriafiamma   138.28   20.20   **

          ** Tomb womb   138.30   38.09   **

Why not bring in HENRY GRATTAN
     139.03+   228.29   599.02

And EDMUND BURKE
     139.03   407.15-408.14 (parody)

TAYLOR, TOM (his American cousin)
  "Our American Cousin"
     139.05   205.07   408.26
  "The Hidden Hand"
     163.38   464.12
  "Vanderdecker, or the Flying Dutchman"
     (478.24)   (479.18)   (636.36)
  See also   297.12   376.26

          ** Like Whiteside   139.08   138.11 **

JOHN PHILPOT CURRAN
     139.13   186.35   523.24

          ** Bushe K. C.   139.15++   100.04 **

And in the PORCHES OF MINE EAR did pour (Hamlet)
     139.26   143.29   194.01   196.38+

How did he find that out? HE DIED IN HIS SLEEP
     139.27   196.40   (425.15)

BEAST WITH TWO BACKS (Othello)
     139.28   197.01   560.06

As contrasted with the earlier MOSAIC CODE
     139.32   464.04

The LEX TALIONIS
     139.33   412.29

          ** Moses   139.33   40.07   **

And he cited the Moses of MICHELANGELO
     139.33   140.12+   142.36   297.08   470.25+

A FEW WELLCHOSEN WORDS
     140.01   465.03

          ** I have often thought   140.06+   37.37   **

          ** That stony effigy   140.12+   139.33 **

That ETERNAL symbol of WISDOM
     140.13   185.18

Of SOULTRANSFIGURED AND OF SOULTRANSFIGURING DESERVES TO LIVE
     140.15   465.07

          ** Muchibus thankibus   140.25   130.24 **

          ** A. E. the master mystic   140.29+   5.13   **

That BLAVATSKY WOMAN started it (THEOSOPHY)
     140.30   185.41
     Isis Unveiled
     191.37   412.32   553.28
     Theosophy
     140.30   185.14   185.29+   191.37+   301.13+   398.05   411.21
     416.26+   420.41   510.14+   521.25   (508.01)
     "Formless spiritual essences"
     185.14   185.29

A. E. has been telling some YANKEE INTERVIEWER
     140.31   185.21

A speech made by JOHN F. TAYLOR
     141.03++   464.35

MR JUSTICE FITZGIBBON, the present lord justice of appeal
     141.04++   397.10   586.25

The REVIVAL OF THE IRISH TONGUE (THE GAELIC LEAGUE)
    141.07++   164.05   194.12   249.21   317.11   412.21   688.20++
    (186.38)
  Corporation meeting on
    165.07   247.17+   310.39+   324.30
  Gaelic League
    193.04   311.02   436.19
  Lovemaking in Irish
    647.18   648.33
  See also   14.30+   194.12

With TIM HEALY . . . on the TRINITY COLLEGE ESTATES COMMISSION
    141.11   397.10   586.25   (297.14) (T)

Upon the new MOVEMENT. It was then a new MOVEMENT
    141.18+   186.38

Had COME there . . . FROM A SICK BED
    141.27   465.03

      ** To and fro   142.02   11.24 **

I was listening to the speech of some HIGHPRIEST of that land (Egypt)
    142.11+   193.39   416.29

      ** The youthful Moses   142.11++   40.07 **

Their SMOKE ASCENDING IN FRAIL STALKS THAT FLOWERED WITH HIS SPEECH
    142.12   218.06+   See also   11.06

AND LET OUR CROOKED SMOKES (Cymbeline)
    142.13   218.11   599.11

THOSE THINGS ARE GOOD WHICH YET ARE CORRUPTED . . . COULD BE CORRUPTED
    142.21+   383.19+   633.36

That's SAINT AUGUSTINE
    142.24   339.03   391.28   See also 186.19(G)   205.30(G)

      ** You jews   142.25++   21.21 **

      ** Child, man, effigy   142.34+   140.12 **

      ** Cradle of bulrushes   142.35   45.08 **

      ** Stonehorned   142.36   139.33 **

      ** Their house of bondage   143.11   122.23 **

The PILLAR OF THE CLOUD by day
    143.11   210.25   480.05   727.20

WITH THE LIGHT OF INSPIRATION SHINING IN HIS COUNTENANCE
    143.14(G)   676.15

** <u>The</u> <u>tables</u> <u>of</u> <u>the</u> <u>law</u>   143.15   (9.22)   **

LAND OF PROMISE
    143.20   149.30   395.34   483.23   734.28

    ** A great future behind him (T)   143.24   (6.37)   **

    ** A troop of bare feet   143.25   128.06   **

    ** Gone with the wind   143.28+   32.19   **

    ** Miles of ears of porches   143.29   139.26   **

    ** The tribune's words   143.29   31.18   **

    ** Scattered to the four winds   143.30   34.13   **

AKASIC RECORDS of all that ever anywhere wherever was
    143.31   145.09

    ** I have money   143.33   11.02   **

My casting vote is: MOONEY'S (pubs)
    144.04   148.23   262.39   518.24

CHIP OF THE OLD BLOCK!
    144.11   212.13

    ** Those blasted keys   144.12   11.35   **

    ** Foot and mouth   144.15   32.01   **

    ** <u>Fuit</u> <u>Ilium</u>!   144.25   88.15   **

    ** Windy Troy   144.25   34.42   50.31   **

    ** The first newsboy   144.28++   128.06   **

    ** I have much, much to learn   144.31   35.14   **

    ** Two Dublin vestals   145.03+   37.34   **

Two Dublin Vestals (PARABLE OF THE PLUMS)
    145.03++   579.12   685.18   See also 75.02   95.10

Two Dublin VESTALS, Stephen said (VESTAL VIRGINS)
    145.03   146.01   193.31   (188.09)

    ** Fumbally's lane   145.04+   47.19   **

    ** Akasic records   145.09   143.31   **

ON now
    145.10   208.42   211.27   260.41   279.17

LET THERE BE LIFE (Artist as creator of life)
    145.10   190.29   391.22++   415.07   666.35   782.04   (137.29)
    (548.23)   (662.23)   See also 207.40

         ** The top of Nelson's pillar   145.12++   95.09   **

WISE VIRGINS, professor MacHugh said
    145.18   521.17++

         ** Twenty ripe plums   145.23   95.10   **

         ** Anne Kearns   145.31++   37.34   **

         ** Florence MacCabe   145.31++   37.34   **

         ** Lourdes water   145.32   81.12   **
                                                    See also   37.36

         ** A bottle of double X   145.34   81.39   **

         ** Vestal virgins   146.01   145.03 **

         ** A bevy of scampering newsboys   146.04++   128.06 **

His HAT AUREOLING his scarlet face
    146.07   458.13

         ** His scarlet face   146.07   125.07 **

         ** Telegraph! Racing special!   146.16+   35.22   **

         ** Rathmines   146.19   116.06 **

         ** Just this ad . . . Mr Keyes   146.21   107.35 **

         ** He wants a par   146.24   117.05 **

         ** I told councillor Nannetti   146.26   118.16 **

         ** From the Kilkenny People   146.26   120.38 **

         ** In the national library   146.27   15.35   **

         ** K. M. A. . . . kiss my arse   146.31   123.23 **

         ** Lenehan's yachting cap   147.02   125.10 **

         ** Has a good pair of boots   147.04   3.01   **

         ** In Irishtown?   147.06   87.40   **

         ** It's worth a short par   147.08   117.05 **

         ** K. M. R. I. A.   147.10   123.23 **

** Rathmines' blue dome   148.01   116.06   **

ADAM AND EVE'S (CHURCH AND TAVERN)
    148.01   297.16   314.16   688.38   See also   14.23   38.06

NELSON, HORATIO
  "Onehandled adulterer"
    148.09+   150.12   276.18   579.12
  Other references
    325.02   433.32
  See also   15.32   95.09

    ** Mooney's (pub)   148.23   144.04   **

    ** SOPHIST WALLOPS HAUGHTY HELEN   148.26+   32.01   **

    ** SPARTANS GNASH MOLARS   148.27   137.24   **

PEN IS CHAMP (PENELOPE)
    148.29   149.04   201.15++   202.08   See also 149.05

You remind me of ANTISTHENES
    148.30   186.13(G)   201.17   242.04   523.12

A disciple of GORGIAS
    148.31   201.17

He took the PALM OF BEAUTY
    149.03   201.18   204.28   See also 415.08

    ** Poor Penelope   149.04   148.28+   **

Poor Penelope.   PENELOPE RICH
    149.05   201.38+   See also 148.29

    ** Rathmines   149.09   116.06   **

    ** Ringsend   149.11   41.09   **

    ** Sandymount Green   149.11+   37.01   **

    ** VIRGILIAN   149.20   88.15   **

    ** OLD MAN MOSES   149.22+   40.07   **

    ** Deus nobis haec otia fecit   149.24   88.15   **

I call it A PISGAH SIGHT OF PALESTINE
    149.25+   685.17   (393.36)

    ** The promised land   149.30   143.20   **

    ** A weary sidelong glance   150.03   (3.41)   **

    ** Sir John Gray's pavement island   150.06   94.08   **

** Onehandled adulterer   150.12   148.09   **

LESTRYGONIANS

PINEAPPLE ROCK
    151.01   167.16   272.05   485.23

Scoopfuls of creams for a CHRISTIAN BROTHER
    151.02   221.07   339.11   617.19

      ** His Majesty the King   151.04   31.15 **

To His Majesty THE KING. GOD. SAVE. OUR
    151.04   597.06   See also 592.09

Sucking red JUJUBES white
    151.05   578.18   590.20   591.17

Among the warm sweet fumes of GRAHAM LEMON's
    151.07   272.05   676.05

A THROWAWAY in a hand of Mr Bloom
    151.07++   676.06   725.26
  Blood of the Lamb
    151.11+   164.25   428.14   436.31   560.14   637.28 (168.19+)
    See also   436.31
  Elijah is coming. Dr John Alexander Dowie
    151.15+   152.28   227.06   250.08   279.19   428.14+ 492.11++
    507.10+   550.12   690.05   (418.37)
    See also   191.32   398.04   505.16
  Restorer of the Church in Zion
    151.16   676.07
  A crumpled paper ball [the throwaway as a skiff]
    152.28   227.06   240.16   249.33   550.12
    See also   44.09   85.42   197.17   325.31

BLOO . . . Me?
    151.10   258.09   647.16+

     ** Kidney burntoffering   151.15   55.04 **

     ** Druid's altars   151.15   11.06 **

     ** Restorer of the church in Zion   151.16   44.09 **

PAYING GAME
    151.20   260.39

     ** Luminous . . . phosphorescence   151.22+ (56.06) **

     ** Iron nails ran in   151.24   81.22 **

Before Rudy was born (MOLLY'S PREGNANCY WITH RUDY)
    151.29   338.07   738.19   760.39   See also 66.25

Dedalus' daughter still there (DILLY DEDALUS)
  General reference
    151.33   152.08   226.38   237.09#   243.06#   253.25   579.15
    581.16   620.20   670.20
  Eyes like Stephen's
    243.17   645.31

     ** Dillon's auctionrooms   151.33   128.30 **

     ** When the mother goes   151.36+   5.16 **

Their butteries and larders (GOOD LIFE OF THE CLERGY)
    151.41+   155.12+

The black fast YOM KIPPUR
    152.01   172.01   487.08

     ** Poor child's dress (Dilly Dedalus)   152.08   151.33 **

CERVANTES, Miguel de (Proof of the pudding) (G)
    152.10   192.30+

     ** Get a pass through Hancock   152.15   67.24 **

     ** The brewery. . . . Vats of porter   152.15+   81.39 **

He saw . . . GULLS
    152.22++   164.22   279.19   453.26+   471.28   598.20
    See also   152.34

     ** Reuben J's son   152.23   4.28   93.41 **

     ** Elijah . . . is com   152.28   151.07 **

     ** Thirtytwo feet per sec   152.29   72.10 **

     ** The Erin's King   152.32   67.03 **

THE HUNGRY FAMISHED GULL/FLAPS O'ER THE WATERS DULL
    152.34+   166.15   552.23   (164.38)   See also 152.22

HAMLET, I AM THY FATHER'S SPIRIT/DOOMED FOR A CERTAIN TERM. . . .
    152.39   188.35   473.02   561.02
    See also   18.37   21.09   188.03

The glazed apples serried on HER STAND
    153.02   (416.04)

Two BANBURY CAKES for a penny
    153.07   453.27+   711.18

SWANS from Anna Liffey swim down here
    153.13   188.22+   (188.24)   See also 188.23
    See also   188.23

Swans from ANNA LIFFEY
    153.14   310.01

       ** Robinson Crusoe had to live on them   153.16   109.36 **

       ** Spread foot and mouth disease   153.19   32.01 **

KINO'S 11/- TROUSERS
    153.25+   523.02   683.32

       ** Which in the stream of life we trace 153.30   86.32 **

That QUACK DOCTOR
    153.31   523.08

Strictly confidential. DR HY FRANKS
    153.33   523.02

Like MAGINNI the dancing master
    153.34   220.24   235.35   253.40   575.17++

POST NO BILLS. POST 110 PILLS
    153.37   523.02

Timeball on the BALLAST OFFICE
    154.04+   167.01   343.25

DUNSINK TIME
    154.05   167.02   344.04   465.30   717.32

Book . . . of Sir Robert Ball's (THE STORY OF THE HEAVENS)
    154.05   465.17   708.27   (166.39)

PARALLAX
    154.06+   167.10   414.16   488.17   512.21   698.33

       ** Met him pikehoses she called it   154.07   50.13 **

** O rocks!   154.09+   64.22   **

** Only big words for ordinary things   154.11   31.12   **

** Ben Dollard. . . . Barreltone   154.14   91.01   **

Number one BASS. Barrel of BASS (BASS'S ALE)
   154.19   283.26   414.40   416.29   417.03   425.09

** Like that priest . . . this morning   154.23   80.28   **

** We have sinned: we have suffered   154.23   81.20   **

H. E. L. Y. S.   Wisdom Hely's
   154.25++   227.22   229.21   253.37   446.06   See also 106.26

They are not Boyl: no: M'Glade's (SANDWICHMEN)
   154.30   618.21   725.25

I suggested to him about a transparent SHOW CART
   154.31   684.19

** Pillar of salt   154.37   44.14   51.04   61.23   **

** Plumtree's potted   154.40   75.02   **

Jones . . . ROBINSON
   154.42   627.31   See also 586.29

** Sold by Hely's Ltd   155.01   106.26 **

TRANQUILLA CONVENT
   155.03   368.09   552.20

Sister? Sister? (SISTER AGATHA)
   155.05++   368.11   552.20   See also 156.02

Feast of Our Lady of MOUNT CARMEL
   155.09   326.20   339.05   552.21

** Fried everything in the best butter   155.12+   151.41+ **

** My heart's broke   155.13   95.22   **

It was a nun they say INVENTED BARBED WIRE
   155.16   369.07   553.23

** Those races are on today   155.18   86.19   **

Year PHIL GILLIGAN died
   155.19+   682.20   704.35

** We were in Lombard street west   155.19   110.15 **

** Was in Thom's   155.20   123.05 **

```
            ** The job in Wisdom Hely's              155.20    106.26  **

VAL DILLON was lord mayor
     155.22      234.05      371.17      465.13    586.19    731.29      750.06

The GLENCREE DINNER
     155.23+     234.03+     371.15     750.04+    774.08    (494.08)

FOR WHAT WE HAVE ALREADY RECEIVED, MAY THE LORD MAKE US
     155.26      169.35      375.41

            ** Milly was a kiddy then                155.27++    21.42  **

Molly had that ELEPHANTGREY DRESS with the braided frogs
     155.27      738.31

SHE DIDN'T LIKE IT
     155.29      156.15

I SPRAINED my ANKLE
     155.29      738.30

CHOIR PICNIC at the Sugarloaf
     155.30      738.31      (755.34)

Choir picnic at the SUGARLOAF (Mountain)
     155.30      343.14      738.31

            ** Old Goodwin's tall hat                155.30      63.05  **

HAPPY, HAPPIER THEN
     155.35      156.30      168.02      176.22    377.03    462.12

DOCKRELL'S WALLPAPER ONE AND NINEPENCE A DOZEN
     155.36      462.13      781.23      See also 713.21

American SOAP I bought: ELDERFLOWER
     155.37      327.10

            ** Now photography                       155.39      21.42  **

            ** Papa's . . . atelier                  155.39      76.26  **

Poor papa's DAGUERROTYPE ATELIER
     155.39      723.26      766.12

            ** Stream of life                        155.42      86.32  **

Pen something. . . . Pen . . . ? (PENROSE)
     156.02      181.32      519.27      586.40    731.25    754.11+
     See also    155.05

            ** Stopped in Citron's                   156.02      60.33  **
```

```
    ** (Nannetti) couldn't remember        156.04      118.16  **

    ** The dayfather's name                156.05      121.31  **

BARTELL D'ARCY was the tenor
    156.06+     234.07     586.24     731.26    745.31     763.12      774.20
    Kissing Molly on the choir stairs
    745.32      763.13

Gave her that song WINDS THAT BLOW FROM THE SOUTH
    156.08      525.03+     763.12

    ** Goodwin's concert                   156.10+      63.05  **

About those LOTTERY TICKETS
    156.11      313.24+     345.08     485.28    630.27     721.24      772.20

    ** Spoils the effect of a night for her  156.15    155.29  **

Shaky ON HIS PINS
    156.16      372.17      660.27

Her BOA nearly smothered old Goodwin
    156.20      234.34     (503.23)

The busk of [MOLLY'S] STAYS
    156.26+     375.02      380.04     465.32    512.08     537.01      755.34

    ** Taking out her hairpins             156.29       64.12  **

    ** Milly tucked up in beddyhouse       156.29       21.42  **

    ** Happy.  Happy                       156.30      155.35  **

    ** Milly . . . down in Mullingar       156.35       21.42  **

    ** Just come from a funeral            157.01       57.11  **

    ** Coming through the rye              157.11        6.28  **

Oh, how do you do, Mrs Breen (JOSIE BREEN)
    156.32+     167.17      240.41     253.32    299.01     321.07+     369.09
    373.15      442.21++    586.27+    722.27    742.34++   761.33      773.12

And your lord and master? (DENIS BREEN)
    157.17++    159.33+     164.19     240.40    253.32+    298.32++    320.25++
    339.19      381.08      446.06+    586.27    744.07++   773.15
    His bath slippers
    298.40      446.07      744.20

ROLYPOLY
    157.24      407.12

Poured out from HARRISON'S
    157.24      159.34
```

PENNY DINNER
        157.29   485.28

DEVILS if they lose sixpence
        157.33   369.17

There must be a NEW MOON out
        157.38   167.17+   349.14   361.40   368.13+   702.10

        ** Trust me   158.02   7.16   **

Said the ACE OF SPADES was walking up the stairs
        158.07+   446.09

U.P.? . . . U.P.: UP
        158.11++   160.03   280.22   299.04++   320.26++   381.09   446.12
        474.08   486.28   744.21

        ** Round to Mr Menton's office   158.16   102.38   **

        ** In Luke Doyle's . . . the charades   158.31   64.24   **

MINA PUREFOY
        158.36   161.06+   163.07   164.20   235.23   280.22   286.07
        373.11   380.10   386.10#   452.12   586.28   599.12   729.09
        742.23

        ** Philip Beaufoy . . . Matcham   158.37   67.39   **

        ** Lying-in hospital in Holles street   159.01   97.29   **

DR [ANDREW] HORN got her in
        159.01   383.03+   385.07++   388.40   392.11   392.25   395.07
        397.19+   403.36   407.01   417.26   420.20   423.16

DTH! DTH!
        159.08   161.22

A bony form (CASHEL BOYLE O'CONNOR FITZMAURICE TISDALL FARRELL)
        159.15++   164.19   215.14   244.40   249.38#   254.22   286.31
        511.26   (725.28)

        ** Denis Breen in skimpy frockcoat   159.33+   157.17   **

        ** Shuffled out of Harrison's   159.34   157.24   **

MESHUGGAH. Off his chump
        159.38   487.10

        ** That other old mosey lunatic   160.01   10.32   **

        ** U.P.: up   160.03   158.11   **

That's ALF BERGAN
        160.03   267.21   298.30#   339.19   446.08+

        ** That's . . . Richie Goulding   160.03   38.34   **

Wrote it for a lark in the SCOTCH HOUSE
        160.04   238.05   332.19

        ** Menton's . . . oyster eyes   160.05   102.38   **

He passed the IRISH TIMES
        160.07   160.20   456.12   638.10   745.09

TO AID GENTLEMAN IN LITERARY WORK
        160.12   165.38   369.32

        ** I called you . . . does your wife   160.12   72.30   **

And the other one LIZZIE TWIGG
        160.16   165.29++   372.20   637.37

        ** The eminent poet A. E.   160.18   5.13   **

        ** Best paper . . . for a small ad   160.20   160.07   **

        ** Our gracious and popular vicereine   161.26   138.03   **

WARD UNION staghounds
        160.28   572.25

        ** That one at the Grosvenor   160.35   73.33   **

        ** That pugnosed driver   160.37   74.29   **

Mrs MIRIAM DANDRADE that sold me her old wraps
        160.39+   536.16+   587.02   See also 268.38

The SHELBOURNE HOTEL
        160.40   536.17

        ** The Express   161.01   125.17   **

        ** Poor Mrs Purefoy!   161.06+   158.36   **

Methodist husband (THEODORE PUREFOY)
        161.06   397.39+   408.25+   421.01++   423.23++   491.23+   586.27
        742.23   See also 421.05

Theodore's cousin in DUBLIN CASTLE
        161.10   246.02   421.19   456.08   646.01

        ** Dog in the manger   161.15   125.21   **

        ** Must look up that ad   161.18   107.35   **

** In the national library   161.18   15.35   **

An eightpenny in the BURTON
    161.19   168.39++   271.07   370.38

** I forgot to tap Tom Kernan   161.21   71.24   **

** Tap Tom Kernan (for the Dignam fund)   161.21   57.11   **

** Dth, dth, dth!   161.22   159.08 **

TWILIGHTSLEEP
    161.28   410.36

** Queen Victoria was given that   161.29   43.13   **

** He was consumptive (Prince Albert)   161.31   102.13 **

** Pensive bosom . . . effulgence   161.32   91.08   **

** Mrs. Moisel   162.02   60.38   **

PHTHISIS retires for the time being
    162.02   464.34   704.35+

** Old Mrs Thornton   162.04   66.23   **

Old Mrs Thornton was a jolly old soul ("OLD KING COLE")
    162.04   658.05

Old TOM WALL's son
    162.07   615.03

** Snuffy Dr Murren   162.08   113.20 **

Before . . . the Irish house of parliament a flock of PIGEONS flew
    162.14   228.20

APJOHN, (PERCY)
    162.16   548.20   667.20   704.34   716.22   737.12

Myself and OWEN GOLDBERG
    162.17   548.19   667.17

MACKEREL they called me
    162.18   548.23

** Policeman's lot is oft a happy one   162.22   38.35   **

** Moore's . . . meeting of the waters   162.29+   45.12   **

Great song of JULIA MORKAN's
    162.33   670.15

** Pupil of Michael Balfe's   162.34   130.28 **

        ** Jack Power   162.36   87.03 **

Jack Power could A TALE UNFOLD
    162.36   285.09   463.20

In the BRIDEWELL
    162.38   615.02

The day JOE CHAMBERLAIN was given his degree in Trinity
    162.40   163.12   457.26

Those medicals (TRINITY MEDICALS)
    163.04   184.20   431.24   764.02   (184.24)

        ** That young Dixon   163.06   97.28 **

        ** Dressed that sting for me   163.06   68.18 **

        ** In the Mater   163.06   8.27 **

        ** In Holles street   163.07   97.29 **

        ** Where Mrs Purefoy   163.07   158.36 **

Up the Boers! (BOER WAR)
    163.10+   205.04   319.32   457.26+   484.01   484.02   596.10+
    640.33   649.09   722.19   748.30   748.43++ 749.17   762.20
    See also   187.22

Three cheers for DE WET!
    163.11   593.09   649.09

        ** We'll hang Joe Chamberlain   163.12   162.40 **

        ** Vinegar hill   163.13   (129.13) **

WHETHER ON THE SCAFFOLD HIGH ("God Save Ireland")
    163.16   425.01+   642.31   (336.04)

        ** Corny Kelleher   163.18   71.15 **

        ** Harvey Duff in his eye   163.19   92.06 **

        ** The invincibles   163.19   81.27 **

        ** Plain clothes men . . . slaveys   163.23   60.02 **

Easily TWIG a man used to uniform
    163.24   372.01   See also 160.16

SQUAREPUSHING up against a backdoor
    163.24   432.03

PEEPING TOM through the keyhole
      163.27   368.27

Are those yours, MARY
      163.30   (409.26)

            ** There are great times coming (T)   163.33+   (111.02)   **

            ** James Stephens idea was the best   163.36   43.25   **

            ** Circles of ten (Fenian Brotherhood)   163.36   31.18   **

            ** Hidden hand   163.38   139.05   **

SINN FEIN
      163.38   190.34   306.22   335.39   337.18   748.37   772.23
      See also   7.33   43.08   57.35

GARIBALDI
      163.41   317.25

            ** Must have a certain fascination   163.42   92.25   **

            ** Parnell   163.42   35.02   **

            ** Arthur Griffith   163.42   43.08   **

DUBLIN BAKERY COMPANY's tearoom (D.B.C.)
      164.03   165.14   198.18   248.31   253.21   744.43++

            ** The language question   164.05   141.07   **

            ** Halffed enthusiasts   164.10+   68.29   **

Penny roll and a walk with the band (CLERICAL BRIBERY)
      164.10   180.27+

            ** Home Rule sun rising   164.14   57.35   **

            ** Things go on the same; day after day 164.17++ (86.32)   **

            ** Loonies (Breen and Farrell) 164.19   157.17   159.15   **

            ** Dignam carted off   164.19   57.11   **

            ** Mina Purefoy swollen belly   164.20   158.36   **

ONE BORN EVERY SECOND SOMEWHERE
      164.21   235.23

            ** Since I fed the birds   164.22   152.22   **

            ** Three hundred kicked the bucket   164.23   113.14   **

            ** Washed in the blood of the lamb   164.25   151.07   **

BABYLON
    164.34   193.23   414.18   627.03

        ** Big stones left   164.34   44.40   **

ROUND TOWERS
    164.34   296.05   See also   3.16

        ** Dull, gloomy: hate this hour   164.38   (152.34)   **

Feel as if I had been EATEN AND SPEWED
    164.39   179.24

PROVOST's house. The reverend DR SALMON
    164.40   170.30+   253.42   586.26   690.04

        ** Hope they have liver and bacon   164.42   55.03   **

NATURE ABHORS A VACUUM
    164.42   208.17   506.29

By which JOHN HOWARD PARNELL passed
    165.02++   170.29   247.18   483.17+   586.26   See also   35.02
    Playing chess
    165.14   230.35   248.15++   253.24   480.10
    Poached eyes on ghost
    165.11   168.42   248.25   See also 102.38   115.04

        ** Now that's a coincidence   165.05   68.24   **

        ** A corporation meeting today   165.07   141.07   **

        ** I have a pain   165.12   17.40   **

        ** Drop into the D.B.C.   165.14   164.03   **

        ** His brother used men as pawns   165.14+   35.02   **

        ** That's the fascination   165.17   92.25   **

Still DAVID SHEEHY beat him for south Meath
    165.19   219.20++

        ** Parnell would come back   165.23   35.02   **

The TWOHEADED OCTOPUS
    165.25   507.11

The ENDS OF THE WORLD . . . with a SCOTCH ACCENT
    165.26+   507.11+

        ** Beard (AE)   165.29+   5.13   **

BICYCLE
     165.29++   510.10+

          ** Young woman (Lizzie Twigg)   165.29++   160.16   **

          ** A coincidence: secondtime   165.30   68.24   **

          ** Coming events cast their shadows   165.31   113.19   **

          ** Albert Edward   165.34   31.15   **

          ** To aid gentleman in literary work   165.38   160.12   **

Only WEGGEBOBBLES and fruit. Don't eat BEEFSTEAK
     165.41   423.40

Her STOCKINGS ARE LOOSE over her ankles
     166.07   372.20   637.37   See also 66.08   74.18

Those literary ETHEREAL people they are all
     166.08   276.02   278.22   552.23   553.08   See also 69.39

DREAMY, cloudy, SYMBOLISTIC
     166.08+   172.31   274.29   276.02   510.23   552.23   (366.11)

          ** The poetical   166.11   69.39   **

          ** The dreamy cloudy gull   166.15   152.34   **

          ** Last year travelling to Ennis   166.26   76.26   **

The tip of his little FINGER BLOTTED OUT THE SUN's disk
     166.36   495.19   (48.26)

Talk about those SUNSPOTS
     166.39   548.14   (154.05)

          ** Lombard street west   166.39   110.15   **

          ** Ball falls at Greenwich time   167.01   154.04   **

          ** An electric wire from Dunsink   167.02   154.05   **

If I could get an introduction to PROFESSOR JOLY
     167.04   586.27

FLATTERY where least expected
     167.06   208.22   371.06

          ** What's parallax   167.10   154.06   **

          ** Like that pineapple rock   167.16   151.01   **

          ** Must be a new moon   167.17+   157.38   **

        ** She said (Josie Breen)   167.17   156.32 **

He went on by LA MAISON CLAIRE
    167.18   246.33

        ** The full moon was the night we were   167.19+   69.27 **

Walking down by the TOLKA
    167.21   740.10   See also 45.12

        ** The young may moon she's beaming   167.21   45.12 **

TOUCH. FINGERS. ASKING. ANSWER. YES
    167.23   501.10

        ** Bob Doran's bottle shoulders   167.29   74.01 **

        ** His annual bend   167.29   74.01 **

        ** M'Coy   167.30   67.24 **

        ** The Coombe . . . with streetwalkers   167.31   78.37 **

        ** His Harp theatre   167.35+   127.13 **

        ** The Queen's (Theatre)   167.36   92.04 **

        ** Dion Boucicault business   167.36   92.06 **

        ** Three Purty Maids from School   167.38   38.35 **

        ** His parboiled eyes   167.42   165.11 **

        ** The harp that once did starve us all 168.01   45.12 **

        ** Happier then   168.02   155.35 **

        ** Or was that I? Or am I now I?   168.02   11.22 **

        ** Lombard street west   168.03   110.15 **

        ** After Rudy   168.04   66.25 **

        ** Not happy . . . little naughty boy   168.07   72.30 **

        ** Write it in the library   168.09   15.35 **

GRAFTON STREET . . . lured his senses
    168.10   170.26   251.15   372.21   752.37

JINGLE OF HARNESSES
    168.11   168.33+   (607.22++) (639.04)   See also 256.15

Thick feet that WOMAN has IN the WHITE STOCKINGS
    168.13   372.21

     ** All the beef to the heels were in   168.14   66.08   **

Bloodhued POPLIN washed in rainwater
     168.19   326.18   480.29   (151.07)

     ** The huguenots   168.20   84.06   **

MEYERBEER, G. (La causa e santa!)
   Les Huguenots
     168.20+   370.22   514.18   661.08   771.19   772.12
   Personal reference
     290.35

PINCUSHIONS
     168.23   (513.26)

     ** Must go back for that lotion   168.26   84.03   **

For her birthday perhaps. . . . september 8 (MOLLY'S BIRTHDAY)
     168.26   181.38   736.05   747.14   751.20

Say it cuts lo (PIN CUTS LOVE)
     168.28   263.35

PETTICOATS on slim brass rails
     168.30   (180.16)

     ** Useless to go back   168.32   67.17   **

     ** Had to be   168.32   66.39   **

     ** Tell me all   168.32   72.30   **

     ** Jingling harnesses   168.33   168.11+   **

     ** Agendath Netaim   168.35   60.16   **

     ** The Burton   168.39++   161.19   **

ALL KISSES, YIELDED: IN DEEP SUMMER FIELDS
     168.42   (176.01)   (224.25+)

New set of MICROBES
     169.16   170.36

A man spitting back on his plate: HALFMASTICATED GRISTLE
     169.19   271.07   370.39

     ** See ourselves as others see us   169.22   6.28   **

That last pagan king of Ireland CORMAC
     169.24   323.13   667.02

Southward of THE BOYNE
    169.25   189.34

      ** Saint Patrick converted him   169.26   80.12 **

      ** Grace after meals   169.35   155.26 **

TEAR IT LIMB FROM LIMB
    170.03   345.20

ROCK, THE BAILIFF
    170.07   245.15

Get a light snack in DAVY BYRNE'S (public house)
    170.19++   279.19   490.06   586.31   676.04

      ** Back towards Grafton street   170.26   168.10 **

      ** Eat or be eaten   170.26   122.29 **

      ** John Howard Parnell example   170.29   165.02 **

      ** The provost of Trinity   170.30+   164.40 **

Don't talk. . . . hares of them all ("FATHER O'FLYNN")
    170.30+   340.17   599.14+

      ** Old queen in a bathchair   170.34   43.13 **

      ** Like Sir Philip Crampton's fountain   170.36   92.12 **

      ** Rub off the microbes   170.37   169.16 **

As big as the PHOENIX PARK
    170.41   252.08   315.37   316.10   467.06   681.02
    See also   81.27

      ** City Arms hotel   170.42   35.27 **

GARLIC . . . IT STINKS ITALIAN
    171.06   241.33   477.20   637.06

ITALIAN ORGANGRINDERS
    171.06   285.37   731.30

Fine flavour of things from the earth . . . TRUFFLES
    171.07   516.10   526.30   531.09

PAIN TO ANIMAL too
    171.07   315.19   (5.31)   (17.39)   (207.41)

Waiting for the POLEAXE to split their skulls open
    171.09   187.29   307.30

STAGGERING BOB
     171.10   420.07++   549.25+

RAWHEAD AND BLOODY BONES. . . . Famished ghosts
     171.12   581.28

He entered Davy Byrne's (BLOOM'S LUNCH)
     171.20++   711.19   728.38

       ** Davy Byrne's   171.20++   170.19 **

But in the LEAPYEAR once in four
     171.21   351.36   362.32   782.16

HE DREW HIS WATCH
     171.23   178.08   See also 191.28

NOSEY FLYNN said
     171.25++   232.18+   253.14   325.37   370.01   470.03   487.25+
     491.01+   765.05

I'll take a glass of BURGUNDY
     171.28++   175.41   179.37   183.16+   290.26   291.06   291.10
     456.03   462.34   615.25

HAM and his descendants mustered and bred there
     171.31   497.14

       ** Plumtree's potted meat   171.32+   75.02 **

       ** Dignam's potted meat   171.34   57.11 **

       ** Cannibals would with lemon and rice 171.35   80.37 **

Who ate or something the somethings of THE REVEREND MR MACTRIGGER
     171.39+   172.30+

       ** Kosher. No meat and milk together 171.42   62.30 **

       ** Yom Kippur fast   172.01   152.01 **

       ** Peace and war depend on some fellow's digestion 172.02 **
                                          See   25.14++

SLAUGHTER OF INNOCENTS
     172.03   423.39

EAT, DRINK AND BE MERRY
     172.04   381.07   526.27

       ** Tom Kernan can dress   172.11   71.24 **

       ** Milly   172.12   21.42 **

Take one SPANISH ONION
       172.13   458.14   652.14   675.19

Take one Spanish onion (RECIPE)
       172.13   175.06

              ** A big tour end of this month   172.24   75.23+   **

              ** Who's getting it up?   172.26+   75.12   **

              ** Mr MacTrigger   172.30+   171.39   **

              ** Dreamy creamy stuff   172.31   166.08   **

He's the ORGANISER in point of fact
       173.09   319.27+   470.06

JACK MOONEY was telling me
       173.13   246.33   314.26
       See also   303.03

That boxing match. . . . (THE KEOGH-BENNETT FIGHT)
       173.14+   318.07++   777.42   See also 250.33

              ** The Gold cup   173.27   85.40   **

              ** Mr Bloom ate . . . with relish   173.31   55.01   **

Nice piece of wood in that counter. . . . Like the way it CURVES there
       173.36   176.25+   182.07   183.26   234.36   546.09   576.14
       734.31   (215.25)
       See also   236.05

LICENSED . . . PREMISES
       173.39   340.29   427.15

              ** Lenehan   174.01   125.10   **

              ** Sceptre   174.02   128.03   **

ZINFANDEL's the favourite, LORD HOWARD DE WALDEN's
       174.02   178.42+   325.36   573.14   648.21+

ROTHSCHILD's filly (St. Amant)
       174.11   495.16   719.31   728.10

              ** Big Ben Dollard   174.12   91.01   **

Bad luck to big Ben Dollard and his JOHN O'GAUNT
       174.13   (210.02)

              ** Lenehan?   174.18   125.10   **

              ** Old Mrs Riordan   174.22   97.25   **

SKYE TERRIER (Mrs Riordan's)
      174.23   681.13   760.39   See also   44.33

         ** The City Arms hotel   174.23   35.27   **

         ** Smell. . . . fruit. . . . Cream   174.39+   (47.07) **

         ** Instinct   174.40   92.16   **

         ** Orangegroves   174.40   60.16   **

         ** Bleibtreustrasse   174.41   60.26   **

OYSTERS . . . SEWAGE they feed on
      174.42+   381.02+

Fizz and RED BANK OYSTERS
      175.02+   516.08   See also   92.21

Oysters. EFFECT ON THE SEXUAL. APHRODIS
      175.02   331.33   742.09   (526.24+)

         ** The Red Bank (Restaurant)   175.03   92.21   **

         ** First catch yur hare (recipe)   175.06   172.13   **

         ** Idea for a poison mystery (Titbits)   175.08   67.39   **

         ** Milly   175.12   21.42   **

ÉLITE. Crème de la crème
      175.17   263.01   660.12

A little more filleted lemon sole, MISS DUBEDAT?
      175.30+   486.04   586.38

         ** Huguenot name   175.31   84.06   **

A miss Dubedat lived in KILLINEY I remember
      175.32   755.34

Stuck on the pane two FLIES buzzed, stuck
      175.39   176.23   515.15

         ** Grapes of Burgundy   175.41   171.28   **

Hidden under wild ferns on Howth (MOLLY AND BLOOM ON HOWTH)
      176.01++   271.20   288.14   377.06+   379.19   550.04   628.11
      782.13#   (168.42)   (748.22)   See also   40.25

         ** The bay purple   176.02   (5.07) **

THE LION'S HEAD
      176.03   537.19   550.15

High on Ben Howth rhododendrons a NANNYGOAT walking surefooted
     176.15   550.04+

          ** She kissed me. I was kissed   176.19+   **
                                               See   48.01

          ** Me. And me now   176.22   155.35   **

          ** Stuck, the flies buzzed   176.23   175.39   **

          ** The silent veining of the oaken slab 176.24   (3.17)   **

          ** Beauty: it curves, curves are beauty 176.25+ 173.36   **

          ** Goddesses . . . library museum   176.25+   80.10   **

Shapely goddesses, VENUS
     176.26   177.01   201.05+   206.25   208.34   371.37   419.03
     466.21   490.14+   (466.21)
     Venus Pandemos
     425.40   490.15+
     Venus Kallipyge
     201.11   490.15
     Venus Metempsychosis
     490.16
     See also   210.08

Shapely goddesses. . . . JUNO
     176.26+   202.11   415.28

          ** Library   176.26   15.35   **

BOTTLE OF ALLSOP
     176.33   328.25+   (325.24)

Nectar, imagine it like DRINKING ELECTRICITY
     176.34   551.04

          ** Like stoking an engine   176.37   118.23   **

          ** They have no. . . . look today   176.38+   80.10   **

          ** A man and ready (G)   176.41   50.31   **

          ** A youth enjoyed her (Venus)   177.01   176.26   **

Isn't he in the insurance line? (DAVID DRIMMIE AND SONS)
     177.05+   370.02   586.40   769.12   772.09

          ** Canvassing for the Freeman   177.07++   57.36   **

That Irish farm dairy JOHN WISE NOLAN's wife has
     177.18   246.13#   253.07   324.27#   484.11+   547.24+   586.36

          ** He's in the craft   177.28+   73.05   **

IIIIIICHAAAAAAACH!
      177.39   490.07

          ** Didn't you see him look at his watch? 178.08   171.23   **

          ** Paddy Leonard . . . came in   178.20++   90.39   **

          ** Bantam Lyons came in   178.20++   74.02   **

TOM ROCHFORD followed
      178.20++   179.28   232.04++   253.13+   267.12   299.16   474.18+
      598.25
   His claret waistcoat
      178.21   232.06   253.16   474.19

I'll take a STONE GINGER, Bantam Lyons said
      178.28   179.18

          ** The Gold cup   178.41   85.40   **

          ** Zinfandel is it?   178.42+   174.02 **

          ** Who gave it to you?   179.10+   86.07   **

We'll take two of your small Jamesons after that (JOHN JAMESON WHISKEY)
      179.17   338.30   341.03   775.22

          ** Stone ginger   179.18   178.28 **

SPINACH
      179.22   462.34

Then with those RÖNTGEN RAYS searchlight you could
      179.22   179.41+   633.31++

          ** Terrier choked up a . . . cud   179.24   164.39 **

          ** Lapped it with new zest   179.25   41.18   **

          ** Mr Bloom coasted warily   179.27   41.04   **

          ** Tom Rochford   179.28   178.20 **

          ** Don Giovanni, a cenar teco   179.35++   63.31   **

          ** Burgundy. Good pick me up   179.37   171.28 **

          ** That Kilkenny People   179.38   120.38 **

          ** In the national library   179.39   15.35   **

          ** Watch it all the way down   180.01   179.22 **

          ** Keyes: two months if I get   180.12   107.35 **

** If I get Nannetti to   180.12   118.16   **

** Three Hynes owes me   180.13   119.33   **

** Hynes   180.13   90.04   **

** Prescott's ad   180.14   83.42   **

Could buy one of those silk PETTICOATS FOR MOLLY
        180.16   261.01   381.15   (168.30)

** Colour of her new garters   180.17   57.30   **

** Those lovely seaside girls   180.21   62.36   **

JOHN LONG'S (public house)
        180.21   181.01

** Gnawing a crusted knuckle   180.22   (114.21) **

WHY I LEFT THE CHURCH OF ROME?
        180.26+   519.26

** Give pauper children soup   180.27+   164.10   **

** Papa went to   180.29   76.26   **

A BLIND STRIPLING stood tapping the curbstone (piano tuner)
        180.31++   250.02++   254.34   263.11   264.12   288.20   289.01+
        289.27   290.41   486.18   538.07   725.27
        See also   250.19   264.12   281.15

** Tapping   180.31#   27.18   **

** Before Drago's   180.41   68.23   **

** (Boylan's) brilliantined hair   180.41   68.24   **

** Just when I was (coincidence)   180.41   68.24   **

** Driver in John Long's   181.01   180.21   **

SLAKING HIS DROUTH
        181.01   216.10   See also   41.05

HAND . . . SENSITIVE
        181.15   264.23

** Like Milly was   181.15   21.42   **

** Behind a bull: in front of a horse   181.18   23.12   **

** How on earth did he know . . . ?   181.25++   37.10   **

** Volume. Weight   181.27   72.05   **

** Bloodless pious face   181.30   27.19   **

** Penrose! That was the chap's name   181.32   156.02   **

** Molly's birthday   181.38   168.26   **

** Dark men they call them   181.39   (47.26)   **

** The curves   182.07   173.36   **

** It was black. . . . feeling of white 182.08   37.04   **

** Post office. Must answer   182.11   72.30   **

Post office. Must answer (BLOOM'S REPLY TO MARTHA CLIFFORD'S LETTER)
    182.11   262.01   275.03   278.05++   286.30   288.17   370.01

Send her a POSTAL ORDER two shillings half a crown
    182.11   280.28   537.33   711.24

Accept my little PRESENT
    182.12   275.04   278.10   279.18+

** The justice being born that way?   182.28   122.29   **

** Burned and drowned in New York   182.29   4.28   **

KARMA they call that
    182.30   185.40   416.30

** Met him pikehoses   182.31   50.13   **

** Sir Frederick Falkiner   182.34+   138.02   **

** Into the freemasons' hall   182.34   73.05   **

Annals of the BLUECOAT SCHOOL
    182.37   484.13

** Reuben J   183.01   93.41   **

MIRUS BAZAAR
    183.05   254.32   365.22   379.06   482.28   526.04   578.03

His excellency the Lord Lieutenant (LORD DUDLEY)
    183.05   248.11   252.03#   270.22+   526.05   579.17
    See also   233.22

In aid of funds for MERCER'S HOSPITAL
    183.06   254.32   379.07

** The Messiah. . . . Yes Handel   183.07   97.21   **

  ** Drop in on Keyes   183.08 107.35 **

  ** Sure to know someone on the gate 183.09 67.24 **

  ** Library   183.11++ 15.35 **

TAN SHOES (BOYLAN'S)
  183.12   227.19   253.42   282.25
  Creaked
  264.36   267.16   276.17   See also 56.16   184.06

TURNEDUP TROUSERS (BOYLAN'S)
  183.12   368.35   (47.11)

IT IS (Boylan)
  183.12+ 263.41

  ** Museum. Goddesses   183.14+ 80.10 **

  ** Wine in my face   183.16+ 171.28 **

  ** Light in his eyes   183.21 (26.01) **

  ** Cream curves of stone   183.26 173.36 **

  ** Agendath Netaim   183.30+ 60.16 **

  ** <u>Freeman</u>   183.35 57.36 **

  ** Potato   183.35 57.02 **

  ** Soap   183.39 85.17 **

  ** Lotion   183.39 84.03 **

SCYLLA AND CHARYBDIS

      ** (National Library)   184.01#   15.35 **

      ** (Stephen's Hamlet theory)   184.01#   16.13 **

Urbane, to comfort them, the quaker librarian purred (THOMAS LYSTER)
    184.01++   190.24++   509.17   598.33

GOETHE, J. W. von (We have . . . Wilhelm Meister)
  Wilhelm Meister's Apprenticeship
    184.02+
  Dichtung und Wahrheit
    196.19
  Faust
    80.26   422.27   429.03

On neatsleather CREAKING (LYSTER'S SHOES)
    184.06+   190.25   193.11   200.25   211.12   (208.37)
    See also   56.16   183.12

      ** Beautiful ineffectual dreamer   184.11(G)   7.30 **

SHELLEY, P. B. (The beautiful ineffectual dreamer)
    184.11   185.17
  "Epipsychidion"
    190.31
  Defense of Poesie
    194.30
  Prometheus Unbound
    201.06
  "Hellas" (G)
    (47.34+)
  "The Sensitive Plant"
    (71.42)

Against HARD FACTS
    184.11   418.15   (510.05)   (621.38)   (643.02)   See also 325.02

He CORANTOED off. . . . Most ZEALOUS (Lyster)
    184.14   509.21

      ** Those six brave medicals   184.20   163.04 **

JOHN EGLINTON asked
    184.20#   509.22+

      ** Paradise Lost   184.21   25.25 **

      ** The Sorrows of Satan   184.22   50.25 **

      ** Smile Cranly's smile   184.23   7.14 **

First he tickled her ("MEDICAL DICK AND MEDICAL DAVY")
    184.24+   209.18+   428.12   (163.04)

      ** The shining seven   184.30   (24.07) **

      ** W. B. calls them   184.30   9.22 **

His GREENCAPPED DESKLAMP
    184.31   510.02

An OLLAV, HOLYEYED
    184.33   510.06

      ** Orchestral Satan, weeping   184.35   25.25 **

      ** Satan   184.35   50.25 **

      ** Del cul fatto trombetta   184.37   20.20 **

      ** Cranly's eleven true Wicklowmen 184.39   7.14 **

      ** Gaptoothed Kathleen   184.40+   9.22 **

HER FOUR BEAUTIFUL GREEN FIELDS
    184.40   400.10

      ** The stranger in her house   184.40   34.42 **

SYNGE, JOHN M. (In the shadow of the glen)
  In the Shadow of the Glen
    185.02
  Riders to the Sea
    205.27
  Tramper
    200.02   412.17
  Other references
    193.03   198.15   200.02+   216.16

Parodies
     199.30-40   412.16-19

He COOEES for them
     185.02   551.21   (279.04)

          ** Mulligan   185.05   3.01 **

Mulligan has my TELEGRAM
     185.05   197.21   199.15+   425.31+

          ** Our young Irish bards   185.07   5.01 **

          ** Saxon   185.08   4.17 **

JONSON, BEN (Though I admire him, as old Ben did. . . .)
     Timber
          185.09   205.16
     "To the Memory of . . . William Shakespeare"
          188.24   203.06   206.06
     "Epitaph on Salomon Pavy"
          (653.01)

          ** All these questions   185.11++   5.13 **

Whether Hamlet is Shakespeare or JAMES I
     185.13   205.01

          ** Formless spiritual essences   185.14   140.30 **

          ** The deepest poetry of Shelley   185.17   184.10 **

          ** The eternal wisdom   185.18   140.13 **

PLATO's world of ideas
     185.19++   186.13   214.04   215.42   394.22   See also 190.28

          ** Some yankee interviewer   185.21   140.31 **

          ** Aristotle   185.24++   25.17 **

          ** Formless spiritual (Theosophy)   185.29++   140.30 **

Father, WORD and Holy Breath
     185.29   358.42   422.42

ALLFATHER
     185.29   423.22

The LOGOS who suffers in us at every moment
     185.31   191.39

I AM THE sacrificial BUTTER
     185.32   510.23

** The plane of buddhi   185.38   (80.10) **

** Karma   185.40   182.30   **

** Our . . . sister H. P. B's elemental   185.41   140.30   **

BEST, RICHARD (Mr Best entered)
     186.02#   509.21+

** That model schoolboy (Aristotle)   186.04+   25.17   **

** Horseness is the whatness 186.13   148.30   185.19   **

** God: noise in the street   186.15   34.33   **

** Space   186.15   (37.06) **

** After Blake's buttocks   186.17   24.07   **

Hold to the now, the here. through which all future (PAST-PRESENT-FUTURE)
     186.19   194.32   515.11   701.24+   See also 142.24(G)

** Haines   186.22   4.13   **

DON'T YOU KNOW
     186.25   187.08+   194.08+   198.36+   209.12+   210.40+   214.03
     509.29

** Hyde's Lovesongs of Connacht   186.25+   48.01   **

** He's gone to Gill's   186.27   95.37   **

** Bound thee forth, my booklet   186.28+   48.01   **

** We feel in England   186.34   20.40   **

** Green twinkling stone   186.35   20.01   **

An emerald set in the ring of the sea ("CUSHLA-MA-CHREE")
     186.35   205.27   287.28   426.02   600.17   (399.34)

The AURIC EGG of Russell
     186.38   See   196.16

** Movements which work revolutions   186.38   141.18   **

** The earth is . . . the living mother   186.40   5.13   **

For them the earth is not an EXPLOITABLE GROUND
     187.01   191.30

** Mallarmé   187.04++   49.12   **

The life of HOMER's Phaeacians
     187.05   216.28

```
        ** Don't you know              187.08+     186.25  **

        ** In Paris                    187.10      12.18   **
```

LE DISTRAIT
    187.17   558.21

PIECE DE SHAKESPEARE
    187.18   570.30

KIPLING, RUDYARD (The absentminded beggar)
   "The Absent-Minded Beggar"
    187.22+   457.30   558.21   589.08   722.15+   748.29   (604.22)
    See also   187.31
   "Recessional"
    (220.04)

GREENE, ROBERT (A deathsman of the soul Robert Greene called him)
   A Groat's Worth of Wit
    187.27   190.41   210.04   (211.21)   (504.16)   See also   41.31
   Friar Bacon and Friar Bungay
    617.29   658.35   See also 617.27

Not for nothing was he a BUTCHER's son
    187.28   213.24   242.17

```
        ** The sledded poleaxe         187.29      171.09   **

        ** Our father who art in purgatory   187.30    6.33   **
```

Khaki Hamlets DON'T HESITATE TO SHOOT
    187.31   316.16   See also 187.22

```
        ** Mr Swinburne                187.33      5.05     **

        ** Cranly                      187.34      7.14     **

        ** I his mute orderly          187.34      6.41     **

        ** Saxon smile                 187.37      23.12    **

        ** Yankee yawp                 187.37      17.05    **

        ** Hamlet is a ghoststory      187.39#     18.12    **

        ** Like the fat boy in Pickwick   188.01    37.37   **
```

LIST! LIST! O LIST! . . . If thou didst ever
    188.03   188.36   196.38   208.40   473.02   See also 152.39

```
        ** What is a ghost?            188.06++    115.04   **

        ** Corrupt Paris               188.09      12.18    **
```

    ** Virgin Dublin   188.09   (145.03)   **

The ghost from <u>LIMBO</u> <u>PATRUM</u>
   188.10   389.22

The BEAR Sackerson . . . Paris GARDEN
   188.16   463.08

    ** The huguenot's house   188.21   84.06   **

    ** The swanmews along the riverbank   188.22+   153.13   **

The PEN CHIVYING HER GAME OF CYGNETS towards the rushes
   188.23   568.11   See also 153.13

    ** The swan of Avon   188.24   185.09   **

    ** Composition of place. (St.) Ignatius 188.25   9.14   **

    ** The castoff mail of a court buck   188.28   3.01   **

A king and no king (BEAUMONT AND FLETCHER)
   188.29   196.32   393.04++

The YEARS OF HIS LIFE WHICH WERE NOT VANITY (Ecclesiastes)
   188.31   700.12

    ** <u>Hamlet, I am thy father's spirit</u>   188.35   152.39   **

    ** Bidding him list   188.36   188.03   **

Son of his body, HAMNET SHAKESPEARE
   188.37+   208.32

ANN SHAKESPEARE, born Hathaway
   189.08#   432.25

    ** As for living, our servants (T)   189.15   9.22   **

    ** Our servants   189.15   6.41   **

    ** <u>Flow over them with your waves</u>   189.20   5.13   **

    ** <u>Mananaan MacLir</u>   189.21   38.24   **

    ** That pound he lent you   189.22+   31.03   **

You spent most of it in GEORGINA JOHNSON's bed
   189.26   433.08   559.21

    ** Agenbite of inwit   189.27   16.07   **

    ** I paid my way   189.33   30.39   **

    ** Beyant Boyne water   189.34   169.25   **

** I am other I now   189.36+   11.22   **

But I, ENTELECHY. form of forms
     189.39   432.20

     ** Form of forms   189.39   25.17   **

I that SINNED AND PRAYED AND FASTED
     189.41   (367.15)

     ** Conmee   190.01   80.03   **

     ** Saved from pandies   190.01   135.18   **

     ** Mother's deathbed   190.13+   5.16   **

     ** Candle   190.13   10.20   **

     ** Liliata rutilantium   190.15   10.23   **

     ** The tangled glowworm of his lamp 190.17   45.12   **

     ** A man of genius   190.21   136.26   **

     ** The quaker librarian   190.24++   184.01   **

     ** Softcreakfooted   190.25   184.06   **

What useful discovery did SOCRATES learn?
     190.28+   202.26   213.15   215.42   217.24   418.01   432.25
     (103.07)   See also 185.19

From XANTHIPPE
     190.28   202.27

     ** How to bring thoughts into the world 190.29   145.10   **

     ** Epipsychidion   190.31   184.10   **

     ** The midwife's lore   190.33   37.37   **

     ** The archons of Sinn Fein   190.34   163.38   **

     ** A good groatsworth of wit   190.41   187.27   **

     ** Romeville   191.01   47.13   **

Whistling THE GIRL I LEFT BEHIND ME
     191.01   589.09

The bedchamber of every LIGHT-OF-LOVE in London
     191.05   432.27   456.20

Antony and CLEOPATRA
      191.08   208.33   297.06

            ** Left her and gained the world of men 191.10   43.27 **

GOLDSMITH, OLIVER (Stooping to conquer)
   She Stoops to Conquer
      191.16   264.34(G)
   The Deserted Village
      567.22
   Other reference
      228.14   406.01-407.14 (parody)

A boldfaced Stratford wench who TUMBLES in a cornfield A LOVER
      191.17+   196.27   512.31

PRETTY COUNTRYFOLK
      191.25   203.32

PARIS
      191.26   347.07

            ** The wellpleased pleaser   191.26   42.34 **

A tall figure . . . unveiled its COOPERATIVE watch
      191.28   510.20   See also 171.23

            ** The Homestead   191.29   35.22 **

            ** Exploitable ground   191.30   18.01 **

MOORE, GEORGE (Shall we see you at Moore's tonight?)
      191.32   192.27+   211.42   214.39+   397.12   405.18
   The Lake
      599.29

PIPER is coming
      191.32+   214.09+   See also 151.07

            ** Isis Unveiled . . . Yogibogeybox   191.37   140.30 **

            ** Logos   191.39   185.31 **

            ** Buddh under plantain   192.03   80.10 **

            ** Hesouls, shesouls . . . they bewail 192.03   (20.20) **

            ** Wide headless caubeen (Stephen's hat) 192.15   17.08 **

CAUBEEN
      192.15   499.11

            ** His ashplanthandle   192.16   17.17 **

            ** Touch. . . . Aristotle's experiment 192.16   25.17 **

```
        ** Necessity is that in virtue of which  192.18      25.17   **

STARKEY
      192.21      193.06

LONGWORTH will give it a good puff
      192.22      216.02      216.20

        ** The Express                      192.23     125.17   **

        ** That queer thing, genius         192.24+    136.26   **

        ** Yeats                            192.25       9.22   **

        ** Malachi Mulligan                 192.26       3.01   **

        ** Moore                            192.27+    191.32   **

        ** Haines                           192.27       4.13   **

Moore is Martyn's WILD OATS
      192.29      195.20      504.07      605.09

        ** Don Quixote and Sancho Panza     192.30+    152.10   **

        ** Lir's loneliest daughter   192.36    45.12      49.04   **

        ** Pigs' paper (The Irish Homestead)  193.02    35.22   **

        ** Bullockbefriending               193.02       5.01   **

        ** Synge                            193.03     185.02   **

An article for DANA
      193.03      214.18

        ** Gaelic League                    193.04     141.07   **

        ** Bring Starkey                    193.06     192.21   **

        ** Mask                             193.09       7.30   **

        ** He creaked                       193.11     184.06   **

        ** To and fro                       193.11      11.24   **

Courtesy or an INWARD LIGHT
      193.16      509.19         See also 412.01

        ** Reconciliation . . . sundering   193.17      38.12   **

        ** Christfox in leather trews       193.20+     26.33   **

        ** From hue and cry                 193.21     129.34   **
```

** Walking lonely in the chase   193.21   49.04   **

** A whore of Babylon   193.23   164.34   **

Bully tapsters' wives (SIR WILLIAM DAVENANT'S MOTHER)
    193.23   202.01

The discreet VAULTED CELL
    193.29   208.39   215.10

** A vestal's lamp   193.31   145.03   **

** What Caesar would have lived to do   193.32   25.14   **

** Possibilities of the possible   193.34   25.17   **

BROWNE, SIR THOMAS (What name Achilles bore when he lived among women)
    Urn Burial
    193.35
    Christian Morals
    393.41   394.03
    Parody of style
    393.41-395.15

What name ACHILLES bore
    193.35   640.35+   658.23   660.26

THOTH, god of libraries
    193.38   510.15

** And I heard the voice   193.39   142.11   **

** Tell me in my ear   194.01   139.26   **

** Others abide our question   194.05   7.30   **

** Don't you know   194.08+   186.25   **

** His private papers   194.12   141.07   **

** In the orginal   194.12   5.08   **

Ta an bad. . . . (Father O'Growney's Simple Lessons In Irish)
    194.12   296.39   See also 141.07

** Malachi Mulligan   194.15   3.01   **

** Miscreant eyes . . . a basilisk   194.21   40.04   **

** Mother Dana   194.23   (186.40)   **

** Weave and unweave   194.23+   21.14   **

** Molecules shuttled   194.24   11.22   **

   ** To and fro   194.24   11.25 **

The MOLE on my right breast
   194.26   194.41   197.07

   ** Shelley says   194.30   184.10 **

   ** In possibility I may come to be   194.31   25.17 **

   ** The future, the sister of the past 194.32   186.19 **

   ** That mole is the last to go   194.41   194.26 **

   ** The birthmark of genius   195.01   136.26 **

Which RENAN admired so much
   195.03   205.06

   ** Reconciliation . . . sundering   195.05+   38.12 **

Like another ULYSSES
   195.14   212.01   (757.10)   (330.18)

The leaning of SOPHISTS towards the bypaths of apocrypha
   195.17   242.04   See also 148.29+

Good BACON: gone musty. Shakespeare BACON's wild oats
   195.20+   634.27   See also 208.12

   ** Wild oats   195.20   192.29 **

TIR NA N-OG
   195.24   734.27

HUGO, VICTOR (The art of being a grandfather)
  L'art d'être grand-père
   195.37
  L'Homme qui Rit
   506.23

   ** That queer thing genius   195.39   136.26 **

The favoured rival is WILLIAM HERBERT, EARL OF PEMBROKE
   196.11   202.18

   ** What ought not to have been   196.13   (25.17) **

AUK'S EGG, prize of their fray
   196.16   737.25   See also 186.38

   ** A saying of Goethe's   196.19   184.02 **

Why does he send . . . a lordling to WOO for him?
     196.24   202.31   210.17   211.32   294.13   351.34   354.37
     377.01

     ** A lord of language   196.24   (6.37)   (50.31) **

     ** Romeo   196.25   108.15 **

     ** Cornfield   196.27   191.17 **

     ** Assumed dongiovannism   196.29   63.31 **

     ** Where love lies ableeding   196.32   188.29 **

DARKENING even his own UNDERSTANDING of himself
     196.35   212.14   (26.01)

     ** They list   196.38   188.03 **

     ** The porches of their ears   196.38+   139.26 **

THOSE THAT ARE DONE TO DEATH IN SLEEP
     196.40   425.15

     ** Done to death in sleep   196.40   139.27 **

     ** The beast with two backs   197.01   139.28 **

     ** His lean unlovely English   197.04   186.31 **

     ** Always turned backward   197.04   44.14   51.04 **

     ** What he would but would not   197.05   63.31 **

     ** With its mole cinquespotted   197.07   194.26 **

     ** Weary   197.08   3.41 **

     ** An old dog licking an old sore   197.09   44.33 **

HIS BEAVER IS UP
     197.12   387.28

     ** He is a ghost, a shadow now   197.12   18.12 **

     ** The wind by Elsinore's rocks   197.13   18.25 **

     ** Son consubstantial with the father   197.15   21.09 **

Hast thou found me, O mine enemy? [Ahab to ELIJAH]
     197.17   339.05   345.27+   See also 151.07

     ** Buck Mulligan   197.19#   3.01 **

     ** My telegram   197.21   185.05 **

** Primrosevested	197.24	18.02	**
** His doffed Panama	197.24	19.01	**
** Brood of mockers	197.28	3.37	**
** Photius	197.28	21.07	**
** Pseudomalachi	197.28	(3.01)	**
** Himself begot 197.29+	20.42	21.11	**
** The Holy Ghost	197.29	135.23	**
** Agenbuyer	197.30	16.07	**
** Crosstree	197.32	51.06	**
** Chap that writes like Synge 198.15	9.22	185.02	**
** Haines missed you	198.17	4.13	**
** At the D.B.C.	198.18	164.03	**
** He's gone to Gill's	198.18	95.37	**
** Hyde's Lovesongs of Connacht	198.18	48.01	**
** The museum	198.20	80.10	**
** The bard's fellowcountrymen	198.22	5.01	**
** An actress played Hamlet	198.24	76.23	**
** Vining . . . the prince was a woman	198.25	76.25	**

JUDGE BARTON . . . is searching for some clues
    198.27   297.10   679.20

** Saint Patrick	198.28	80.12	**

He swears . . . BY SAINT PATRICK
    198.28   595.06

** That story of Wilde's	198.29+	6.37	**
** Who am I?	198.34	11.22	**
** Don't you know	198.36+	186.25	**
** The very essence of Wilde	198.38+	6.37	**

Three drams of USQUEBAUGH you drank
    199.01   334.26

** Dan Deasy's ducats   199.02   11.02   27.25   **

** Lineaments of gratified desire   199.06   24.07   **

IN PAIRING TIME
     199.07   549.17

** Eve   199.09   14.23   **

** Wheatbellied sin   199.09   38.08   **

** Fang in's kiss   199.09   14.23   42.38   **

** The mocker   199.11+   3.37   **

** Folded telegram   199.15+   185.05   **

A PAPAL BULL!
     199.19   399.32++

MEREDITH, GEORGE (The sentimentalist is he who would enjoy. . . .)
   The Ordeal of Richard Feverel
     199.21   202.09   412.29   425.31   See also 256.42   257.24
   Personal reference
     211.42

** The four quid (Stephen's pay)   199.24   11.02   **

** The aunt   199.24   5.16   **

** Your unsubstantial father   199.25   21.09   **

** The Ship, lower Abbey street   199.26+   6.19   **

** O, you peerless mummer!   199.26   5.26   **

** You priestified kinchite   199.27   3.08   **

** It's what I'm telling you   199.30+   185.02   **

** Haines   199.31   4.13   **

** The tramper Synge   200.02   185.02   **

** Patrick   200.12   80.12   **

HIS IMAGE . . . HE MET. I MINE
     200.14   213.19   369.24   See also 213.14   377.01

His image WANDERING, he met
     200.14   214.33   217.31   249.02
     See also   9.22   34.05   83.27

** The Freeman   200.21+   57.36   **

** The <u>Kilkenny</u> <u>People</u>   200.22+   120.38   **

** Creaked, asked   200.25   184.06   **

** Voluble pains of zeal   200.28   184.14   **

** Ikey Moses?   201.01   57.38   **

** Collector of prepuces   201.03   13.33   **

** In the museum   201.04   80.10   **

** The foamborn Aphrodite   201.05+   176.26   **

The Greek mouth that has never been TWISTED IN PRAYER
     201.05   206.26   See also   3.38

** <u>Life</u> <u>of</u> <u>life,</u> <u>thy</u> <u>lips</u> enkindle   201.06   184.10   **

HE KNOWS YOUR OLD FELLOW
     201.09   207.04   See also 38.11

** His pale Galilean eyes   201.10   5.05   **

** Upon her mesial groove   201.11   80.10   **

** Venus Kallipyge   201.11   176.26   **

** <u>The</u> <u>god</u> <u>pursuing</u> <u>he</u> <u>maiden</u> <u>hid</u>   201.12   5.05   **

** Penelope   201.16++   149.04   **

** Antisthenes   201.17   148.30   **

** Pupil of Gorgias   201.17   148.31   **

** The palm of beauty   201.18   149.03   **

** Kyrios Menelaus   201.18   34.41   **

** Argive Helen   201.18   32.01   **

** The wooden mare of Troy   201.19   34.42   **

** Walt Whitman   201.23   17.05   **

SIR WALTER RALEIGH
     201.26   478.09

The GOMBEEN woman
     201.28   244.04

Eliza Tudor (QUEEN ELIZABETH I)
     201.28   202.05   204.41   205.08+

HER OF SHEBA
    201.29   297.19

You know MANNINGHAM's story of . . . Burbage . . . and . . . Shakespeare
    201.31+   211.32

      ** Took the cow by the horns   201.34   32.01 **

And the gay lakin, MISTRESS FITTON
    201.37   202.17+

      ** Lady Penelope Rich   201.38   149.05 **

      ** Davenant of Oxford's mother   202.01   193.23 **

Harry of six wives (HENRY VIII)
    202.05   328.09   400.35++

      ** Harry of six wives' daughter   202.05   201.28 **

      ** Lawn Tennyson, gentleman poet   202.06   50.31 **

      ** Poor Penelope   202.08   148.29 **

The DIAMOND PANES
    202.08   542.11

DO AND DO
    202.09+   280.27   See also 256.42   257.24

      ** Thing done   202.09   199.21 **

In a rosery of FETTER LANE of GERARD, herbalist
    202.09   280.26   661.39

He walks, GREYEDAUBURN
    202.10   280.26

      ** Lids of Juno's eyes   202.11   176.26 **

ONE LIFE IS ALL. One body
    202.11   280.27

      ** Reek of lust and squalor   202.12   28.03 **

WHOM DO YOU SUSPECT?
    202.15   338.14

      ** The court wanton   202.17+   201.37 **

      ** Spurned him for a lord   202.18   196.11 **

      ** His dearmylove   202.18   (4.12) **

```
        ** Love that dare not speak its name      202.19        6.37  **

        ** Socrates                               202.26      190.28  **
```

The holy office an OSTLER does for the stallion
    202.26   204.38   213.24

```
        ** He had a midwife to mother             202.27       37.37  **

        ** A shrew to wife                        202.27      190.28  **

        ** Once a wooer twice a wooer             202.31      196.24  **
```

MARY (ARDEN SHAKESPEARE)
    202.39   207.11+

Her goodman JOHN (SHAKESPEARE)
    202.39   207.11+

Susan, her husband too (SUSANNAH SHAKESPEARE HALL)
    202.42   212.13

While Susan's daughter, ELIZABETH (HALL)
    203.01   213.11+

WED HER SECOND, HAVING KILLED HER FIRST
    203.01   568.25

SHAKESPEARE'S WILL (His swansong, too)
    203.06++   206.15   212.19   393.24   543.20   See also 185.09

```
        ** Satan                                  203.14       50.25  **

        ** Mocker                                 203.15        3.37  **

        ** Pretty countryfolk                     203.32      191.25  **

        ** That Stagyrite schoolurchin            204.05+      25.17  **
```

Don't forget NELL GWYNN Herpyllis
    204.09   370.16

Don't forget . . . HERPYLLIS
    204.09   432.26

I must tell you what Dowden said (EDWARD DOWDEN)
    204.14+   214.08   393.16

```
        ** The bard                               204.20        5.01  **
```

You cannot EAT YOUR CAKE and have it
    204.27   215.41

```
        ** Will they wrest from us, from me       204.28       14.19  **
```

** From me the palm of beauty   204.28   149.03   **

And the SENSE OF PROPERTY
    204.30++   See also 505.03

He drew SHYLOCK out of his own long pocket
    204.30+   313.11

    ** Ten tods of corn hoarded   204.33   29.40   **

    ** Aubrey's ostler and callboy   204.38   202.26   **

GRIST TO HIS MILL
    204.39   632.15

    ** The queen   204.41   201.28   **

    ** A Scotch philosophaster   205.01   185.12   **

    ** The lost armada   205.02   41.02   **

    ** Mafeking enthusiasm   205.04   163.10   **

Warwickshire Jesuits are tried (GUNPOWDER PLOT)
    205.04   231.18

    ** Renan   205.06   195.03   **

    ** Patsy Caliban   205.07   6.37   **

    ** Our American cousin   205.07   139.05   **

The sugared sonnets follow SIDNEY's
    205.08   211.37

    ** Fay Elizabeth, . . . carroty Bess   205.08+   201.08   **

    ** Mixture of theolologicophilolological 205.13   39.38   **

    ** Sufflaminandus sum   205.16   185.09   **

    ** Coleridge   205.19   57.18   **

    ** Saint Thomas (Aquinas)   205.23++   17.40   **

ORA PRO NOBIS
    205.24   356.25+   358.22   377.35+   498.23++   (229.39)

    ** Pogue mahone!   205.27   123.23   **

    ** Acushla machree!   205.27   186.35   **

    ** It's destroyed we are   205.27   185.02   **

    ** Saint Thomas   205.30   17.40   142.24   **

** In the original	205.31	5.08 **
** Hoards	205.39	29.40 **
** Old Nobodaddy	205.41	24.07 **
** Gentle Will	206.06	185.09 **
** What of all the will to do?	206.13	5.13 **
** That secondbest bed	206.15	203.06 **

IT SKILLS NOT to ask
    206.20   433.15

** Venus	206.25	176.26 **
** Twisted her lips in prayer	206.26	201.05 **
** Agenbite of inwit	206.26	16.07 **
** Russell	206.32	5.13 **
** The unco guid	206.36	6.28 **

A sire in ULTONIAN ANTRIM
    206.38   509.27

** Give me my Wordsworth . . . Matthew	206.40+	113.19 **
** Clauber of ten forests	207.02	9.22 **
** A wand of wilding in his hand	207.03	113.19 **
** He knows your old fellow	207.04	201.09 **
** Her squalid deathlair (May Dedalus)	207.05	5.16 **
** Gay Paris	207.05	12.18 **

On the quayside I touched his hand (SIMON'S HAND)
    207.06   208.06

A father . . . is a NECESSARY EVIL
    207.10   500.02   595.05   633.18   See also 208.03

** His father	207.11+	202.39 **
** Mezzo del cammin di nostra vita	207.12	20.20 **
** Boccaccio's Calendrino	207.19	45.31 **

The first and last MAN WHO FELT HIMSELF WITH CHILD
    207.19   208.24

** From only begetter to only begotten   207.22   20.42 **

** The madonna   207.23   47.39 **

** Founded . . . upon the void   207.26   21.13 **

Upon INCERTITUDE
    207.26   697.26+   734.04

** Amor matris   207.27   27.38 **

** Sundered   207.35   38.12 **

** Loves that dare not speak their name   207.38   6.37 **

OVID, Metamorphoses (Queens with prize bulls)
  Pasiphaë, Minotaur
    207.40   411.29   569.08
  Dedalus, Icarus
    210.35+   572.02
  Dedal, Dedale
    394.29   423.05
  Dragon's teeth
    598.33
  See also   3.37   38.31   47.05   50.24   145.10

PAIN (OF CHILDBIRTH)
    207.41   389.02   392.01   408.20   (5.31)   (17.40)   (171.07)

IN RUE MONSIEUR-LE-PRINCE I THOUGHT IT
    208.03   595.05   See also 207.10

** Shrunken uncertain hand   208.06   207.06 **

** Sabellius, the African   208.07   21.11 **

** Heresiarch   208.07   21.06 **

** The bulldog of Aquin   208.09   17.40 **

Rutlandbaconsouthamptonshakespeare (RUTLAND THEORY)
    208.12   214.10   See also 195.20

** The father of his own grandfather   208.16   18.10 **

** Nature . . . abhors perfection   208.17   164.42 **

** Through twisted eglantine   208.20   25.25 **

** Flatter. Rarely. But Flatter   208.22   167.06 **

** I am big with child   208.24   207.19 **

** His mother's name . . . Arden   208.28   202.39 **

** Cleopatra   208.33   191.08   **

** Fleshpot of Egypt   208.33   41.32   **

** Venus   208.34   176.26   **

** Member of his family (fratricide)   208.35   100.05   **

** Quaking, tiptoed in, quake   208.37+   (184.06)   **

** His mask   208.37   7.30   **

** Cell   208.39   193.29   **

** They list   208.40   188.03   **

** Come, mess   208.42   145.10   **

He had three brothers, Gilbert, EDMUND, RICHARD
     209.02++   211.14+

WHAT'S IN A NAME?
     209.10   210.05   211.31   370.15   377.09   622.43

        ** Don't you know   209.12+   186.25   **

        ** Medical Dick   209.18+   184.24   **

RICHARD CROOKBACK
     209.22   211.30   407.27

        ** Painter of old Italy (Browning) (G)   209.33   (43.27)   **

        ** Like John O'Gaunt   210.02   (174.13)   **

As dear as the COAT OF ARMS he toadied for
     210.02   715.31

        ** Greatest shakescene in the country   210.04   187.27   **

        ** What's in a name?   210.05   209.10   **

STAR . . . rose at his birth
     210.07   698.31   700.36   See also   48.18

A DAYSTAR
     210.07   414.30

Brighter than VENUS in the night (star)
     210.08   376.24   See also 176.26

        ** Delta in Cassiopeia   210.09   48.18   **

        ** To be wooed. . . . Who will woo you? 210.17   196.24   **

BOUS STEPHANOUMENOS
    210.19   415.06

       ** A pillar of the cloud by day   210.25   143.11 **

       ** His hat   210.27+   17.08 **

       ** His stick (ashplant)   210.27   17.17 **

       ** His boots   210.27+   3.01 **

       ** Handkerchief too   210.29   4.37 **

       ** Your own name   210.32   3.37 **

       ** Fabulous voyager . . . Icarus   210.35   207.40 **

       ** Newhaven-Dieppe, steerage passenger   210.36   42.12 **

       ** Paris and back   210.36   12.18 **

LAPWING . . . Lapwing you are. Lapwing he
    210.36+   211.20+   (24.07(T))

       ** Fallen   210.37   50.24 **

       ** Don't you know   210.40+   186.25 **

GRIMM, JAKOB and WILHELM
  "The Sleeping Beauty"
    210.42+
  "The Boy Who Could not Shiver and Shake"
    561.07

The THIRD BROTHER
    211.01   412.32

FATHER DINEEN wants
    211.10   215.17

       ** Rectly creaking rectly rectly   211.12   184.06 **

       ** What do you have to say of Richard   211.14+   209.02+ **

       ** What . . . of Edmund   211.15+   209.02 **

       ** Nuncle Richie   211.17   39.02 **

       ** Lapwing   211.20+   210.36 **

My WHETSTONE
    211.21   504.16

       ** Then Cranly   211.22   7.14 **

** They mock to try you   211.23   3.37   **

The VOICE OF ESAU
    211.25   473.04   See also   38.11   76.29

** On   211.27   145.10   **

** Richard the conqueror   211.32   201.31   **

** Woos and wins her   211.32   196.24   **

** What's in a name?   211.31   209.10   **

** Richard, a whoreson crookback   211.30   209.22   **

** Sidney's Arcadia   211.37   205.08   **

** A novel by George Meredith   211.42   199.21   **

** Moore would say   211.42   191.32   **

** Ulysses   212.01   195.14   **

** Aristotle   212.01   25.17   **

** The usurping . . . brother   212.04   23.23   **

** Buries it certain fathoms   212.09   (21.28)   **

** His married daughter Susan   212.13   202.42   **

** Chip of the old block   212.13   144.11   **

It was the ORIGINAL SIN
    212.14+   365.25   383.19

** Darkened his understanding   212.14   196.35   **

My lords bishops of MAYNOOTH
    212.16   330.41   332.23   519.10

** His last written words   212.19   203.06   **

** His mind from his mind's bondage   212.26   (122.23)   **

He is ALL IN ALL
    121.29   213.24   365.04

He is BAWD AND CUCKOLD
    212.31   213.25   242.17   470.21

Like José he kills the real CARMEN
    212.33   527.04

CUCKOO! CUCKOO!
   212.36   335.37   382.23++   469.23+   542.26   See also 256.40

Dumas _fils_ (or is it DUMAS PÈRE?) is right
   212.40   505.03

He RETURNS AFTER A LIFE OF ABSENCE
   213.01+   See also 505.03

   ** Gravediggers bury Hamlet   213.04   109.14   **

   ** Betrayed   213.07+   14.05   **

   ** Lizzie (Elizabeth Hall)   213.11   203.01   **

   ** Grandpa's lump of love   213.11   39.13   **

   ** Nuncle Richie   213.11   39.02   209.02   **

   ** The place where the bad niggers go   213.12   111.02   **

   ** In his world within as possible   213.14   25.17   **

MAETERLINCK, MAURICE (Maeterlinck says: If _Socrates_. . . .)
   Wisdom _and_ _Destiny_
      213.14   217.14   505.02+   See also 200.14   377.20
   Personal reference
      215.34

   ** Socrates   213.15   190.28   **

   ** Life is many days   213.17   50.29   **

   ** Brothers-in-love   213.19   (333.20)   **

   ** Always meeting ourselves   213.19   200.14   **

THE LORD OF THINGS AS THEY ARE . . . _DIO BOIA_
   213.22+   304.35   581.28

   ** All in all in all of us   213.24   212.29   **

   ** Ostler   213.24   202.26   **

   ** Butcher   213.24   187.28   **

   ** Bawd and cuckold too   213.25   212.31   **

In the economy of heaven . . . are NO MORE MARRIAGES
   213.26+   395.36

MAN . . . BEING A WIFE UNTO HIMSELF
   213.27   216.35

EUREKA! Buck Mulligan cried.   EUREKA! (ARCHIMEDES)
   213.28   378.17+   See also   72.05

      ** Take some slips from the counter   213.33   15.35 **

Mr Best, DOUCE herald
   213.34   215.41

      ** Don't you know   214.03   186.25 **

      ** Platonic dialogues Wilde   214.04   6.37   185.19 **

      ** Why you should expect payment   214.07+   16.16 **

      ** Dowden   214.08   204.14 **

      ** Herr Bleibtreu   214.09   (60.26) **

      ** Piper   214.09+   191.32 **

      ** That Rutland theory   214.10   208.12 **

      ** Dana   214.18   193.03 **

      ** Pieces of silver   214.18+   (14.05) **

      ** Fred Ryan   214.19+   31.02 **

      ** I called upon the bard Kinch   214.27#   3.08 **

In upper MECKLENBURGH STREET
   214.28   432.22

      ** The Summa contra Gentiles   214.29   17.40 **

FRESH NELLY and ROSALIE, the coalquay whore
   214.30   217.11+   (430.29)

      ** Wandering Aengus   214.33   9.22   200.14 **

      ** You have eaten all we left   214.34   17.13 **

      ** Ay, I will serve you your orts   214.34   6.41 **

      ** Life is many days. This will end   214.37   50.29 **

      ** Notre ami Moore says   214.39+   191.32 **

      ** Mulligan flaunted his . . . panama   214.40   19.01 **

Monsieur Moore, lecturer on FRENCH LETTERS to the youth of Ireland
   214.41   370.39   393.21   405.16   721.20   772.33

      ** The bards must drink   215.01   5.01 **

**	Irish nights' entertainment	215.04	47.05	**
**	A lubber jester	215.09	25.09	**
**	The vaulted cell	215.10	193.29	**
**	What have I learned?	215.12	35.14	**
**	Haines	215.13	4.13	**
**	Cashel Boyle . . . Farrell	215.14	159.15	**
**	A priesteen in booktalk	215.17	211.10	**
**	The curving balustrade	215.25	(173.36)	**
**	Smoothsliding Mincius	215.25	25.25	**
**	Panamahelmeted	215.26	19.01	**
**	John Eglinton, my jo	215.28	6.28	**
**	O, the chinless Chinaman!	215.31	96.40	**

The chinless CHINAMAN!   CHIN CHON EG LIN TON
    215.31   509.23

**	Haines	215.32	4.13	**
**	M. Maeterlinck	215.34	213.14	**
**	He has his cake	215.41	204.27	**
**	The douce youngling	215.41	213.34	**
**	Phedo's toyable fair hair 215.42	185.19	190.28	**
**	Fair hair	215.42	(3.17)	**
**	Longworth	216.02	192.22	**

Longworth and McCURDY ATKINSON were there
    216.02+   519.02

**	I hardly hear the purlieu cry	216.04	9.22	**
**	To slake his drouth	216.10	181.01	**
**	Jest on 216.14	25.09	(24.07)	**
**	Mournful mummer	216.16	5.26	**
**	Synge	216.16	185.02	**
**	Longworth	216.20	192.22	**

** You inquisitional drunken jew jesuit	216.22	3.08 **
** The Yeats touch?	216.23+	9.22 **
** Most beautiful book. . . . Homer	216.27	9.22 **
** One thinks of Homer	216.28	187.05 **
** A play for the mummers	216.30	5.26 **
** The pillared Moorish hall	216.32	(47.05) **
** The nine men's morrice	216.33	28.11 **
** His tablet	216.34	40.07 **
** Everyman His own Wife	216.35	213.27 **

CRAB (a bushranger)
    217.06   496.11+

** MEDICAL DICK	217.07	209.18 **
** MOTHER GROGAN (a watercarrier)	217.10	12.33 **
** FRESH NELLY and ROSALIE	217.11	214.30 **
** To and fro	217.14	11.24 **

When the DAUGHTERS OF ERIN had to lift their skirts
    217.17   393.34   498.17+

Your MULBERRYCOLOURED, MULTICOLOURED, MULTITUDINOUS vomit
    217.19   729.21

** The most innocent son	217.20	25.01 **
** If Socrates leave his house today	217.24	213.24 **
** Socrates	217.24	190.28 **
** If Judas go forth tonight	217.25	14.05 **
** Ineluctably	217.26	25.17 **
** Here I watched the birds for augury	217.31	48.19 **
** Aengus of the birds 217.31	9.22	200.14 **
** I flew (Stephen's dream)	217.32+	47.05 **
** The wandering jew	217.35	34.05 **
** With clown's awe	217.36	25.09 **

** Did you see his eye?   217.36   101.36 **

SERMON ON THE MOUNT (He looked upon you to lust after you)
    217.36   326.08   457.19   468.26

** I fear thee, ancient mariner   217.37   57.18 **

** Manner of Oxenford   217.39   4.19 **

** Step of a pard   218.01   4.23 **

** Offend me still   218.04   8.42 **

** No birds   218.05   48.19 **

** Frail . . . two plumes of smoke   218.06+   142.12 **

** The druid priests   218.08   11.06 **

OUR CROOKED SMOKES CLIMB . . . FROM OUR BLESSED ALTARS
    218.11   599.11

WANDERING ROCKS

```
    ** The Very Reverend John Conmee        219.01#      80.03   **

    ** Steps (of St. Francis Xavier)        219.03       82.08   **

    ** Artane                               219.03      101.41   **

    ** That boy's name. . . . Dignam        219.04      101.02   **

    ** Mr Cunningham                        219.06       80.13   **

A ONELEGGED SAILOR . . . growled some notes
      219.08      225.15#      248.36      579.08     725.27      747.35   (418.38)
      See also      15.32

    ** Mr David Sheehy M. P.                219.20++    165.19   **

Were they getting on well at BELVEDERE?
      219.25      220.06     (223.25+)

    ** Father Bernard Vaughan               219.29++     82.10   **

    ** Pilate!                              219.41       82.10   **

    ** A zealous man                        219.42     (184.14)  **

    ** Lest he forget                       220.04     (187.22)  **

    ** They were from Belvedere             220.06      219.25   **

    ** Mr Denis J. Maginni                  220.24      153.34   **

    ** Walking with grave deportment        220.27       37.37   **
```

He passed LADY MAXWELL
    220.28   224.17

Was that not MRS M'GUINNESS?
    220.30+   226.26+   586.31

D. V. (DEO VOLENTE)
    220.39   223.09

        ** Wonder that there was not a tramline 221.03   58.03 **

        ** Christian brother boys   221.07   151.02 **

        ** Dreadful catastrophe in New York   221.20   4.28 **

An ACT OF perfect CONTRITION
    221.23   741.40

Father Conmee went by DANIEL BERGIN's publichouse
    221.24   613.29

        ** Corny Kelleher   221.28   71.15 **

A constable on his beat saluted Father Conmee (CONSTABLE 57C)
    221.29   225.05+

        ** A turfbarge . . . a bargeman   221.35   99.09 **

        ** Saint Francis Xavier's church   222.01   82.08 **

        ** Pray for me   222.39 (205.24) **

        ** Mr Eugene Stratton   202.41   92.05 **

        ** Grinned with thick niggerlips   222.42   80.19 **

        ** Saint Peter Claver . . . mission   223.02+   80.04 **

        ** D. V.   223.09   220.39 **

        ** At the Howth road stop   223.13 (40.25) **

        ** Gay Malahide   223.16   43.27 **

        ** First countess of Belvedere   223.25+ 219.25 **

        ** A listless lady   223.26+   18.05 **

EIACULATIO SEMINIS INTER VAS NATURALE MULIERIS
    223.31   736.08+

        ** Don John Conmee   223.38   63.31 **

        ** Cabbages, curtseying to him   224.05 (13.22) **

A flock of muttoning clouds over RATHCOFFEY
    224.10   231.12

      ** Clongowes field   224.11   11.22   **

      ** Lady Maxwell   224.17   220.28   **

      ** The <u>Pater</u>   224.19   6.33   **

A flushed young man (LYNCH)
  His tryst with Kitty
    224.25+   231.16   405.28+   415.39++   (169.01)
  Other references
    388.20#   430.35#   615.30+
  His jockey cap
    431.11   502.23   503.27++
  Lecherous Lynx
    433.08   560.02

Wild nodding DAISIES in her hand
    224.26   263.36

      ** Corny Kelleher   224.33#   71.15   **

      ** Father John Conmee   225.01   80.03   **

      ** Constable 57C   225.05+   221.29   **

A GENEROUS WHITE ARM . . . FLUNG FORTH A COIN
    225.10   226.02   747.34

      ** What's the best news?   225.12   85.25   **

      ** A onelegged sailor   225.15#   219.08   **

Skirting RABAIOTTI'S icecream car
    225.16   429.05   434.06   (621.23)

      ** Towards Larry O'Rourke   225.17   57.40   **

      ** <u>For England</u>   225.19++   15.32   **

KATEY AND BOODY DEDALUS
    225.20   226.07#   620.25   747.32

      ** J. J. O'Molloy   225.23   124.32   **

      ** Mr Lambert   225.23   90.03   **

With a visitor (REV. HUGH C. LOVE)
    225.24   230.10++   245.08   245.26+   252.35   270.10   282.04
    579.14   599.16+   (16.29)

A card <u>UNFURNISHED APARTMENTS</u> slipped from the sash and fell
    225.39   234.10

```
        ** Taut shiftstraps                    226.02      92.33  **

        ** A woman's hand flung forth a coin   226.02     225.10  **

        ** Katey and Boody Dedalus             226.07#    225.20  **

MAGGY (DEDALUS) at the range
     226.10#     243.24      620.25

        ** Father Conmee                       226.13      80.03  **

        ** Clongowes fields                    226.13      11.22  **

        ** M'Guinness's                        226.16+    220.30  **

The lacquey rang his bell (LACQUEY AT DILLON'S)
     226.31      237.06++    539.32+     579.07

        ** Where's Dilly?                      226.38     151.33  **

        ** Our father who art not in heaven    227.03       6.33  **

        ** Crumpled throwaway.  Elijah is coming 227.06   151.07  **

The CUSTOMHOUSE old dock
     227.09      343.25      433.15      615.36      619.24

Bedded the WICKER BASKET WITH RUSTLING FIBRE
     227.11      675.13

The bottle swathed in pink tissue paper (Bottle of PORT WINE)
     227.12      675.15      741.31      747.28

        ** A small jar (of Plumtree's)         227.13      75.02  **

She bestowed fat PEARS . . . PEACHES
     227.17      675.14

        ** Blazes Boylan . . . in new tan shoes 227.19   183.12  **

        ** H.E.L.Y.'s                          227.22     154.25  **

A darkbacked figure . . . scanned books (BLOOM'S BOOKHUNT)
     227.27      233.27      235.18#     729.02

It's for an INVALID
     227.35      675.15

[Boylan] took a RED CARNATION from the tall stemglass
     228.02+     251.15      254.07      265.26      265.40      266.20      564.13
     741.24

ALMIDANO ARTIFONI
     228.13#     249.37      255.06      518.06+
```

** At Goldsmith's knobby poll   228.14   191.16 **

** Where pigeons roocoocooed   228.20   162.14 **

** Swaying his ashplant   228.26   17.17 **

CI RIFLETTA
  228.28+   518.09

** The stern stone hand of Grattan   228.29   139.03 **

An Inchicore tram unloaded straggling HIGHLAND soldiers of a BAND
  228.30   229.07   254.10   See also 479.34

** The rout of barekneed gillies   229.07   228.30 **

** The Capel street library   229.10   64.42 **

COLLINS, WILKIE
  The Woman in White
    229.10+
  The Moonstone
    756.18

THE DISK SHOT DOWN THE GROOVE, WOBBLED A WHILE, CEASED AND OGLED THEM
  229.15   232.07   474.26

16 JUNE 1904
  229.18   711.09

WOLFE TONE's statue
  229.20   297.02   305.34   593.04   599.02

** H.E.L.Y.'s   229.21   154.25 **

The large poster of MARIE KENDALL, CHARMING SOUBRETTE
  229.23+   232.37   251.05   253.17   536.05   (418.37)

** Listlessly lolling   229.24   18.05 **

** Sport   229.38   128.02 **

** Mr Lenehan   230.01   125.10 **

He said he'll be in the ORMOND at four
  230.02   232.23   246.08   252.29+   257.27#   376.09   564.02
  729.04

** Ned Lambert   230.04#   90.03 **

RINGABELLA AND CROSSHAVEN
  230.05   278.39+

** Hello, Jack   230.07   124.32 **

** In the clergyman's uplifted hand   230.10++   225.24   **

The historic council chamber of SAINT MARY'S ABBEY
    230.15+   688.37

    ** Silken Thomas   230.16+   45.26   **

    ** O'Madden Burke   230.17   131.30   **

    ** The time of the union   230.19   31.20   **

    ** Beard . . . hung on chessboard   230.35   165.02   **

    ** Trespass on your valuable time   230.37   (32.01)   **

    ** Rathcoffey   231.12   224.10   **

    ** The Fitzgeralds   231.14+   45.26   **

    ** The young woman with slow care   231.16   224.25   **

    ** Gunpowder plot   231.18   205.04   **

    ** The earl of Kildare   231.21   45.26   **

    ** Poor little . . . what do you call   232.02   157.01   **

    ** Tom Rochford . . . claret waistcoat   232.04++   178.20   **

    ** It shot down the groove, wobbled   232.07   229.15   **

    ** Richie Goulding   232.10+   38.34   **

    ** Goulding, Collis and Ward   232.11   88.23   **

AN ELDERLY FEMALE with false teeth smiling incredulously
    232.13   236.29   252.25

    ** Nosey Flynn   232.18   171.25   **

    ** In the Ormond   232.23   230.02   **

    ** Lenehan   232.23   125.10   **

Tell him I'm BOYLAN WITH IMPATIENCE
    232.25   263.25   267.09   269.42   276.23

    ** M'Coy   232.27#   67.24   **

    ** He's a hero   232.34++   4.29   **

DAN LOWRY'S MUSICHALL . . . THE EMPIRE
    232.37+   312.32

```
        ** Marie Kendall, charming soubrette    232.37     229.23  **
At the DOLPHIN [HOTEL]
     233.09      260.42

        ** Sceptre                              233.12+    128.03  **

MARCUS TERTIUS MOSES' sombre office
     233.14      449.23

THE VICEREGAL CAVALCADE
     233.22      252.03#     257.27++
  Passes out Parkgate
     239.04      252.08
  Outriders, leaping, leaping
     241.17      248.07      573.16
  Hoofirons steelyringing
     256.01      257.28      258.38      270.22
  Imperthnthn thnthnthn
     256.01      258.24      259.32
  See also       183.05

        ** Bantam Lyons                         233.25      74.02  **

        ** Darkbacked figure . . . scanned books 233.27    227.27  **

Leopoldo or the Bloom is on the Rye ("WHEN THE BLOOM IS ON THE RYE")
     233.31      256.06      262.02      266.10      286.34

He bought a BOOK . . . ASTRONOMY it was about
     233.34+     543.09      709.11+

MANGAN'S, LATE FEHRENBACH'S
     234.01      250.21

        ** Master Patrick Aloysius Dignam       234.01     101.02  **

Master . . . Dignam . . . carrying a pound an  a half of PORKSTEAKS
     234.02      250.22      251.19      254.30     568.16

        ** Glencree reformatory                 234.03+    155.23  **

        ** The lord mayor . . . Val Dillon      234.05     155.02  **

And sir CHARLES CAMERON
     234.05      586.23

        ** Dan Dawson spoke                     234.06      91.08  **

        ** Bartell D'Arcy sang                  234.07     156.06  **

        ** Benjamin Dollard                     234.07      91.01  **

        ** My missus sang there once            234.08      75.05  **
```

    ** Unfurnished <u>Apartments</u>   234.10   225.39 **

But WAIT TILL I TELL YOU (Lenehan)
   234.14+   259.14

    ** The year my missus was there   234.20   75.05 **

It was a gorgeous winter's night on the FEATHERBED MOUNTAIN
   234.25   371.15   750.05   See also 50.13   155.23

    ** Chris Callinan   234.26++   137.31 **

    ** <u>Lo, the early beam of morning</u>   234.28   130.28 **

She has a FINE PAIR, God bless her
   234.31   425.21   (513.18)

    ** Settling her boa   234.34   156.20 **

    ** Moulded ample curves of air   234.36   173.36 **

    ** His yachtingcap   235.12   125.10 **

There's A TOUCH OF THE ARTIST ABOUT OLD BLOOM
   235.17   653.07

    ** Mr Bloom turned over idly pages   235.18++   227.27 **

ARISTOTLE'S <u>MASTERPIECE</u>
   235.19   411.06   772.37   (715.18)

    ** Child born every minute somewhere 235.23   164.21 **

    ** Mrs Purefoy   235.23   158.36 **

SACHER MASOCH, LEOPOLD VON (<u>Tales of the Ghetto</u>)
  <u>Tales of the</u> Ghetto
    235.25
  <u>Venus im Pelz</u>
    466.21   565.23

    ** The grave deportment   235.34   37.37 **

    ** Mr Denis J. Maginni   235.35   153.34 **

<u>Fair Tyrants</u> by JAMES LOVEBIRCH
  <u>Fair Tyrants</u>
    235.37   751.41+   756.03+   777.11
  Other references
    465.25   468.11   (327.05)

SWEETS <u>OF</u> SIN
  Title
    236.05#   258.10   260.04+   261.01   288.18   437.07   452.30
    498.29   586.38   652.19   688.11   735.22   765.10   769.32

Frillies for Raoul
   236.09++   236.25   258.11+   260.42   263.40   274.15   288.18
   382.15   565.21
Hands felt for the opulent curves inside her deshabille
   236.13   274.19   368.29   373.24   439.09   653.06   653.27
Heaving embonpoint
   236.18+   286.11   382.15   462.07   653.30
Mouth glued on his in a . . . kiss
   (48.01)

ARMPITS' oniony sweat
   236.25   375.06   501.13   511.07   535.24   540.31

      ** An elderly female   236.29   232.13 **

The case . . . of the . . . LADY CAIRNS VERSUS the . . . barque MONA
   236.33   638.13

      ** The lacquey by the door   237.06++   226.31 **

      ** Dillon's auctionrooms   237.06++   128.30 **

      ** Dilly Dedalus   237.098   151.33 **

      ** The halfmile wheelmen   237.16   86.19 **

W. E. WYLIE
   237.17   349.33

      ** Your uncle John the cornetplayer 237.24   38.35 **

      ** Mr Kernan   238.03   71.24 **

      ** In the Scotch house   238.05   160.04 **

      ** Your poor mother   238.14   5.16 **

      ** Jack Power   238.34   87.03 **

      ** A shave for the funeral   238.35   57.11 **

      ** The viceregal cavalcade passed out 239.04   233.22 **

      ** Mr Kernan   239.13#   71.24 **

The order he had booked for PULBROOK ROBERTSON
   239.14   726.35   729.33

      ** General Slocum explosion   239.22+   4.28 **

You know why? PALMOIL
   239.29+   639.34

      ** Father Cowley   239.39   76.07 **

    ** Kildare street club   240.06   86.29 **

    ** Must dress the character   240.10   17.03 **

COWPER, WILLIAM (The cup that cheers but not inebriates)
  The Task
    240.12   249.18   284.40

    ** Cup that cheers (George Berkeley)(G)   240.12   48.26 **

    ** Sir John Rogerson's quay   240.14   71.01 **

    ** A crumpled throwaway . . . Elijah   240.16   151.07 **

    ** Lambert   240.20   90.03 **

    ** Down there Emmet was hanged   240.27   114.18 **

    ** Dogs licking the blood   240.28   44.33 **

Is he buried in SAINT MICHAN's?
    240.30   293.38+   297.39   339.29   344.10

    ** In Glasnevin   240.31   100.22 **

    ** Dignam is there now   240.32   57.11 **

    ** Guinness's   240.35   81.39 **

    ** Denis Breen   240.40   157.17 **

    ** Weary of having waited   240.40   (3.41) **

    ** John Henry Menton   240.41   102.38 **

    ** Led his wife   240.41   156.32 **

    ** The office of Messrs Collis and Ward   240.42   88.23 **

    ** Ned Lambert   241.02   90.03 **

    ** A kind of retrospective arrangement   241.04   91.07 **

    ** Lord Edward Fitzgerald   241.07+   45.26 **

    ** That sham squire (Francis Higgins)   241.11   126.26 **

INGRAM, J. K. (They rose in dark and evil days)
  "The Memory of the Dead"
    241.12   257.17+(T)   285.13   290.36   305.12   306.17

    ** Ben Dollard   241.14   91.01 **

    ** Masterly rendition   241.14   91.04 **

** <u>At the siege of Ross</u>   241.16   91.01   **

** Outriders leaping   241.17   233.22   **

** With their vulture nails   241.26   47.03   **

** Winedark stones   241.27   5.07   **

Born all in the DARK WORMY EARTH
   241.29   257.03   283.15+

** Born all in the dark . . . wrest them 241.29+   (25.25)   **

** Lights shining in the darkness   241.30   26.01   **

** Where gum burns with garlic   241.33   171.06   **

A SAILORMAN . . . EYES HER. A long and seafed silent rut
   241.34   361.41

** A stolen hoard   242.02   29.40   **

**   The brainsick words of sophists   242.04   195.17   **

** Antisthenes   242.04   33.07   148.30   **

** Orient and immortal wheat   242.05   38.08   **

** Two old women   242.07+   37.34   **

** Through Irishtown   242.08   87.40   **

** A midwife's bag   242.09   37.37   **

** Between two roaring worlds   242.14   (7.30)   **

SHATTER THEM, ONE AND BOTH
   242.15   583.03+   (24.07)

** Bawd and butcher, were the words   187.28   212.31   **

** Not yet awhile   242.17   115.08   **

Not yet awhile (STEPHEN'S FEAR OF DESTRUCTION BY GOD)
   242.17   394.36+

A LOOK AROUND
   242.18   453.08

** The handle of the ash   242.21   17.17   **

A faded 1860 print of HEENAN BOXING SAYERS
   242.23   318.23

** Heroes' hearts   242.26   4.29   **

My pawned SCHOOLPRIZES
   242.31   768.29

      ** Father Conmee   242.33   80.03 **

      ** Eighth and ninth book of Moses   242.36   40.07 **

      ** Who has passed here before me?   242.37   40.38 **

<u>Se</u> <u>el</u> <u>yilo</u> <u>NEBRAKADA</u> <u>FEMININUM</u>!
   242.41++   440.02   553.21

      ** Joachim's. Down, baldynoddle   243.03   39.37 **

      ** Dilly   243.06#   151.33 **

      ** A Stuart face   243.09   29.25 **

LANK LOCKS falling
   243.09   243.28   579.28

She crouched FEEDING THE FIRE with broken boots (Dilly)
   243.10   670.09

      ** I told her of Paris   243.11   12.18 **

      ** Maggy   243.24   226.10 **

      ** She is drowning. . . . Save her 243.27+   4.28 **

      ** Agenbite   243.27+   16.07 **

      ** Lank coils   243.28   243.09 **

SEAWEED HAIR around me
   243.29   281.26

MISERY! Misery!
   243.32   382.12   456.28   462.33   725.33

      ** Father Cowley   243.33#   76.06 **

      ** What's the best news?   243.38   85.25 **

      ** A certain gombeen man   244.04   201.28 **

      ** Reuben of that ilk   244.07++   93.41 **

      ** Ben Dollard   244.08#   91.01 **

      ** Long John (Fanning)   244.09   119.20 **

      ** Arse and pockets   244.17   123.23 **

Square hat above large SLOPS (Dollard's)
    244.19+   267.35   See also 91.01   268.22

        ** Cashel Boyle . . . Farrell   244.40   159.15   **

        ** The Kildare street club   244.41   86.29   **

        ** The reverend Hugh C. Love   245.08   225.24   **

        ** Attended by Geraldines   245.10   45.26   **

Towards the THOLSEL beyond the Ford of Hurdles
    245.11   324.36

        ** The subsheriff's office   245.14   119.20   **

        ** Rock   245.15   170.07   **

        ** John Henry Menton   245.17   102.38   **

        ** Your landlord (Love)   245.26   225.24   **

The LANDLORD has the PRIOR CLAIM
    245.30   282.04

        ** Tell Barabbas (Reuben J. Dodd)   245.35   93.41   **

        ** The youngster (Master Dignam)   246.01+   101.02   **

        ** Martin Cunningham   246.01#   80.13   **

        ** The Castleyard   246.02   161.10   **

BRONZE BY GOLD
    246.07   252.30   256.01   257.09   257.26#   564.08

Miss KENNEDY's head by Miss DOUCE's head
    246.07   252.30   257.26#   564.03+   566.20+

Above the CROSSBLIND of the Ormond hotel
    246.08   252.29   257.27   268.06   564.03

        ** The Ormond hotel   246.08   230.02   **

        ** Cunningham . . . fingering his beard   246.09   80.13   **

        ** Father Conmee   246.10   80.03   **

        ** Mr Power   246.11#   87.03   **

        ** John Wyse Nolan   246.13#   177.18   **

        ** Reading the list (of contributors)   246.13+   57.11   **

        ** Councillor Nannetti   246.15   118.16   **

      ** Bloom . . . down for five shillings   246.21   57.11 **

There's JIMMY HENRY
    246.30#   487.11+
  His corns
    246.40   247.30   586.32

Just heading for KAVANAGH'S
    246.31+   253.07

      ** Outside la Maison Claire   246.33   167.18 **

      ** Jack Mooney   246.33   173.13 **

      ** Mooney's brother-in-law (Bob Doran) 246.34   74.01 **

      ** The liberties   246.34   37.38 **

MICKY ANDERSON's watches
    246.39   253.10

      ** The assistant town clerk's corns   246.40   246.30 **

      ** Long John Fanning   247.04#   119.20 **

He removed his large HENRY CLAY [cigar] decisively
    247.11   471.11   485.21

      ** About their damned Irish language 247.17+   141.07 **

      ** The marshal (J. H. Parnell)   247.18   165.02 **

And HUTCHINSON, the LORD MAYOR
    247.21   254.41   480.13

And little LORCAN SHERLOCK doing locum tenens
    247.21   479.07+

      ** Cunningham . . . his beard   247.25   80.13 **

      ** What Dignam was that?   247.28#   57.11 **

      ** O, my corns!   247.30   246.30 **

      ** Menton's office   247.40   102.38 **

      ** Leaping leaders, rode outriders   248.07   233.22 **

      ** The lord lieutenant general   248.11   183.05 **

      ** Buck Mulligan   248.13#   3.01 **

      ** Buck Mulligan . . . his panama   248.14   19.01 **

```
** Haines                              248.14#        4.13   **

** Parnell's brother                   248.15++     165.02   **

** Ghostbright                         248.25       165.11   **

** We call it D.B.C.                   248.31       164.03   **

** You missed Dedalus on Hamlet        248.32        16.13   **

** His newbought book                  248.33        48.01   **

** The onelegged sailor                248.36       219.08   **

** England expects                     248.37        15.32   **

** Buck Mulligan's primrose waistcoat  248.38        18.02   **

** Wandering Aengus          249.02      9.22      200.14   **

** The Attic note                      249.08         3.38   **

** Swinburne                           249.08         5.05   **

** He can never be a poet              249.10        39.38   **

** I tackled him . . . on belief       249.12        19.33   **

** The cheerful cups                   249.18       240.12   **

** The sense of destiny                249.19        66.39   **

** Your movement                       249.21       141.18   **
```

Slit a steaming SCONE. . . . its SMOKING pith
   249.23   580.06   See also 755.25

```
** Elijah . . . throwaway              249.33       151.07   **

** Threemasted schooner Rosevean       249.36        51.05   **
```

From BRIDGWATER with bricks
   249.36   625.14   631.16   647.12

```
** Almidano Artifoni                   249.37       228.13   **

** Cashel Boyle . . . Farrell          249.38#      159.15   **

** A blind stripling                   250.02++     180.31   **

** Tapped his way                      250.02#       37.18   **

** Elijah                              250.08       151.07   **
```

COACTUS VOLUI
    250.12   520.01

He strode past MR BLOOM'S DENTAL WINDOWS
    250.14   337.35   455.05   586.34

God's curse on you, . . . you BITCH'S BASTARD!
    250.19   263.20   284.14   286.02

       ** Master Patrick Aloysius Dignam   250.20#   101.02 **

       ** Pound and a half of . . . porksteak   250.22   234.02 **

Sitting in the parlour with MRS STOER
    250.24   251.07   351.28

And MRS QUIGLEY
    250.24   385.12

And MRS MACDOWELL (GERTY'S MOTHER)
    250.24   (253.01)

The SUPERIOR TAWNY SHERRY
    250.26   251.36   473.18   568.09

       ** Uncle Barney (Corrigan)   250.26   101.25 **

Bought from TUNNEY'S
    250.27   355.20   See also 250.26

Sergeantmajor BENNETT, the Portobello bruiser
    250.33+   451.21   603.13+   See also 173.14

       ** Myler Keogh   250.33+   173.14 **

       ** Marie Kendall, charming soubrette   251.05   229.23 **

One of the MOTS
    251.06   606.15

       ** Stoer   251.07   250.24 **

       ** In Grafton street   251.15   168.10 **

       ** Flower in a toff's mouth   251.15   228.02 **

       ** The drunk (Bob Doran)   251.17   74.01 **

       ** Sandymount tram   251.18   37.01 **

       ** The porksteaks   251.19   234.02 **

       ** Uncle Barney (Corrigan)   251.25+   101.25 **

       ** Get it into the paper   251.25   57.11 **

** His face . . . red like it was   251.28   57.11   **

** Bawling out for his boots   251.36   57.11   **

** To Tunney's   251.36   250.26   **

He went to confession to FATHER CONROY
    252.01   358.29++   359.39+   361.29   362.10   363.27   365.10
    377.40   382.27   469.19

** William Humble   252.03#   183.05   233.22   **

** Lady Dudley   252.03#   138.03   **

** The honourable Mrs   252.06   73.40   **

The honourable GERALD WARD
    252.07#   257.34+

** The lower gate   252.08   233.22   **

** Phoenix Park   252.08   170.41   **

** Mr Thomas Kernan   252.12   71.24   **

** Broadstone terminus   252.20   74.13   **

** Richie Goulding   252.21   38.34   **

** Goulding, Collis and Ward   252.22   88.23   **

** Reuben J. Dodd   252.23   93.41   **

** An elderly female about to enter   252.25   232.13   **

Under TOM DEVAN's office
    252.28   766.34+

** Above the crossblind   252.29   246.08   **

** The Ormond Hotel   252.29   230.02   **

** Gold by bronze   252.30   246.07   **

** Miss Kennedy's head by Miss Douce's   252.30   246.07   **

** For the subsheriff's office   252.32+   119.20   **

** The reverend Hugh C. Love   252.35   225.24   **

** Lenehan   252.38   125.10   **

** M'Coy   252.38   67.24   **

GERTY MACDOWELL
    253.01   333.28   348.02#   442.06+   471.30   722.29   735.16
    (250.24)

    ** Cork lino   253.02   113.16   **

    ** Couldn't see . . . because the tram   253.03   74.28   **

    ** Kavanagh's winerooms   253.07   246.31   **

    ** John Wyse Nolan   253.07   177.18   **

    ** Micky Anderson's . . . watches   253.10   246.39   **

    ** Tom Rochford   253.13+   178.20   **

    ** Nosey Flynn   253.14   171.25   **

    ** His claret waistcoat   253.16   178.20   **

    ** A charming soubrette, Marie Kendall   253.17   229.23   **

    ** The D.B.C.   253.21   164.03   **

    ** Buck Mulligan   253.22   3.01   **

    ** Haines   253.22   4.13   **

    ** John Howard Parnell   253.24   165.02   **

    ** Dilly Dedalus   253.25   151.33   **

    ** John Henry Menton . . . Oyster eyes   253.28+   102.38   **

    ** King Billy's horse   253.31   31.23   **

    ** Mrs Breen   253.32   156.32   **

    ** Her hastening husband   253.32+   157.17   **

    ** H. . . . E.L.Y.'s   253.37   154.25   **

    ** Mr Denis J. Maginni   253.40   153.34   **

    ** Gravely walked   253.41   37.37   **

    ** Provost's wall   253.42   164.40   **

Came JAUNTILY BLazes Boylan
    253.42   256.15   262.17   263.26   263.41+   264.29   267.42
    269.09   271.17   273.03   274.16   276.19   579.14   (341.26)
    See also   56.27   748.15

    ** In tan shoes   253.42   183.12   **

SOCKS WITH SKYBLUE CLOCKS (Boylan's)
        254.01   282.26   368.34   749.40

The refrain of MY GIRL'S A YORKSHIRE GIRL
        254.01++   574.10++   575.11++   576.02++   598.29   (500.06)

High action a SKYBLUE TIE (Boylan's)
        254.04   266.15   368.34   749.40

A SUIT OF INDIGO SERGE (Boylan's)
        254.05   279.35

            ** The red flower between his lips   254.07   228.02   **

            ** Unseen brazen highland laddies   254.10   228.30   **

            ** The quartermile flat handicappers   254.19+   86.19   **

            ** Cashel Boyle . . . Farrell   254.22   159.15   **

            ** Hornblower   254.26   86.23   **

Hornblower, touched his TALLYHO cap
        254.27   428.03   578.21   586.10

            ** Master Patrick Aloysius Dignam   254.28+   101.02   **

            ** Greased by porksteak paper   254.30   234.02   **

            ** The Mirus bazaar   254.32   183.05   **

            ** Mercer's hospital   254.32   183.06   **

            ** A blind stripling   254.34   180.31   **

            ** A pedestrian in a brown macintosh   254.35   109.29   **

            ** Mr Eugene Stratton   254.37   92.05   **

            ** His blub lips agrin   254.38   80.19   **

            ** Two sanded women   254.39   37.34   **

            ** The lord mayor   254.41   247.21   **

            ** The late queen   255.05   43.13   **

            ** Almidano Artifoni   255.06   228.13   **

SIRENS

** Hoofirons, steelyringing imperthnthn 256.01   233.22 **

** Bronze by gold heard the hoofirons   256.01#   246.07 **

CHIPS, PICKING CHIPS OFF ROCKY THUMBNAIL, CHIPS
    256.03   261.04   261.36

HORRID! AND GOLD FLUSHED MORE
    256.04   260.34+

A HUSKY FIFENOTE BLEW
    256.05   261.31

** Blue bloom is on the   256.06   233.31 **

Gold PINNACLED HAIR (Miss Kennedy's)
    256.07   260.15   260.28   270.25   273.27

A jumping ROSE (Miss Douce's)
    256.08   258.27   260.32   265.07   266.19   273.26   281.01
    286.11   287.01   287.27   290.29

SATINY BREASTS OF SATIN (Miss Douce's)
    256.08   261.16   265.21   277.35   284.12   286.10   287.01

** Rose of Castille   256.08   130.28 **

"THE SHADE OF THE PALM" (Trilling, trilling: Idolores)
    256.09   261.38+   265.39   266.02+   269.31   275.27   286.40

PEEP! WHO'S IN THE . . . PEEPOFGOLD
   256.10   262.13   356.38   486.21

TINK CRIED TO BRONZE IN PITY
   256.11   263.21

And A CALL, PURE, LONG AND THROBBING. LONGINDYING CALL
   256.12   264.11+

DECOY
   256.13   264.27

BUT LOOK!
   256.13   286.14

The bright stars fade. . . . ("GOODBYE, SWEETHEART, GOODBYE")
   256.13+   264.19++ 286.14   774.19   (210.13)

      ** O rose! . . . Castille   256.13+   130.28 **

NOTES CHIRRUPING ANSWER
   256.14   264.22

JINGLE JINGLE jaunted JINGLING
   256.15   256.20   261.25   262.17   263.26   264.01   264.29
   267.42+   269.09   269.40   271.17   272.06   273.03   274.13+
   276.18   277.34   279.21   279.38
   See also   56.27   168.11   253.42

      ** Jaunted   256.15   253.42 **

COIN RANG
   256.16   265.31   266.01

CLOCK CLACKED
   256.16   265.41+   266.02

AVOWAL. . . . AVOWAL
   256.17+   266.22

<u>SONNEZ</u> . . . SMACK. <u>LA</u> CLOCHE. THIGH SMACK. WARM
   256.17   266.25+   274.07   276.20   289.35
   See also   264.41   274.06

      ** Jingle   256.20   256.15 **

BOOMED CRASHING CHORDS
   256.21   270.03

When love absorbs. War! War! ("LOVE AND WAR")
   256.21   268.04   270.01++   522.03

The TYMPANUM (associated with Ben Dollard)
   256.22   270.13   521.23

A SAIL! A VEIL AWAVE UPON THE WAVES (A LAST FAREWELL -- painting)
    256.23   271.28+

LOST. . . . ALL IS LOST NOW (Song from Bellini's La Sonnambula)
    256.24   272.09   272.32++   289.37   415.27   484.05   523.04

        ** Throstle fluted   256.24   93.28 **

HORN. HAWHORN
    256.25   256.36   267.15   270.01+   279.21   289.35   290.10
    564.07   See also 447.13

        ** When first he saw   256.26+   117.35 **

Full TUP
    256.27   274.37+

Full THROB
    256.27   274.30+

WARBLING
    256.28   275.25

AH, LURE! ALLURING
    256.28   275.28   277.25

CLAPCLOP. CLIPCLAP. CLAPPYCLAP
    256.30   276.09+

GOODGOD HENEV ERHEARD INALL
    256.31   272.24   276.39+   447.11

DEAF BALD PAT
  Deaf-bald
    256.32   278.36   283.42
  Deaf-bothered
    283.11
  Bald-bothered
    263.22   264.17   267.27   267.39   280.36+   447.05+
  Deaf
    278.08   280.31   283.13   286.38
  Bald
    266.11   267.39   268.10   268.28   271.09   273.35   278.07
    278.36

BROUGHT PAD KNIFE TOOK UP
    256.32   278.36+

A MOONLIGHT NIGHTCALL: FAR: FAR
    256.33   279.04

        ** I feel so sad   256.34   49.04 **

I feel so sad. P.S. So lonely
    256.34   257.15   280.10   See also 49.04

     ** So lonely blooming   256.34   45.12   117.34 **

LISTEN!
   256.35   281.06

The spiked and winding cold seahorn (MISS DOUCE'S SHELL)
   256.36+   259.05   267.05   281.03++

     ** Have you the?   256.36   256.25 **

PLASH AND SILENT ROAR
   256.37   281.18

PEARLS
   256.38   282.32+   294.27

LISZT'S RHAPSODIES
   256.38   282.32

HISSS
   256.38   282.09   282.33

YOU DON'T? DID NOT
   256.39+   277.38+

LIDlyd (George Lidwell)
   256.40   257.17   261.40   271.01#   586.32

WITH A COCK WITH A CARRA
   256.40   257.11   282.36+   284.24   286.25   See also 212.36

BLACK. DEEPSOUNDING
   256.42   283.06

DO, BEN, DO
   256.42   282.42   See also 199.21   202.09   257.24

     ** Ben (Dollard)   256.42++   91.01 **

WAIT WHILE YOU WAIT
   257.01   275.09   280.37+   283.13   447.09

HEE HEE. Wait while you HEE. . . . BUT WAIT!
   257.01+   280.38+   283.13+   291.01   447.09   567.02   606.21

     ** In dark middle earth. Embedded ore   257.03   241.29 **

     ** Naminedamine   257.04   103.27 **

     ** All gone. All fallen   257.04   45.12 **

Tiny, her TREMULOUS FERNFOILS OF MAIDENHAIR
   257.05   261.35   286.13   287.03

** Amen! He gnashed in fury   257.06   137.24   **

** Fro. To, fro   257.07   11.24   **

A BATON COOL PROTRUDING (the beerpull)
    257.07   269.29   284.18   286.18+   288.13

ONE RAPPED
    257.11   282.35+

** One tapped   257.11#   37.18   **

** With a carra, with a cock   257.11   256.40   **

PRAY FOR HIM! PRAY, GOOD PEOPLE!
    257.12   287.06+

His GOUTY FINGERS NAKKERING (Ben Dollard's)
    257.13   267.37   287.19   522.02

** Big Benaben   257.14   91.01   **

** Last rose Castille   257.15   130.28   **

** Last rose . . . alone   257.15   45.12   117.35   **

** So sad alone   257.15   256.34   **

PWEE! LITTLE WIND PIPED WEE
    257.16   288.36

** True men. . . . Like you men   257.17+   241.12   **

** Lid (George Lidwell)   257.17   256.40   **

** Ker (Mr. Kernan)   257.17   71.24   **

** Cow (Father Cowley)   257.17   76.07   **

WILL LIFT YOUR TSCHINK WITH TSCHUNK (Song: "Thirty-Two Counties")
    257.18   290.27   290.40   See also 241.12(T)   308.13

FFF! OO! . . . PFRWRITT (Fart)
    257.19+   290.01   291.05+   370.20

Where bronze from ANEAR? Where gold from AFAR? Where hoofs?
    257.20   258.37   264.37   267.07   279.04   281.20   290.27

KRAA. KRAANDL (Tramcar sound)
    257.22   291.09+

** Then, not till then. My eppripfftaph 257.23+   114.18   **

** Bronze by gold. Miss Douce . . . Kennedy
                                     256.01#   246.07   **

DONE
    257.24   291.13   See also 199.21   202.09   256.42

      ** The crossblind   257.27   246.08 **

      ** The Ormond bar   257.27#   230.02 **

      ** Viceregal hoofs . . . ringing steel 257.27+   233.22 **

      ** Is that her? (Lady Dudley)   257.29   138.03 **

Pearl grey and EAU DE NIL
    257.30   268.12   273.27   (394.16)   (41.32)   See also 268.12

EXQUISITE CONTRAST, Miss Kennedy said
    257.32   258.30   268.11   289.04   See also 263.12

      ** Fellow in the tall silk (Gerald Ward) 257.34+   252.07 **

O WEPT! AREN'T MEN frightful idiots?
    258.01   266.40

      ** Bloowho   258.09   151.10 **

      ** The sweets of sin   258.10+   236.05 **

THE BOOTS to them
    258.12+   287.09+   564.02+

      ** Imperthnthn thnthnthn   258.24   233.22 **

      ** On her flower   258.27   256.08 **

      ** In exquisite contrast   258.30   257.32 **

      ** Anear . . . afar   258.37   257.20 **

      ** Steelhoofs ringhoof ringsteel   258.38   233.22 **

The BARMIRROR . . . WHERE HOCK AND CLARET GLASSES SHIMMERED
    259.03   267.04

      ** In their midst a shell   259.05   256.36 **

      ** Wait till I tell you   259.14   234.14 **

NO, DON'T, SHE CRIED
    259.17   288.34

      ** Antient Concert Rooms   259.25   91.40 **

      ** Imperthnthn   259.32   233.22 **

YOUR OTHER EYE
      259.36   260.07+   279.06

        ** Bloowhose dark eye   259.37++   101.36   **

Read AARON FIGATNER's name
      259.37   586.01

        ** Huguenot name   259.39   84.06   **

        ** By Bassi's blessed virgins   259.39+   47.39   **

        ** Goddess. . . . could not see   259.41   80.10   **

        ** That fellow . . . might be Mulligan 259.41   3.01   **

        ** The sweets of sin   260.04+   236.05   **

        ** Sweet are the sweets   260.04   236.05   **

        ** Your other eye   260.07+   259.36   **

        ** Fair pinnacles of hair   260.15   256.07   **

GREASY -- GREASABLOOM (O greasy eyes!)
      260.19++   291.03   See also 101.36

        ** Peal after peal, ringing in changes 260.25   (50.31) **

        ** Pinnacled   260.28   256.07   **

        ** Her jumping rose   260.32   256.08   **

I FEEL ALL WET
      260.33   270.36

        ** Horrid thing! And flushed yet more 260.34+   256.04   **

        ** Nannetti   260.38   118.16   **

Wheedling at doors as I (BLOOM AS COMMERCIAL TRAVELLER)
      260.39   336.08   413.12   667.23   See also 505.03

        ** Religion pays   260.39   151.20   **

        ** Keyes's par   260.40   107.35   **

        ** Par   260.40   117.05   **

        ** On. . . . On   260.41   145.10   **

        ** The Clarence   260.41   135.33   **

        ** Dolphin   260.42   233.09   **

** For Raoul	260.42	236.05 **
** The violet silk petticoats	261.01	180.16 **
** The sweets of sin	261.01	236.05 **
** Chips, picking chips	261.04	256.03 **
** Of satin	261.16	256.08 **
** Jingle	261.25	256.15 **

With the greatest ALACRITY
    261.26+   263.23

** Cantrell and Cochrane's	261.27	76.21 **
** Two husky fifenotes	261.31	256.05 **

I often wanted to see the MOURNE MOUNTAINS
    261.32   263.07   343.15

** Her maidenhair	261.35	257.05 **
** Chips	261.36	256.03 **
** Gaily . . . trilling . . . Idolores	261.38+	256.09 **
** Was Mr Lidwell in today?	261.40	256.40 **
** In came Lenehan	261.41	125.10 **
** To Martha I must write	262.01	182.11 **

DALY'S
    262.01   263.33++   289.28

** Blue Bloom is on the rye	262.02	233.31 **
** Peep! Who's in the corner?	262.13	256.10 **
** Jingle . . . jingle	262.17	256.15 **
** Jaunty	262.17	253.42 **
** Ah fox met ah stork	262.21	125.21 **
** Stephen, the youthful bard	262.31	5.01 **
** Select company (Simon on Stephen)	262.35	88.31 **
** Mooney's en ville . . . sur mer	262.39	144.04 **
** He had received the rhino	262.40	11.02 **

He had received the RHINO
   262.40   300.16

For THE LABOUR OF HIS MUSE
   262.40   391.15   See also 11.02

** The élite of Erin	263.01	175.17 **
** The ponderous pundit	263.02	123.18 **
** Most brilliant scribe and editor	263.02	125.07 **
** That minstrel boy of the . . . west	263.03	45.12 **
** O'Madden Burke	263.04	131.30 **
** Mourning mountain eye 263.07	261.32	(42.18) **
** The tuner was in today	263.11+	180.31 **

I never heard such an EXQUISITE PLAYER
   263.12   289.04   See also 257.32

** God's curse on bitch's bastard	263.20	250.19 **
** Tink . . . cried a diner's bell	263.21	256.11 **
** Came bald Pat, came bothered Pat	263.22	256.32 **
** Without alacrity	263.23	261.26 **
** Boylan with impatience	263.25	232.25 **
** Jingle	263.26	256.15 **
** Jaunty	263.26	253.42 **
** In Wisdom Hely's	263.33	106.26 **
** In Daly's	263.33++	262.01 **
** Henry Flower	263.33	72.31 **
** Are you not happy in your home?	263.34	72.30 **
** Flower (Martha's)	263.34	73.11 **

TO CONSOLE ME
   263.34   409.42

** A pin cuts lo	263.35	168.28 **
** Language of flow	263.35	78.15 **
** Was it a daisy?	263.36	224.26 **

** Respectable girl meet after mass   263.36   78.27 **

** Tanks awfully muchly   263.37   78.27   130.24 **

A POSTER, A SWAYING MERMAID . . . coolest whiff of all
   263.38+   289.28+

** For Raoul   263.40   236.05 **

** On a jauntingcar   263.41+   253.42 **

** It is. Third time   263.41   183.12 **

** Third time. Coincidence   263.42   68.24 **

** Jingling   264.01   256.15 **

On SUPPLE RUBBERS (Tyres)
   264.01   269.09   269.42

TWO PENCE, the shopgirl dared to say
   264.04   711.21

BLOO SMI QUI GO. TERNOON
   264.07   279.12

** A call came, long in dying   264.11+   256.12 **

That was a TUNINGFORK the tuner had that he forgot
   264.12   271.39   288.40

** The tuner   264.12   180.31 **

** Bald and bothered   264.17   256.32 **

** The bright stars fade   264.19++   256.13 **

** Birdnotes chirruped . . . answer   264.22   256.14 **

** Under sensitive hands   264.23   181.15 **

THE STRAIN OF DEWY MORN, OF LOVE'S LEAVETAKING, LIFE'S, LOVE'S MORN
   264.24   (367.03+)

** A low whistle of decoy   264.27   256.13 **

** Rose of Castille   264.28+   130.28 **

** Jingle   264.29   256.15 **

** Jaunted   264.29   253.42 **

** No questions . . . no lies   264.34   191.16 **

      ** Blazes Boylan's smart tan shoes   264.36   183.12 **

      ** Gold from anear by bronze from afar 264.37   257.20 **

      ** The conquering hero   264.39+   4.29   97.21 **

The SEAT he sat on: WARM
    264.41   269.42   See also 256.17

      ** Richie Goulding   256.01#   38.34 **

      ** A rose   265.07   256.08 **

A SLOEGIN for me
    265.10++   267.02   741.24

      ** Cowley's red lugs   265.12   76.07 **

BEST VALUE IN DUBLIN
    265.16   271.09   272.18   447.04   528.26   See also 113.25

DINNER FIT FOR A PRINCE
    265.18   269.38   271.19   272.06   283.08   294.32   528.27
    (606.07)

      ** Her satin arm   265.21   256.08 **

      ** Flower in his coat   265.26   228.02 **

      ** Coin rang   265.31   256.16 **

      ** Sceptre will win   265.34   128.03 **

I plunged a bit. . . . Fancy of a friend of mine (BOYLAN'S BET ON SCEPTRE)
    265.35   325.34   675.32+   749.43+   (778.19)

      ** Her lips had trilled. Idolores 265.39   256.09 **

      ** Flower, wonder who gave   265.40   228.02 **

      ** Clock clacked. Coin . . . clanged 265.41+   256.16 **

      ** Fair one of Egypt   266.02+   256.09   (41.32) **

      ** Goulding, Collis, Ward   266.10   88.23 **

      ** Ryebloom   266.10   233.31 **

      ** Bald Pat   266.11   256.32 **

      ** Blazure's skyblue bow   266.15   254.04 **

      ** Communing with her rose   266.19   256.08 **

      ** Blazes Boylan's flower   266.20   228.02 **

** Phrases of avowal   266.22   256.17   **

** Sonnezlacloche!   266.25+   256.17   **

Found it again, LOST CHORD, and lost (Song: "The Lost Chord")
     266.30   268.28   288.31

** Wept! Aren't men?   266.40   258.01   **

** Tossed . . . his chalice   267.01   81.37   **

** The last fat violet syrupy drops   267.02   265.10   **

** Hock and claret glasses   267.04   259.03   **

** A spiky shell   267.05   256.36   **

** From anearby   267.07   257.20   **

** Boylan with impatience   267.09   232.25   **

** Tom Rochford   267.12   178.20   **

** Got the horn or what?   267.15   256.25   **

** The hasty creaking shoes   267.16   183.12   **

** Mr Dollard   267.18#   91.01   **

** Father Cowley   267.20#   76.07   **

** Alf Bergan   267.21   160.03   **

** The long fellow   267.21   119.20   **

** That Judas Iscariot   267.22   14.05   93.41   **

POWER for Richie
     267.27   267.40   272.08   272.19   276.26

** Bald Pat, bothered waiter   267.27   256.32   **

** Black. . . . refracts (is it?) heat 267.29   57.10   **

CIDER. Yes, bottle of cider
     267.30+   272.08   276.27   288.10   290.26   370.21

** Bulky slops . . . hold that fellow   267.35   244.19   **

** His gouty paws   267.37   257.13   **

** Bald Pat. . . . bothered   267.39   256.32   **

** Power and cider   267.40   267.27   **

```
      ** Jingle                              267.42+      256.15   **

      ** Jaunted                             267.42       253.42   **

      ** Love and war                        268.04       256.21   **

      ** From the crossblind                 268.06       246.08   **

      ** Pensive                             268.07+       91.08   **

      ** Where bald stood                    268.10       256.32   **

      ** Contrast inexquisite nonexquisite   268.11       257.32   **
```

Slow cool dim SEAGREEN SLIDING DEPTH OF SHADOW
     268.12   269.29   287.03   See also 257.30

```
      ** Eau de Nil                          268.12       257.30   **

      ** Poor old Goodwin                    268.14+       63.05   **
```

By Japers I had no wedding garment (BEN DOLLARD'S TIGHT TROUSERS)
     268.22++   270.33++   283.39   521.28   774.08+
     See also   91.01   244.19   270.36

```
      ** The lost chord                      268.28       266.30   **

      ** Bald Pat                            268.28       256.32   **

      ** I knew he was on the rocks          268.36        93.21   **
```

In the COFFEE PALACE
     268.37   373.14   634.38+   753.22

```
      ** Gave me the wheeze                  268.38       134.19   **
```

[Molly] was doing THE OTHER BUSINESS (SELLING CLOTHING)
     268.39   753.21   See also 160.39

We had to search all Holles street (BLOOM'S HOME IN HOLLES STREET)
     268.40   369.40   385.22+   386.17   536.07   632.28   692.32
     753.20   757.37   772.11   773.03   774.09

```
      ** Mrs Marion                          269.07+       61.37   **

      ** Jingle                              269.09       256.15   **

      ** Haunted down the quays              269.09       253.42   **

      ** On bounding tyres                   269.09       264.01   **

      ** Liver and bacon                     269.11#       55.03   **
```

STEAK AND KIDNEY PIE
         269.11   269.35   272.06   447.08   528.27

         ** Met him pike hoses   269.13   50.13   **

         ** Smell of burn   269.13   55.04   **

         ** Paul de Kock. Nice name he   269.13   64.39   **

         ** Daughter of the regiment   269.20   111.02   **

         ** The old drummajor   269.21   56.32   **

         ** The rock of Gibraltar   269.28   56.29   **

         ** They pined in depth of ocean shadow   269.29   268.12   **

         ** Gold by the beerpull   269.29   257.07   **

         ** Idolores, a queen, Dolores   269.31   256.09   **

AS SAID BEFORE
         269.33   271.06   276.17+

         ** He ate with relish the inner organs   269.34   55.01   **

         ** Richie Goulding, Collis, Ward   269.35   88.23   **

         ** Steak and kidney, steak then kidney   269.35   269.11   **

         ** Dinners fit for princes   269.38   265.18   **

         ** Jogjaunty   269.40   253.42   **

         ** Jingled Blazes Boylan   269.40   256.15   **

         ** On bounding tyres: sprawled   269.42   264.01   **

         ** Warmseated   269.42   264.41   **

         ** Boylan impatience   269.42   232.25   **

         ** Ardentbold. . . . When love absorbs   270.01++   256.21   **

         ** Horn. . . . Haw haw horn   270.01+   256.25   **

         ** Booming over bombarding chords   270.03   256.21   **

         ** Your landlord   270.10   225.24   **

         ** Burst the tympanum   270.13   256.22   **

TWO GENTLEMEN WITH TANKARDS
         270.19+   276.14++   287.36++

```
** The lord lieutenant                270.22+    183.05   **

** Heard steelhoofs ringhoof ring     270.22     233.22   **

** Her outspread Independent          270.25     125.19   **

** Her pinnacles of hair              270.25     256.07   **

** Gold by bronze                     270.28     256.01   **

** Trousers tight as a drum           270.33++   268.22   **
```

With all his BELONGINGS ON SHOW
    270.36   283.40   284.34   371.37   See also 268.22

```
** I'm drenched                       270.36     260.33   **

** The base barreltone                270.38      91.01   **

** For instance eunuchs               270.39+     82.22   **

** Suave solicitor, George Lidwell    271.01#    256.40   **

** Bloom ate liv                      271.06      55.01   **

** As said before                     271.06     269.33   **

** In the Burton                      271.07     161.19   **

** Gummy with gristle                 271.07     169.19   **

** To and fro                         271.08      11.24   **

** Bald Pat                           271.09     256.32   **

** Best value in Dub                  271.09     265.16   **
```

NIGHT WE WERE IN THE BOX
    271.13   284.26   769.10   (465.26)
    See also   92.09   284.26   284.38

```
** Jiggedy jingle                     271.17     256.15   **

** Jaunty jaunty                      271.17     253.42   **

** Only the harp                      271.18+    127.13   **
```

POOP of a lovely. . . . GOLDEN SHIP. Erin
    271.19   341.29   See also   67.03

```
** Fit for a [prince]                 271.19     265.18   **

** The harp that once or twice        271.20      45.12   **

** Ben Howth, the rhododendrons       271.20     176.01   **
```

** Listless	271.22	18.05	**
** M'Appari	271.25++	117.35	**
** A Last Farewell	271.28+	256.23	**
** My dancing days are done	271.38	86.19	**
** Beside the tuningfork	271.39	264.12	**
** In the original	271.41	5.08	**
** Graham Lemon's pineapple rock	272.05	151.01	**
** By Elvery's elephant	272.05	94.01	**
** Jingle jogged	272.06	256.15	**
** Steak, kidney	272.06	269.11	**
** Fit for princes	272.06	265.18	**
** Power	272.08	267.27	**
** Cider	272.08	267.30	**
** Sonnambula	272.09	256.24	**
** Backache he	272.14	39.26	**

BRIGHT'S bright eye
        272.14   447.15   See also   39.26   125.03

Next item on the programme.   PAYING THE PIPER
        272.15   446.31

** Best value in	272.18	265.16	**
** Power	272.19	267.27	**

Fresh VARTRY WATER
        272.20   613.07

** Dribs and drabs	272.21	58.27	**
** Never would Richie forget	272.24	256.31	**

In the gods of THE OLD ROYAL [THEATRE]
        272.25   465.27   508.12   767.09   (272.25)

** Little Peake	272.25	91.17	**
** All is lost now	272.32++ 256.24	(434.01)	**

** A thrush. A throstle   272.34   93.28   **

** Echo. How sweet the answer   272.38   45.12   **

** Jingle   273.03   256.15   **

** Jaunty   273.03   253.42   **

** Wise child that knows her father   273.08   88.19   **

** Crosseyed Walter sir I did sir   273.12   38.36   **

** A heart bowed down   273.24   130.28   **

** Her . . . rose   273.26   256.08   **

** Eau de Nil   273.27   257.30   **

** Her pinnacles of gold   273.27   256.07   **

** When first I saw   273.30++   117.35   **

** Bald Pat   273.35+   256.32   **

** Whatdoyoucallthem   273.41   61.02   **

** Dulcimers   273.42   57.32   **

** Love's old sweet song   274.06   63.31   **

Bloom wound slowly the ELASTIC BAND OF HIS PACKET
    274.06+   274.34   277.16   277.32   278.09   See also 256.17

** Sonnez la   274.07   256.17   **

TENORS GET WOMEN BY THE SCORE
    274.12   281.11   742.09

INCREASE THEIR FLOW
    274.12   370.21

** When will we meet   274.13   72.30   **

** My head it simply . . . swurls   274.13+   62.36   **

** Jingle   274.13+   256.15   **

** Perfumed for him   274.15   236.05   **

** What perfume does your wife   274.15   72.30   **

** Jing   274.16   253.42   **

KISSING COMFITS, in her satchel
    274.18   675.09   770.03

```
    ** Hands felt for the opulent            274.19      236.05   **

    ** Could have made oceans of money       274.24+      93.21   **

    ** For creamy dreamy                     274.29      166.08   **

    ** Full it throbbed. . . . Throb         274.30+     256.27   **

    ** Bloom looped, unlooped, noded         274.34      274.06   **

    ** Tup                                   274.37+     256.27   **

    ** Martha it is.  Coincidence            275.03+      68.24   **

    ** Just going to write                   275.03      182.11   **

    ** Lovely name you have                  275.04       72.30   **

    ** Accept my little pres                 275.04      182.12   **

    ** I called you naughty boy              275.06       72.30   **

    ** Waiting, to wait                      275.09      257.01   **

    ** In Drago's                            275.13       68.23   **

    ** At Mat Dillon's in Terenure           275.17      106.19   **

    ** Fate.  After her.  Fate               275.19+      66.39   **

Singing.  WAITING she sang
     275.23       351.35       365.01     755.21     757.06    (283.12)

    ** What perfume does your                275.24       72.30   **

    ** Your lilactrees                       275.24      106.19   **

    ** Throat warbling                       275.25      256.28   **

    ** Spanishy eyes                         275.26       84.40   **

Under a peartree alone patio this hour IN OLD MADRID
     275.27       652.32       755.21     758.32     775.23+     782.41

    ** Dolores shedolores                    275.27      256.09   **

    ** Luring.  Ah, alluring                 275.28      256.28   **

DOMINANT to love to RETURN
     275.31+      504.22+

    ** In cry of . . . loneliness            275.32       49.04   **

    ** Soar silver orb                       275.40       91.08   **
```

** In the effulgence symbolistic   276.02   126.04   **

** Symbolistic, high, of the ethereal   276.02   166.08   **

** Of the eternal bosom   276.03   91.08   **

** All clapped. . . . Bravo! Clapclap   276.09+   256.30   **

TO ME, TO HIM, TO HER, YOU TOO, ME US
      276.09   (453.20)

** Two gentlemen with two tankards   276.14++   270.19   **

** Boylan's smart tan shoes creaked   276.17   183.12   **

** Said before   276.17+   269.33   **

** Jingle   276.18   256.15   **

** Sir John Gray   276.18   94.08   **

** By monuments of . . . Nelson   276.18   95.09   **

** Horatio onehandled Nelson   276.18   148.09   **

** Reverend Father Theobald Matthew   276.19   95.39   **

** Jaunted   276.19   253.42   **

** Cloche. Sonnez la   276.20   256.17   **

** By the Rotunda   276.22   95.42   **

** Impatience Boylan   276.23   232.25   **

** His Power   276.26   267.27   **

** His cider   276.27   267.30   **

** His Guinness   276.27   81.39   **

** Like a garden thrush   276.32   93.28   **

** Tom Kernan   276.34#   71.24   **

** 'Twas rank and fame   276.39+   130.28   **

** In Ned Lambert's 'twas   276.39+   90.03   **

** Good God he never heard. . . .   276.39   256.31   **

** A flush struggling in his pale   277.03   125.03   **

** Rift in the lute   277.10   50.31   **

** Plucked the slender catgut thong   277.16   274.06 **

While Goulding talked of BARRACLOUGH's voice production
    277.17   663.26

** A retrospective sort of arrangement   277.18   91.07 **

** Thou lost one   277.23   117.35 **

** Lure them on   277.25   256.28 **

** Dignam   277.26   57.11 **

** That rat's tail wriggling!   277.27   114.13 **

** Five bob I gave   277.27   57.11 **

** Corpus paradisum   277.27   80.34 **

** Corncrake croaker   277.28   103.25 **

** Belly like a poisoned pup   277.28   103.31 **

** Big Spanishy eyes   277.30   84.40 **

** He stretched more, more   277.32   274.06 **

** Are you not happy in your?   277.33   72.30 **

** Jingle   277.34   256.15 **

** Her satiny arm   277.35   256.08 **

** Miss Douce. . . . did not believe   277.38+   256.39 **

** Better write it here   278.05+   182.11 **

** Bald Pat . . . deaf Pat   278.07+   256.32 **

** Teasing the curling catgut fine   278.09   274.06 **

** My present   278.10   182.12 **

** Grandest number in the whole opera   278.14   39.29 **

** Symmetry under a cemetery wall   278.20   121.15 **

** The ethereal   278.22   166.08 **

** Milly no taste   278.34   21.42 **

** Bald deaf Pat . . . pad . . . fork   278.36+   256.32 **

** Ringabella, Crosshaven, Ringabella   278.39+   230.05 **

QUEENSTOWN harbour full
      278.40   328.02   624.17   658.08

      ** Cooed a . . . nightcall   279.04   256.33   (185.02)   **

      ** Clear from anear, a call from afar   279.04   257.20   **

      ** His Freeman baton   279.06+   57.36   **

      ** Your other eye   279.06   259.36   **

      ** Callan, Coleman, Dignam, Fawcett   279.07   91.16   **

      ** Dignam Patrick   279.08   57.11   **

      ** Heigho! Heigho!   279.08   57.09   **

CUTE AS A RAT
      279.10   341.14

GREEK EES
      279.11+   280.04

      ** Bloo mur: dear sir   279.12   264.07   **

      ** Dear Henry wrote   279.12++   72.31   **

      ** Got your lett   279.13   72.30   **

      ** Got your . . . flow   279.13   73.11   **

      ** On   279.17   145.10   **

      ** My poor little pres enclos   279.18+   182.12   **

      ** Five Dig   279.18   57.11   **

      ** Penny the gulls   279.19   152.22   **

      ** Elijah is com   279.19   151.07   **

      ** Davy Byrne's   279.19   170.19   **

      ** Write me a long   279.21   72.30   **

      ** Jingle   279.21   256.15   **

      ** Have you the?   279.21   255.25   **

      ** Why do you call me naught?   279.22   72.30   **

      ** O, Mairy lost the pin of her 279.23+   78.38   **

      ** Will tell you . . . exhaust   279.23+   72.30   **

| ** Card | 279.29 | 56.41 | ** |

| ** In my high grade ha | 279.29+ | 56.40 | ** |

SAUCE FOR THE GANDER
    279.31   542.29

A HACKNEY CAR. . . . A GALLANTBUTTOCKED MARE
    279.32+   563.26+

| ** An indigoblue serge suit | 279.35 | 254.05 | ** |

| ** George Robert Mesias | 279.35 | 100.17 | ** |

| ** Bought of John Plasto | 279.37 | 56.40 | ** |

This is the jingle that joggled and jingled ("THE HOUSE THAT JACK BUILT")
    279.38   391.36   394.29   427.23

| ** Jingle | 279.38 | 256.16 | ** |

| ** By Dlugacz' porkshop | 279.39 | 56.11 | ** |

| ** Agendath | 279.40 | 60.16 | ** |

| ** Greek ee | 280.04 | 279.11 | ** |

| ** How will you pun? . . . punish me? | 280.06 | 72.30 | ** |

| ** Crooked skirt swinging | 280.07 | 59.04 | ** |

| ** Tell me I want to. Know | 280.07 | 72.30 | ** |

Trails off there sad in MINOR. Why MINOR sad?
    280.09   518.04   691.08

| ** P.P.S. | 280.10 | 256.34 | ** |

| ** So sad today. . . . So lonely | 280.10 | 49.04 | ** |

| ** Messrs Callan, Coleman and Co | 280.13 | 91.16 | ** |

DOLPHIN'S BARN LANE
    280.17   372.37   492.32   See also 64.24

| ** Prize titbit . . . laughing witch | 280.19+ | 67.39 | ** |

| ** Poor Mrs Purefoy | 280.22 | 158.36 | ** |

| ** U.p.: up | 280.22 | 158.11 | ** |

| ** Too poetical | 280.23 | 69.39 | ** |

| ** That about the sad | 280.23 | 49.04 | ** |

CONGREVE, WILLIAM (Music hath charms)
  The Mourning Bride
       280.23   284.32
  Love for Love
       369.29
  The Way of the World
       371.22   372.16

TO BE OR NOT TO BE (Hamlet)
    280.25   499.17   555.25   641.25   (668.18)

        ** In Gerard's rosery of Fetter Lane   280.26   202.09   **

        ** He walks, greyed-auburn   280.26   202.10   **

        ** One life is all   280.27   202.11   **

        ** Do. But do   280.27   202.09   **

        ** Postal order stamp   280.28   182.11   **

BARNEY KIERNAN'S
    280.29   293.24#   339.20   372.29   380.23   657.11   662.29
    676.03   729.05   735.14

PROMISED TO MEET THEM (about Dignam's insurance)
    280.29   288.12   337.14++   See also 57.09

        ** Pat. . . . Deaf   280.31   256.32   **

        ** Bald Pat . . . bothered   280.36+   256.32   **

        ** Waits while you wait. Hee hee   280.37+   257.01   **

        ** Bronze and rose   281.01   256.08   **

        ** The lovely shell she brought   281.03++   256.36   **

        ** Listen!   281.06   256.35   **

        ** Tenors get wom   281.11   274.12   **

        ** Tap   281.15#   37.18   **

        ** Plash of waves . . . silent roar   281.18   256.37   **

        ** By a weary gold   281.20   3.41   **

        ** Anear, afar   281.20   257.20   **

        ** Lovely seaside girls   281.22+   62.36   **

        ** That lotion musn't forget   281.24   84.03   **

** With seaweed hair?   281.26   243.29   **

** And Turks   281.26   108.13   **

** Her eyes over the sheet   281.27   84.40   **

A YASHMAK
     281.27   289.26   439.11   (84.40)

Find the way in. A cave. No admittance except on business (BLOOM'S DREAM)
     281.27   370.41   381.11+   397.27   439.09
     See also   47.05   381.12

** Find the way in   281.27   (47.05) **

** The sea . . . corpuscle islands   281.29-30   47.37   **

** Larry O'Rourke's . . . Bold Larry O' 281.38   57.40   **

** She was not so lonely   281.41   49.04   **

** The landlord has the prior   282.04   245.30   **

** Long John (Fanning)   282.04   119.20   **

** Hisss   282.09   256.38   **

** Ruttledge's door: ee creaking   282.10   116.30   **

** Minuet of Don Giovanni   282.11+   63.31   **

** Misery   282.12   243.32   **

** M'Coy valise   282.19   67.24   **

** Qui est homo   282.22   82.09   **

** Mercadante   282.22   82.16   **

** Dandy tan shoe of dandy Boylan   282.25   183.12   **

** Boylan socks skyblue clocks   282.26   254.01   **

CHAMBER MUSIC . . . It is a kind of music I often thought when she
     282.27   770.05++

** As the weight of the water is equal   282.30+   72.05   **

** The law of falling water   282.31   (72.10) **

** Rhapsodies . . . Pearls . . . Hiss   282.32+   256.38   **

** One rapped on a door   282.35+   257.11   **

** Paul de Kock, . . . proud knocker   282.36   64.39   **

    ** With a cock carracarracarra cock   282.36+   256.40 **

    ** Qui sdegno   282.39   63.31 **

    ** The Croppy Boy   282.40++   91.01 **

    ** Our native Doric   282.41   126.01 **

    ** Ay do, Ben   282.42   256.42 **

    ** The black deepsounding chords   283.06   256.42 **

    ** Prince Bloom told Richie prince   283.08   265.18 **

    ** A razzle backache spree   283.09   39.26 **

    ** Deaf, bothered   283.11   256.32 **

    ** Waiting, waiting   283.12   (275.23) **

    ** Hee hee. . . . Wait while they wait   283.13+   257.01 **

    ** Deaf   283.13   256.32 **

LUGUGUGUBRIOUS
    283.14   434.01

    ** The dark middle earth. Embedded ore   283.15+   241.29 **

    ** Ben Dollard's voice barreltone   283.21   91.01 **

    ** Croak of vast . . . Marsh   283.22   (103.25) **

    ** Other comedown   283.22   93.21 **

    ** Now in the Iveagh home   283.25   79.24 **

    ** Number one Bass   283.26   154.19 **

    ** The youth had entered   283.31   290.32 **

A LONELY HALL
    283.32   290.32   See also 49.04

SCOTT, SIR WALTER (Lay of the last minstrel)
  Lay of the Last Minstrel
    283.37
  The Bride of Lammermoor
    297.09   See also 111.02

    ** No eunuch yet   283.39   82.22 **

    ** With all his belongings   283.39   270.36 **

** Deaf Pat, bald Pat   283.42   256.32   **

** In nomine Domini   284.03   103.27   **

** Latin. . . . holds them like birdlime 284.06   80.35   **

** Priest with the communion corpus   284.06   80.28   **

** Coffey   284.08   103.25   **

** Corpusnomine   284.08   103.27   (91.01) **

** That rat   284.08   114.13   **

** Fullbusted satin   284.12   256.08   **

** You bitch's bast   284.14   250.19   **

** Listening by the beerpull   284.18   257.07   **

** Cockcarracarra   284.24   256.40   **

Night MICHAEL GUNN gave us the box
    284.26   636.35   678.29   769.10   (678.37)
    See also   67.24   92.09   271.13   284.38

** The box (Gaiety Theatre)   284.26   92.09   271.13   **

SHAH OF PERSIA liked that best. . . . WIPED HIS NOSE IN CURTAIN too
    284.27   290.02

Remind him of HOME SWEET HOME
    284.27   290.15

** Music hath jaws   284.32   280.23   **

** Like Goodwin's name   284.32   63.05   **

** Belongings on show   284.34   270.36   **

Told her WHAT SPINOZA SAYS IN THAT BOOK
    284.36   342.25   687.33   708.26   769.15

** That book of poor papa's   284.36   76.26   **

CHAP IN DRESSCIRCLE, STARING DOWN INTO HER WITH HIS OPERA GLASS
    284.38   731.31   769.14   (465.26)   See also 271.13   284.26

** God made the country man the tune   284.40   240.12   **

** Met him pike hoses   284.41   50.13   **

** O rocks!   284.41   64.22   **

** We are the boys of Wexford   285.02   129.13   **

```
** Milly                          285.04+      21.42    **

** Young student (Bannon)         285.04       21.41    **

** Rudy.  Too late now            285.05+      66.25    **

** His voice unfolded             285.09      162.36    **

** A flush struggling in his pale 285.10      125.03    **

** Who fears to speak of . . . ?  285.13      241.12    **

** Time to be shoving             285.13       83.30    **

** Bless me, father               285.15     (103.27)   **

** Those girls, those lovely      285.20       62.36    **

** By the sad sea waves           285.20       92.06    **

** Henry                          285.23       72.31    **

** The lovely name you            285.23       72.30    **

** Goddess I didn't see           285.34       80.10    **
```

MENDELSSOHN-BARTHOLDY, FELIX (Songs without words)
   "Songs Without Words"
      285.37   498.30
   Personal reference
      342.24   661.29   687.33

```
** That hurdy gurdy boy           285.37      171.06    **
```

Or because so like the Spanish (MOLLY'S SPANISH BACKGROUND)
      285.38   637.13   652.06   749.12   See also 84.40   373.23

```
** Bitch's bastard                286.02      250.19    **

** Poor Mrs Purefoy               286.07      158.36    **

** Satiny heaving bosom's wave    286.10      256.08    **

** Her heaving embon              286.11      236.05    **

** Red rose rose slowly, sank red rose 286.11  256.08   **

** Fernfoils trembled             286.13      257.05    **

** But look.  The bright stars fade 286.14    256.13    **

** O rose! Castille               286.14      130.28    **

** The smooth jutting beerpull    286.18+      257.07    **
```

** Fro, to: to, fro   286.19   11.24   **

** A cool firm white enamel baton   286.23   257.07   **

** With a cock with a carra   286.25   256.40   **

** Amen. He gnashed in fury   286.27   137.24   **

THANKS, THAT WAS HEAVENLY
    286.29   382.05

** Can leave that Freeman   286.30   57.36   **

** Letter I have   286.30   182.11   **

Suppose she were the? (MARTHA'S IDENTITY)
    286.31   372.35

WALK, WALK, WALK
    286.31   688.04

** Cashel Boylo . . . Farrell   286.31   159.15   **

** O'er ryehigh blue   286.34   233.31   **

** Soap feeling rather sticky   286.35   85.17   **

** That lotion, remember   286.36   84.03   **

** High grade   286.37   56.40   **

** Card inside, yes   286.37   56.41   **

** Deaf Pat   286.38   256.32   **

** Dolor! O, he dolores   286.40   256.09   **

** By rose, by satiny bosom   287.01   256.08   **

** Maidenhair   287.03   257.05   **

** Bronze and faint gold   287.03   257.09   **

** In deepshadow   287.03   268.12   **

** I feel so lonely   287.04   49.04   **

** Pray for him   287.06+   257.12   **

** Eavesdropping boots   287.09+   258.12   **

** Most trenchant rendition   287.15   91.03   **

** Gouty fingers nakkering   287.19   257.13   **

```
       ** Big Benaden Dollard.  Big Benben      287.21       91.01   **
You're looking RUBICUND
     287.26       521.26

       ** Miss Douce composed her rose          287.27      256.08   **

       ** Ben machree                           287.28       91.01   **

       ** Rift in the lute                      287.33       50.31   **

       ** Goulding, Collis, Ward                287.33       88.23   **

       ** To ear of tankard one                 287.36++    270.19   **

       ** Last rose of summer        288.05+    45.12       117.35   **

       ** That cider                            288.10      267.30   **

       ** Near Reuben J's one and eightpence    288.11       93.41   **
Dodge round by GREEK STREET
     288.12       297.37

       ** Promised to meet                      288.12      280.29   **

       ** To meet [Martin Cunningham]           288.12       80.13   **

       ** Beerpull                              288.13      257.07   **
Her HAND THAT ROCKS THE CRADLE ("What Rules the World?" by W. R. Wallace)
     288.13       500.25      551.18     (118.23)   (516.31)   (624.37)

       ** Ben Howth                             288.14      176.01   **

       ** Lionelleopold                         288.17      117.35   **

       ** Naughty Henry              288.17     72.30        72.31   **

       ** With letter for Mady                  288.17      182.11   **

       ** With sweets of sin                    288.18      236.05   **

       ** With met him pike hoses               288.18       50.13   **

       ** Blind walked tapping                  288.20      180.31   **
THE WAY OF A MAN WITH A MAID
     288.23       288.34

       ** Enthusiasts                           288.24+      68.29   **

       ** Old Glynn                             288.29       82.06   **
```

** Seated all day at the organ	288.31	266.30 **
** No don't she cried 288.34	259.17	288.23 **
** Pwee! A wee little wind piped eeee	288.36	257.16 **
** This morning at . . . Dignam's	288.38	57.11 **
** A tuningfork	288.40	264.12 **
** That must be the tuner	289.01+	180.31 **
** To simonlionel first I saw	289.01	117.35 **
** Played so exquisitely, treat to hear	289.04	263.12 **
** Exquisite contrast	289.04	257.32 **
** One lonely . . . Bloom alone	289.13	49.04 **
** Last sardine of summer 289.13	45.12	117.35 **

That WONDERWORKER if I had
      289.16   546.18   721.38++   758.08

LOVE ONE ANOTHER
      289.18   See   333.20

** Goulding, Collis, Ward	289.19	88.23 **
** Yashmak	289.26	281.27 **
** I mean kismet	289.26	66.39 **
** Fate	289.26	66.39 **
** A stripling, blind	289.27	180.31 **
** By Daly's window	289.28	262.01 **
** A mermaid	289.28+	261.35 **
** Coolest whiff of all	289.30	263.39 **
** Molly in her shift	289.33	92.33 **
** In Lombard street west	289.33	110.15 **
** Horn. Haw. Have you the?	289.35	256.25 **
** Cloche. Sonnez la!	289.35	256.17 **
** All is lost now	289.37	256.24 **

BUMBAILIFF
    289.38   303.03

      ** Long John (Fanning)   289.38   119.20 **

Long John. Waken the dead (Song: "JOHN PEEL")
    289.38   427.19

      ** Dignam   289.39   57.11 **

      ** Poor little nominedomine   289.39   103.27 **

      ** Fff   290.01   257.19 **

      ** Custom shah of Persia   290.02   284.27 **

      ** Breathe a prayer, drop a tear   290.02+   91.01 **

      ** Chap at the grave in the brown mackin 290.05   109.29 **

A FROWSY WHORE WITH BLACK STRAW SAILOR HAT ASKEW
    290.07++   538.08   632.12++

      ** When first he saw   290.08   117.35 **

      ** I feel so lonely   290.09   49.04 **

      ** Horn. Who had the? Heehaw   290.10   256.25 **

      ** Never, well hardly ever   290.14   38.35 **

      ** Home sweet home   290.15   284.27 **

      ** Lionel Leopold   290.19   117.35 **

      ** Dear Henry Flower   290.19   72.31 **

      ** Cheap   290.21+   34.01 **

      ** Must be the cider   290.26   267.30 **

      ** Or perhaps the burgund   290.26   171.28 **

      ** Anear . . . gold from afar   290.27   257.20 **

      ** Chinked their clinking glasses all 290.27   257.18 **

      ** Lydia's tempting . . . rose   290.29   256.08 **

      ** Last rose of summer   290.29   45.12   117.35 **

      ** Rose of Castille   290.29   130.28 **

      ** Ormond hall   290.32   49.04   91.01   283.32 **

** Robert Emmet's last words	290.34++	114.18	**
** Seven last words	290.34	82.16	**
** Of Meyerbeer that is	290.35	168.20	**
** True men like you men	290.36	241.12	**
** Tschink. Tschunk	290.40	257.18	**
** An unseeing stripling	290.41	180.31	**
** Hee hee hee hee. He did not see	291.01	257.01	**
** Greaseabloom	291.03	260.19	**
** Prrprr	291.05+	257.19	**
** Must be the bur	291.06	171.28	**
** Fff. Oo. Rrpr	291.07+	257.19	**
** Tram. Kran, kran, kran	291.09	257.22	**
** I'm sure it's the burgund	291.10	171.28	**
** Done	291.13	257.24	**

CYCLOPS

THE NAMELESS ONE (Narrator of Cyclops)
    292.01++   339.21   470.04   586.21   See also 293.38

With old TROY of the D.M.P.
    292.01+   586.42

      ** Joe Hynes   292.06++   90.04 **

MOSES HERZOG over there near Heytesbury street
    292.20++   544.19   586.41

An old plumber named GERAGHTY
    292.24++   293.36   294.34   586.41

How are the mighty fallen! (KING DAVID)
    292.27   504.04   528.22

Collector of BAD AND DOUBTFUL DEBTS
    292.27   725.22

I DARE HIM . . . AND I DOUBLEDARE HIM
    292.30   294.33

For TRADING WITHOUT A LICENCE
    292.33   293.37   335.35

      ** Till he's fit to burst   292.34   103.30 **

      ** Barney Kiernan's   293.24#   280.29 **

I want to see THE CITIZEN
    293.25#   436.20   487.01+   490.02   498.13+   498.30   586.21
    593.10+   729.05

His dropsy
   342.01   490.02

     ** Meeting in the City Arms   293.28   35.27 **

     ** About the foot and mouth disease   293.31   32.01 **

     ** That bloody foxy Geraghty   293.36   292.24 **

     ** For trading without a licence   293.37   292.33 **

MANGAN, JAMES C. (In Inisfail the fair there lies a land. . . .)
  "Prince Alfred's Itinerary" (G)
    293.38++
  "My Dark Rosaleen"
    297.10
  "The Fair Hills of Eire, O"
    326.41
  "The Time of the Barmecides"
    332.12
  "The Time of the Roses"
    (421.07)
  "The Nameless One"
    (470.05)   (586.21)   See also 292.01

     ** The land of holy Michan   293.38   240.30 **

Their FIRST CLASS foliage
   294.04   452.07   661.11

     ** To woo them   294.13   196.24 **

From EBLANA to Slievemargy
   294.13   319.06   388.40   619.24

     ** The sons of kings   294.16   31.30 **

A SHINING PALACE (DUBLIN MUNICIPAL FISH AND VEGETABLE MARKET)
   294.18   679.02

PALACE whose CRYSTAL glittering roof (Crystal Palace, London)
   294.18   394.26   484.26

     ** Pearls of the earth   294.27   256.38 **

     ** Fit for princes   294.32   265.18 **

     ** I dare him . . . doubledare him   294.33   292.30 **

     ** Geraghty   294.34   292.24 **

     ** Cuffe's   294.38   59.21 **

     ** Prime springers   294.38   97.40 **

M'GILLICUDDY'S REEKS
     295.05   343.17

GARRYOWEN
     295.13#   339.21   352.24   453.05   453.31+   586.22   662.28

          ** With his cruiskeen lawn   295.15   92.06   **

STAND AND DELIVER
     295.22   425.29

Doing the rapparee and RORY of the hill
     295.27   297.40

          ** It's the Russians   295.34   58.11   **

          ** Thirst on me   295.36   41.05   **

          ** Wine of the country   295.38   81.39   **

          ** Seated on a large boulder   296.05   44.40   **

          ** The foot of a round tower   296.05   164.34   **

A BROADSHOULDERED DEEPCHESTED. . . .
     296.06+   428.16+   521.26+

          ** Hero   296.09   4.29   **

          ** A tear and a smile   296.18   45.12   **

          ** Heroes and heroines   296.35   4.29   **

CONN OF HUNDRED BATTLES
     296.35   323.11

          ** Brian of Kincora   296.36   99.25   **

          ** The Ardri Malachi   296.37   45.13   **

PATRICK SARSFIELD
     296.38   330.17

RED HUGH O'DONNELL
     296.38   495.33

          ** Red Jim MacDermott   296.39   (31.22)   **

          ** Soggarth Eoghan O'Growney   296.39   194.12   **

          ** Francy Higgins   296.40   126.26   **

LONGFELLOW, HENRY W. (the Village Blacksmith)
   "The Village Blacksmith"
     296.41

"The Wreck of the Hesperus"
   636.18

     ** Dante Alighieri   296.42   20.20   **

S. FURSA
   297.01   339.27

S. BRENDAN
   297.01   339.26

     ** Theobald Wolfe Tone   297.02   229.20   **

COOPER, JAMES FENIMORE (The Last of the Mohicans)
   297.03   660.05

     ** The Rose of Castille   297.03   130.28   **

The Man that BROKE THE BANK AT MONTE CARLO
   297.04   718.11

THE MAN IN THE GAP
   297.05   408.33   614.42

NAPOLEON BONAPARTE
   297.06   445.19   456.02   515.02   526.09   550.23   568.06
   571.04   622.41   708.38   (659.26)

     ** Cleopatra   297.06   191.08   **

     ** Julius Caesar   297.07   25.14   **

WILLIAM TELL
   297.08   377.01(T) 626.19

     ** Michelangelo   297.08   139.33   **

HAYES
   297.08   (586.40)

     ** Muhammed   297.08   77.26   **

     ** The Bride of Lammermoor   297.09   283.37   (111.02)   **

Peter the Packer (Lord PETER O'BRIEN)
   297.09   488.06

     ** Dark Rosaleen   297.10   293.38   **

     ** Patrick W. Shakespeare   297.10   198.27   **

VERNE, JULES (Captain Nemo)
   297.11   382.01

WAGNER, RICHARD
  Tristan and Isolde
    297.12   332.17
  The Flying Dutchman
    (478.24)   (479.18)   (636.36)
    See also   376.26
  The Twilight of the Gods
    560.26
  The Valkyrie
    560.29(G)
  The Ring of the Nibelung
    583.02
  Other references
    661.05

** The first Prince of Wales	297.12	(31.15)	**
** The Bold Soldier Boy	297.13	63.01	**
** Arrah na Pogue	297.13	92.06	**
** The Colleen Bawn	297.14	92.06	**

DOLLY MOUNT (DOLLYMOUNT)
    297.15   630.12   718.35

** Ben Howth		297.15	40.25	**
** Adam and Eve	297.16	14.23	38.06	148.01	**

ARTHUR WELLESLEY (Duke of Wellington)
    297.16   332.24   434.03   596.27

** Gautama Buddha	297.17	80.10	**
** The Lily of Killarney	297.18	92.06	**
** The Queen of Sheba	297.19	201.29	**

Acky NAGLE, Joe NAGLE (Pubkeepers)
    297.19   618.30

THE PRUDENT MEMBER gave me the wheeze
    297.34+   304.04

** Gave me the wheeze	297.35	119.27	134.19	**

Sloping around by PILL LANE
    297.36   374.01

** Greek street	297.37	288.12	**

With his COD'S EYE
    297.37   303.15   304.21   315.15

** Through Michan's land   297.39   340.30   **

** The son of Rory   297.40+   76.26   295.27   **

** The old woman of Prince's street   297.42   57.36   **

** The Irish Independent   298.03+   125.19   **

** Founded by Parnell   298.03   35.02   **

** Elder of noble gait and countenance   298.32++   157.17   **

** His lady wife   298.34   156.32   **

** Little Alf Bergan   298.35#   160.03   **

** Bob Doran   298.38++   74.01+ **

** U.p.: up   299.04++   158.11   **

** In John Henry Menton's   299.15   102.38   **

** To Collis and Ward's   299.16   88.23   **

** Tom Rochford   299.16   178.20   **

** To the subsheriff's   299.17+   119.20   **

** I've a pain   299.18   17.40   **

** The foaming ebon ale   299.31+   81.39   **

** Bungiveagh   299.32   79.24   **

** Bungardilaun   299.32   79.27   **

** Cup to him that thirsted   299.40   41.05   **

** A queen . . . Victoria her name   300.05   43.13   **

** From the rising of the sun   300.10   30.35   **

** Chucking out the rhino   300.16   262.40   **

I saw him just now in CAPEL STREET
       300.28   340.08   368.27   See also 64.42

** With Paddy Dignam   300.29++   57.11   **

** You saw his ghost   300.40   (19.34) **

** Whatdoyoucallhim's   301.01   61.02   **

** In the darkness spirit hands   301.13++   140.30   **

The apparition of the ETHERIC DOUBLE
    301.16   416.32   487.16   518.29   (56.06)

Equipped with every modern HOME COMFORT
    301.31   639.14

       ** Mind C.K. doesn't pile it on   301.42+   71.15 **

       ** The dear son Patsy   302.06+   101.02 **

       ** He's a bloody ruffian   302.35   88.32   213.22 **

Mooney, the bumbailiff's daughter (POLLY MOONEY DORAN)
    303.03   314.23   586.35   See also 74.01   173.13

       ** The bumbailiff   303.03   289.38 **

       ** Bantam Lyons   303.05   74.02 **

       ** With his cod's eye   303.15   297.37 **

       ** Martin Cunningham   303.16   80.13 **

H. RUMBOLD, MASTER BARBER
    303.35   308.19+   471.15   593.23+

       ** A prudent member   394.04   297.34 **

TWO FELLOWS WAITING . . . WHEN HE GETS THE DROP
    304.11   594.02

THE WHY AND THE WHEREFORE
    304.20   655.20

       ** The codology of the business   304.21   297.37 **

       ** Joe Brady   304.30   136.12 **

       ** The invincible   304.30   81.27 **

After the drop IT WAS STANDING UP IN THEIR FACES like a poker
    304.32   594.06

POPE, ALEXANDER (Ruling passion strong in death)
  "Moral Essays"
    304.33
  The Rape of the Lock
    424.41+
  The First Satire of the Second Book of Horace Imitated
    601.05
  "Essay on Criticism"
    664.40

It's only a NATURAL PHENOMENON, don't you see
    304.35++   305.38+   306.15   343.04   395.15++   418.14   419.22
    529.04   549.18   634.10   673.29   692.30   694.35   697.20+
    701.11   705.04

      ** About the invincibles   305.11   81.27 **

      ** Who fears to speak of ninetyeight   305.12   241.12 **

GIVE US THE PAW! GIVE THE PAW, DOGGY!
    305.22+   454.04

Out of the bottom of a Jacob's tin (JACOB'S BISCUITS)
    305.29   311.18   342.35++   473.27   586.15

He golloped it down like OLD BOOTS
    305.30   635.35

      ** Wolfe Tone   305.34   229.20 **

      ** Robert Emmet   305.35   114.18 **

      ** The Tommy Moore touch   305.35   45.12 **

      ** Phenomenon!   305.38+   304.35 **

      ** The City Arms   305.40   35.27 **

PISSER BURKE told me
    305.40++   315.12   320.21   335.30   338.16   488.09   586.20
    731.32   765.06

      ** There was an old one there   305.41+   97.25 **

Playing BÉZIQUE
    306.01   681.13

MRS O'DOWD that kept the [City Arms] hotel
    306.09   315.13   586.20   680.23   See also 35.27

      ** Phenomenon!   306.15   304.35 **

      ** The memory of the dead   306.17   241.12 **

      ** Sinn Fein!   306.22   163.38 **

      ** The friends we love are by our side 306.22   45.12 **

      ** Last farewell was affecting 306.24++ 114.18   377.23 **

      ** L–n–h–n   307.03   125.10 **

      ** M–ll–g–n   307.03   3.01 **

FRIENDS OF THE EMERALD ISLE (F. O. T. E. I.)
   307.18   307.39

Countess Marha VIRÁGA Kisászony Putrápesthi
   307.25   See   337.37

    ** Ali Baba Backsheesh   307.26   47.05 **

    ** Pan Poleaxe Paddyrisky   307.30   171.09 **

    ** Among F. O. T. E. I.   307.39   307.18 **

    ** Ireland's patron saint   307.40   80.12 **

In his thirtytwo pockets (representing the THIRTYTWO COUNTIES OF IRELAND)
   308.13   484.24   See also 257.18

    ** Rumbold stepped on to the scaffold 308.19++ 303.35 **

    ** The hero martyr   308.39   4.29 **

Sheila, MY OWN
   309.34   427.41

    ** The banks of Anna Liffey   310.01   153.14 **

    ** Touched to the inmost core   310.08   105.31 **

    ** Oxford graduate   310.14++   4.19 **

I thinks of my old MASHTUB
   310.37   579.17

    ** The Irish language   310.39+   141.07 **

    ** She could get up on a truss of hay 311.07   63.01 **

    ** A lot of colleen bawns   311.10   92.06 **

IRELAND SOBER IS IRELAND FREE
   311.13   (518.17++)

    ** The tin was empty   311.18   305.29 **

I'D TRAIN HIM BY KINDNESS, SO I WOULD
   311.19   311.40   453.31

    ** Ancient Celtic bards   312.05   5.01 **

    ** The writer . . . Little Sweet Branch 312.06   48.01 **

    ** The canine original   312.18   (5.08) **

    ** After Lowry's lights   312.32   232.37 **

With old GILTRAP's dog
    312.39   348.13   352.23   355.32

    ** Martin Cunningham   313.05   80.13   **

    ** This insurance of poor Dignam's   313.06+   57.11   **

    ** If old Shylock is landed   313.11   204.30   (93.41) **

Well, that's a point . . . for the WIFE'S ADMIRERS
    313.12   449.16   731.19++   (759.21)

    ** Royal Hungarian privileged lottery   313.24+   156.11   **

    ** About the funeral   313.29   57.11   **

    ** Overstepped the limits of reserve   313.39   73.40   **

    ** Paddy Leonard   314.10   90.39   **

    ** In Bride street   314.12   37.39   **

    ** Serving mass in Adam and Eve's   314.16   148.01   **

    ** His little concubine of a wife   314.23   303.03   **

    ** Jack Mooney's sister   314.26   173.13   **

SLAN LEAT
    314.32   436.19

    ** The long fellow (Fanning)   314.36   119.20   **

    ** Nannon? . . .   The mimber?   314.39+   118.16   **

    ** The meeting . . . cattle traders   314.41+   35.27   **

    ** William Field, M.P.   314.42   35.26   **

    ** Hairy Iopas   315.01   88.15   **

    ** About the foot and mouth disease   315.03+   32.01   **

A HOOSE drench for coughing calves
    315.06   399.21

Remedy for TIMBER TONGUE
    315.07   399.21

    ** Joe Cuffe   315.10   59.21   **

    ** Pisser Burke   315.12   305.40   **

    ** In the hotel the wife used to be   315.13   35.27   **

** Mrs O'Dowd	315.13	306.09	**
** Old Cod's eye	315.15	297.37	**

Gob, he'd have a SOFT HAND UNDER A HEN
    315.20+   388.13

BLACK LIZ is our hen
    315.21   563.06+

** Field	315.26+	35.26	**
** Nannetti	315.26+	118.16	**
** Irish games in the park	315.37	170.41	**

The SLUAGH NA H-EIREANN
   315.38   316.42

** The Phoenix park	316.10	170.41	**
** Don't hesitate to shoot	316.16	187.31	**
** James Stephens	316.22	43.25	**

DAVIS, THOMAS OSBORNE (building up a nation once again)
  "A Nation Once Again"
    316.33   317.21
  "The Green Above the Red"
    593.04

** Sluagh na h-Eireann	316.42	315.38	**
** The cause of our old tongue	317.11	141.07	**
** Mr Joseph M'Carthy Hynes	317.11#	90.04	**

Practised morning and evening by FINN MACCOOL
    317.14   323.12

** A nation once again	317.22	316.33	**
** The Irish Caruso-Garibaldi	317.25	163.41	**
** That Keogh-Bennett match	318.07++	173.14	**
** Heenan and Sayers	318.23	242.23	**
** Eblanite	319.06	294.13	**
** He's running a concert tour	319.21+	75.23	**

The bright PARTICULAR STAR
    319.25   656.12

** An excellent man to organise   319.27+   173.09   **

** Says I to myself, says I   319.28   (38.35)   **

** Doing the tootle on the flute   319.30   42.18   **

[BOYLAN'S FATHER] SOLD THE SAME HORSE TWICE OVER to the government
     319.31   741.23   749.18

** To fight the Boers   319.32   163.10   **

The RAVENHAIRED daughter of Tweedy
     319.37   382.16   439.13

** Tweedy   319.38   56.32   **

The gardens of ALAMEDA knew her step
     319.39   371.13   756.10   762.37   783.03

** One of the clan of the Molloy's   319.42#   124.32   **

** A comely hero   320.01   4.29   **

** Heir of the noble line of Lambert   320.03#   90.03   **

** With Pisser (Burke)   320.21   305.40   **

** That bloody lunatic Breen   320.25++   157.17   **

** U.p. up   320.26++   158.11   **

He wanted RIGHT GO WRONG
     320.28   347.09

** Corny Kelleher   320.29   71.15   **

** I mean his wife   321.07+   156.32   **

A HALF AND HALF (Bloom)
     321.09   338.15   493.29

Nor GOOD RED HERRING
     321.13   659.05

A PISHOGUE
     321.14   566.02

IF YOU KNOW WHAT THAT IS
     321.14   326.11

The signor BRINI . . . the eyetallyano, papal zuave to the Holy Father
     321.24   495.21+

** Corny Kelleher   321.41   71.15   **

```
    ** That Canada swindle case              322.03+    127.08  **

    ** Recorder (Sir Frederick Falkiner)     322.15++   138.02  **

    ** Reuben J. was bloody lucky            322.21      93.41  **

    ** Poor little Gumley                    322.22     136.18  **

SCANDALOUS!
     322.29      471.03

    ** Of the tribe of Patrick               323.10      80.12  **

    ** Of the tribe of Conn                  323.11     296.35  **

    ** Of the tribe of Finn                  323.12     317.14  **

    ** Of the tribe of Dermot                323.13      34.42  **

    ** Of the tribe of Cormac                323.13     169.24  **

Of the tribe of Kevin (ST. KEVIN)
     323.14      339.26

    ** That little matter                    323.32     119.33  **

    ** Just say a word (about Keyes ad)      323.33+    107.35  **

    ** Mr Crawford                           323.33     125.07  **

    ** Strangers . . . paramour   323.40++     9.22     34.42  **

    ** The Saxon robbers                     324.05      4.17  **

DECREE NISI
     324.06      654.15+

GIVE US A SQUINT at her, says I
     324.15      659.15

    ** Corny Kelleher                        324.17      71.15  **

NORMAN W. TUPPER . . . OFFICER TAYLOR
     324.18+     333.34

THERE'S HAIR
     324.25      425.29

Queer old TAILEND of corned beef
     324.25      378.33      382.17

    ** John Wyse Nolan                       324.27#    177.18  **

    ** In came . . . Lenehan                 324.27#    125.10  **
```

** What did those tinkers . . decide   324.30   141.07   **

** In tholsel   324.36   245.11   **

** The bloody brutal Sassenachs   324.42   4.17   **

And BLINKING FACTS
     325.02   418.15   See also 184.11

** The Nelson policy   325.02   148.09   **

** A bill of attainder   325.04   43.08   **

** Kevin Egan of Paris   325.15   41.17   **

** Full many a flower   325.19   46.39   **

CONSPUEZ LES ANGLAIS!
     325.21   330.25

PERFIDE ALBION!
     325.21   330.23

** Lamh Dearg Abu   325.24   176.33   **

** Rulers of the waves   325.25   18.33   **

** A race of mighty valorous heroes   325.25   4.29   **

** Gold Cup   325.29++   85.40   **

THROWAWAY, says he, at twenty to one
     325.31+   335.13   335.26   415.26   426.21   534.12   604.09
     647.20   648.20+   750.02
   Twenty to one
     325.31+   335.19+   341.14   345.20   470.10   534.11   604.10
     648.23   (630.20)
   Outsider
     325.31   534.11   648.24   717.30   750.02
     See also   86.07   151.07

** Bass's mare (Sceptre)   325.33+   128.03   **

STILL RUNNING
     325.34   648.32   (338.04)

** Boylan plunged two quid   325.34   265.35   **

** Zinfandel . . . de Walden's   325.36   174.02   **

** Mr Flynn gave me   325.37   171.25   **

FRAILTY, THY NAME IS. . . .
     325.40   546.21

```
        ** The mote in others' eyes           326.08      217.36   **

        ** If you know what that means        326.11      321.14   **

WHERE ARE OUR MISSING. . . .
     326.11++    640.16+

        ** Our Huguenot poplin                326.18       84.06   **

        ** Poplin                             326.18      168.19   **

        ** The Carmelite convent              326.20      155.09   **

        ** Gibraltar                          326.22       56.29   **

CONNEMARA MARBLE
     326.25      707.22

YELLOWJOHNS
     326.29      592.21

As treeless as PORTUGAL we'll be soon
     326.33      387.17      719.22

If something is not done TO REAFFOREST THE LAND
     326.34      547.26

The chieftain ELM OF KILDARE
     326.39      726.30

        ** On the fair hills of Eire, O       326.41      293.38   **

        ** Mrs Barbara Lovebirch              327.05     (235.37)  **

        ** Miss Priscilla Elderflower         327.10      155.37   **

        ** Miss O. Mimosa San                 327.11       96.40   **

        ** Senhor Enrique Flor                327.27       72.31   **

        ** Saint Fiacre in Horto              327.31       42.08   **

        ** On the winedark waterway           327.40        5.07   **

OUR HARBOURS THAT ARE EMPTY
     328.01++    639.23+

        ** Queenstown                         328.02      278.40   **

        ** The earl of Desmond                328.06       45.26   **

        ** Your Henry Tudor's harps           328.09      202.05   **

The three SONS OF MILESIUS
     328.12      393.30
```

MOYA
      328.13   333.25

            ** A hands up . . . bottle of Allsop   328.25+   176.33   **

            ** To drown him in the sea   328.34   4.28   **

            ** Crucify him   328.25   41.08   **

            ** That never will be slaves   329.15   18.33   **

COTTONBALL barons
      329.17   650.28

            ** The great empire they boast about   329.18+   73.02   **

            ** On which the sun never rises   329.20   30.35   **

            ** The unfortunate yahoos   329.22   39.38   **

            ** They believe in rod, the scourger   329.23+   20.42   **

            ** In the black 47   329.38+   31.19   **

            ** Whitelivered Saxons. . . . Sassenach 329.41+   4.17   **

            ** The land of bondage   330.05   122.23   **

The sons of Granuaile (GRACE O'MALLEY)
      330.07   628.12

            ** Kathleen ni Houlihan   330.07   9.22   **

            ** The poor old woman   330.11   14.03   **

            ** The French were on the sea   330.11   17.37   **

            ** The royal Stuarts   330.13   29.25   **

            ** The Williamites   330.14   31.23   **

            ** They betrayed us   330.14   14.05   **

            ** The wild geese   330.16   41.17   **

            ** Sarsfield   330.17   296.38   **

Fieldmarshal to MARIA TERESA
      330.18   724.27

Aren't they trying to make an ENTENTE CORDIALE now
      330.22+   571.03

            ** Tay Pay's dinnerparty   330.23   137.27   **

** Perfidious Albion . . . <u>Conspuez</u>   330.23   325.21   **

The HANOVERIANS
     330.26+   590.22

          ** The German lad (Prince Albert)   330.28   102.13   **

          ** The flatulent old bitch that's dead   330.29+   43.13   **

          ** Come where the boose is cheaper   330.35   (111.02)   **

Edward the PEACEMAKER
     330.37   590.26   See also   31.15

          ** Maynooth   330.41   212.16   **

          ** His Satanic Majesty   330.42   50.25   **

          ** Persecution . . . world is full of it 331.17#   36.10   **

          ** Perpetuating national hatred   331.18++   21.21   **

          ** What is your nation . . . ? Ireland   331.31   118.30   **

          ** A Red bank oyster   331.33   175.02   **

Ancient Irish facecloth attributed to . . . authors of the BOOK OF BALLYMOTE
     331.40   688.34

The SLIGO illuminators
     332.11   400.30   480.15   658.25

          ** In the time of the Barmecides   332.12   293.38   **

The lovely LAKES OF KILLARNEY
     332.13   726.32

          ** Brewery of . . . Guinness   332.16   81.39   **

LOUGH NEAGH's banks
     332.17   726.27   (45.12)

          ** The vale of Ovoca   332.17   45.12   **

          ** Isolde's tower   332.17   297.12   **

          ** The Scotch house   332.19   160.04   **

          ** Jury's Hotel   332.22   93.38   **

          ** S. Patrick's Purgatory   332.22   80.12   **

The SALMON LEAP
     332.22   726.31   (474.25)

** Maynooth college refectory   332.23   212.16   **

** The first duke of Wellington   332.24   297.16   **

** Plundered. Insulted. Persecuted   332.36+   36.10   **

** The new Jerusalem?   332.40   122.21   **

** I'm talking about injustice   332.41   122.29   **

** See if Martin is there   333.16   80.13   **

** A new apostle to the gentiles   333.20   29.27   **

UNIVERSAL LOVE
     333.20   405.04   489.22+   (213.19)   See also 289.18

LOVE YOUR NEIGHBOURS
     333.22   338.24

BEGGAR MY NEIGHBOUR is his motto
     333.24   686.04   See also 80.24   122.29

** Moya!   333.25   328.13   **

** A nice pattern of a Romeo and Juliet 333.25   108.15   **

LOVE LOVES to love love
     333.27++   380.15

** Gerty MacDowell   333.28   253.01   **

The boy that has the bicycle (REGGY WYLIE)
     333.28   349.27++   351.06+   351.22++   358.04   362.15++   363.39

** The man in the brown macintosh   333.33   109.29   **

** His Majesty the King (Edward VII)   333.33   31.15   **

** Mrs . . . Tupper loves officer Taylor 333.34   324.18   **

** Patrick   333.41   80.12   **

What about sanctimonious CROMWELL and his ironsides
     334.03+   342.01   644.04

** In the United Irishman   334.06   72.41   **

** That Zulu chief   334.07++   7.11   **

By GOLD STICK in Waiting
     334.13   480.38

The reverend ANANIAS Praisegod Barebones
    334.18   686.31

        ** The British Empire   334.20   73.02 **

        ** The great squaw Victoria   334.24++   43.13 **

        ** Usquebaugh   334.26   199.01 **

        ** By Griffith   334.38   43.08 **

        ** P [suggesting Parnell]   334.40   35.02 **

        ** On <u>Throwaway</u>   335.13   325.31 **

Is it that WHITEYED KAFFIR?
    335.14   443.25

        ** Bantam Lyons   335.16   74.02 **

        ** I put him off it   335.17   125.10 **

        ** Bloom gave him the tip   335.18   86.07 **

        ** A hundred shillings to five   335.19+   325.31 **

        ** Pisser Burke   335.30   305.40 **

        ** Trading without a licence   335.35   292.33 **

        ** Ireland my nation   335.35   118.30 **

        ** Jerusalem   335.37   122.21 **

        ** Cuckoos   335.37   212.36 **

        ** Bloom gave the idea of Sinn Fein 335.39   163.38 **

        ** To Griffith   335.39   43.08 **

        ** God save Ireland   336.04 (163.16) **

Old METHUSALEM Bloom
    336.06   679.35

        ** Bloom, the robbing bagman   336.07   76.26 **

Poisoned himself with PRUSSIC ACID
    336.08   492.04   See also 76.26

        ** Swamping the country with his baubles 336.08   260.39 **

        ** Martin Cunningham   336.14#   80.13 **

And a fellow named crofter or CROFTON, pensioner out of the collector general's
    336.16   337.28+   338.31   341.02   341.24   489.14   586.33
    (93.36)

    ** Jack Power   336.16#   87.03 **

    ** Asking where was Bloom   337.14++   280.29 **

    ** Sinn Fein   337.18   43.08   163.38 **

    ** Quite sure which country it is   337.24   118.30 **

    ** Crofton   337.28+   336.16 **

    ** Bloom the dentist   337.35   250.14 **

His name was Virag (BLOOM AS VIRAG)
    337.37   338.27   342.39   See also 76.26   307.25   378.36

    ** Father's name that poisoned himself 337.37   76.26 **

That is a NEW MESSIAH for Ireland!
    337.39+   495.02   497.20   521.23

    ** Island of saints   337.39   40.19 **

EXPECTING EVERY MOMENT WILL BE HIS NEXT, says Lenehan
    338.04   388.07   (648.32)

    ** That son of his   338.06   66.25 **

    ** Before the wife was delivered   338.08   151.29 **

    ** And who does he suspect?   338.14   202.15 **

Gob, there's many a TRUE WORD spoken in jest
    338.15   436.04   759.36

    ** One of those mixed middlings   338.15   321.09 **

    ** The hotel   338.16   35.27 **

    ** Pisser (Burke)   338.16   305.40 **

Lying up in the hotel (BLOOM'S ILLNESS AT THE CITY ARMS HOTEL)
    338.16   738.03

    ** Charity to the neighbour   338.24   333.22 **

    ** A wolf in sheep's clothing   338.26   125.21 **

    ** Virag from Hungary!   338.27   337.37 **

    ** Ahasuerus. . . . Cursed by God   338.27   34.05 **

```
        ** J.J. and S (Jameson Whisky)        338.30     179.17   **

        ** Crofton?                           338.31     336.16   **

        ** Saint Patrick                      338.32      80.12   **

The blessed company DREW NIGH
      338.41      341.31

        ** Augustine                          339.03     142.24   **

        ** From Carmel mount                  339.05     155.09   **

        ** Elijah prophet                     339.05     197.17   **

And the sons of DOMINIC
      339.09      338.35

        ** Ignatius his children              339.10       9.14   **

        ** The christian brothers             339.11     151.02   **

        ** S. Martin (Cunningham)             339.18      80.13   **

        ** S. Alfred (Bergin)                 339.19     221.24   **

        ** S. Joseph (Hynes)                  339.19      90.04   **

S. DENIS
      339.19      357.08

        ** S. Denis (Breen)                   339.19     157.17   **

        ** S. Cornelius (Kelleher)            339.20      71.15   **

        ** S. Bernard (Barney Kiernan)        339.20     280.29   **

S. BERNARD
      339.20      356.31      391.19++

        ** S. Edward (Lambert)                339.21      90.03   **

        ** S. Owen Caniculous (Garryowen)     339.21     295.13   **

        ** S. Anonymous (Narrator)            339.21     292.01   **

And S. CELESTINE
      339.25      666.40

        ** S. Kevin                           339.26     323.14   **

        ** S. Brendan                         339.26     297.01   **

        ** S. Columbanus                      339.27      27.39   **
```

** S. Fursey (St. Fursa)	339.27	297.01	**
** S. Fiacre	339.28	42.08	**
** S. Thomas Aquinas	339.29	17.40	**
** S. Michan	339.29	240.30	**

And . . . S. ALOYSIUS GONZAGA
    339.30   686.36

And S. BRIDE
    339.33+   726.30

** S. Canice of Kilkenny	339.33	44.03	**

And S. BARBARA
    339.39   599.09

** S. Ursula with . . . virgins	339.40	6.34	**
** Nelson's pillar	340.08	95.09	**
** Capel Street	340.08	300.28	**
** The reverend Father O'Flynn	340.17	170.30	**
** Malachi	340.17	45.13	**
** Patrick	340.17	80.12	**
** Licensed . . . premises	340.20	173.39	**
** Crofton	341.02	336.16	**
** His John Jameson	341.03	179.17	**
** Scut	341.12	86.08	**
** Cute as a . . . rat	341.14	279.10	**
** Hundred to five	341.14	325.31	**
** Crofton	341.24	336.16	**
** The bloody jaunting car	341.26	(253.42)	**
** In the golden poop	341.29	271.19	**
** A many comely nymphs	341.31+	65.11	**
** Drew nigh to starboard	341.31	338.41	**

Blowing with the DROPSY (The Citizen)
    342.01   490.02

```
          ** The curse of Cromwell                342.01      334.03  **

THREE CHEERS FOR ISRAEL!
     342.08      380.29

          ** The parliamentary side of your arse  342.09      123.23  **

          ** Mendelssohn was a jew                342.24      285.37  **

          ** Mercadante                           342.24       82.16  **

          ** Spinoza                              342.25      284.36  **

And THE SAVIOUR WAS A JEW AND HIS FATHER WAS A JEW
     342.25      380.25      643.03      658.20+

          ** I'll crucify him                     342.34       41.08  **

          ** That biscuitbox                      342.35++    305.29  **

          ** A large and appreciative gathering   342.37++   (118.33) **

          ** Nagyaságos uram Lipóti Virag         342.39      337.37  **

          ** Messrs Alexander Thom's, printers    342.40      123.05  **

          ** The distinguished phenomenologist    343.04      304.35  **

The wellknown strains of COME BACK TO ERIN
     343.11      642.38

          ** The Hill of Howth                    343.14       40.25  **

THREE ROCK MOUNTAIN
     343.14      755.10

          ** Sugarloaf (Mountain)                 343.14      155.30  **

          ** Bray Head                            343.15        7.39  **

          ** The mountains of Mourne              343.15      261.32  **

          ** The reeks of M'Gillicuddy            343.17      295.05  **

          ** Slieve Bloom                         343.18       58.37  **

          ** The Ballast office                   343.25      154.04  **

          ** Custom House                         343.25      227.09  **

          ** The Pigeonhouse                      343.26       41.13  **

          ** The Queen's royal theatre            343.32       92.04  **
```

** The sun was in his eyes   343.40   (26.01)   **

** The observatory of Dunsink   344.04   154.05   **

** Silken Thomas   344.07   45.26   **

** Saint Michan   344.10   240.30   **

The much respected clerk of the crown and peace Mr GEORGE FOTTRELL
     344.20   461.21+

** Sir Frederick Falkiner   344.23   138.02   **

The GIANT'S CAUSEWAY
     344.26   726.28

** Those faithful departed   344.38   113.41   **

** The lottery ticket   345.08   156.11   **

** The gold cup   345.09   84.40   **

** Moses   345.12   40.07   **

LUGS BACK
     345.19   586.14   See also 432.12

** Tear him limb from limb   345.20   170.03   **

** Hundred to five!   345.20   325.31   **

** A great brightness   345.22+   26.01   **

** Elijah! Elijah!   345.27+   197.17   **

NAUSICAA

   ** [Sandymount Strand]   346.04#   37.01 **

   ** Dear old Howth   346.04   40.25 **

The quiet CHURCH ("STAR OF THE SEA")
   346.07#   469.18+

LITANY OF OUR LADY OF LORETO (the voice of prayer to . . . Mary)
   346.08+   354.08   354.26   356.23+   358.22+   359.37   377.35
   391.25   498.23+   See also   47.39

CISSY CAFFREY
   346.15#   430.14++   574.03+   587.17

EDY BOARDMAN
   346.15#   431.26+

The BABY in the pushcar (BABY BOARDMAN)
   346.16++   352.41++   356.37++   363.08+   367.37   486.13+

TOMMY CAFFREY
   346.16#   433.17   437.01+   (541.07)
   See also   187.22

JACKY CAFFREY
   346.17#   433.19   437.01+

Their big coloured ball (THE CAFFREY TWINS' BALL)
   346.24   352.41+   355.37++   359.11   360.16   363.09   372.41

   ** Rocking . . . to and fro   346.25   11.24 **

The GOLDEN RULE
   347.07   642.06

** The apple of discord   347.07   191.26 **

** Right go wrong   347.09   320.28 **

** The Martello tower   347.10   (3.10) **

** Irishman's house is his castle   347.13   110.07 **

Edy Boardman . . . with . . . her SHORTSIGHTED EYES
   348.01   349.26   360.34   368.06

     ** Gerty (MacDowell)   348.02#   253.01 **

Cissy's quick MOTHERWIT
   348.04   423.17

As fair a specimen of WINSOME Irish GIRLHOOD
   348.11   360.21   521.06

     ** A Giltrap   348.13   312.39 **

Her FIGURE WAS SLIGHT AND GRACEFUL
   348.14   350.15   362.21   366.38   See also 61.32

     ** The waxen pallor of her face   348.18+   (84.38) **

BERTHA SUPPLE
   348.25   352.09   364.02   365.40   431.26

     ** A languid queenly _hauteur_   348.31   49.36 **

     ** Fate   348.33   66.39 **

To try EYEBROWLEINE
   349.06   364.07

Her WEALTH OF WONDERFUL HAIR
   349.12   360.21
  Haircut
   349.13   361.40

     ** On account of the new moon   349.14   157.38 **

     ** A young May morning   349.25   (45.12) **

     ** Squinty Edy   349.26   348.01 **

     ** The boy that had the bicycle   349.29++   333.28 **

     ** His brother W. E. Wylie   349.33   237.17 **

     ** Saint Joseph   349.40   41.15 **

With the instinctive taste of a votary of Dame Fashion (GERTY'S INSTINCT)
    350.07   358.07   364.33

A piece of cottonwool scented with her favourite perfume (GERTY'S PERFUME)
    350.13   367.25   374.25++   See also 72.30

      ** Her slim graceful figure   350.15   348.14 **

      ** Clery's summer sales   350.20   76.22 **

      ** Her wellturned ankle   350.31   74.14 **

      ** Brought him in to study   351.06   333.28 **

      ** Mrs Reggy Wylie T.D.C.   351.22++ 333.28 **

In the FASHIONABLE INTELLIGENCE
    351.23   715.35

He was TOO YOUNG TO UNDERSTAND
    351.26   362.23

      ** In Stoers'   351.28   250.24 **

      ** Who would woo and win   351.34   196.24 **

      ** Waiting, always waiting to be asked 351.36   275.23 **

      ** It was leap year   351.36   171.21 **

Rather a MANLY MAN
    351.39   See   321.09   358.14

His affianced bride . . . to this day forward (CATHOLIC MARRIAGE SERVICE)
    352.04   442.09   539.02

They could TALK . . . TILL they went BLUE IN THE FACE
    352.09   499.09   508.21

      ** Bertha Supple   352.09   348.25 **

      ** Something poetical like violets   352.21   69.39 **

      ** Grandpa Giltrap   352.23   312.39 **

      ** Lovely dog Garryowen   352.24   295.13 **

      ** Clery's summer jumble sales   352.26   76.22 **

      ** With glistening white teeth   352.28   3.28 **

      ** That baby   352.41++ 346.16 **

      ** Playing with the ball   352.41+   346.24 **

The reverend JOHN HUGHES S.J.
     354.02   356.30   382.28   469.20

The men's temperance retreat . . . ROSARY, sermon and benediction
     354.03#   462.18   524.05   779.09

      ** This weary world   354.07   3.41 **

      ** The litany of Our Lady of Loreto   354.08   346.08 **

      ** In supplication to the Virgin   354.26   346.08 **

Or the GENTLEMAN OFF SANDYMOUNT GREEN . . . passing along the strand
     354.29+   375.38+   See also 376.04

      ** Tell me, Mary, how to woo thee   354.37   196.24 **

      ** My love and cottage near Rochelle   354.37   130.28 **

      ** The moon hath raised   354.40   92.06 **

      ** With Mr Dignam that died   354.40+   57.11 **

      ** And Mrs . . . Dignam   355.01   349.10 **

      ** And Patsy . . . Dignam   355.01   101.02 **

FREDDY DIGNAM
     355.02   568.17+

      ** Catesby's cork lino   355.08   113.16 **

      ** Mr Tunney the grocer   355.20   250.26 **

The picture of HALCYON DAYS
     355.21   355.33   548.15+

      ** Grandpapa Giltrap   355.32   312.39 **

      ** The halcyon days   355.33   355.21 **

      ** The ball   355.37++   346.24 **

Under the brim of HER NEW HAT
     356.19   360.26   369.36

      ** Open window . . . fragrant names   356.23   346.08 **

      ** Original sin   356.25   212.14 **

      ** Their daily bread   356.28   6.33 **

Many who had ERRED AND WANDERED
     356.28   367.15   (189.41)

** The reverend father Hughes   356.30   354.02 **

** Saint Bernard   356.31   339.20 **

** Baby Boardman   356.37+   346.16 **

** Peep she cried   356.38   256.10 **

HAJA JA JA HAJA
   357.05   486.16

** Holy saint Denis   357.08   339.19 **

But Ciss . . . gave him in his mouth the TEAT OF THE SUCKINGBOTTLE
   357.16   373.10

The BAILEY LIGHT
   357.24   376.14   550.19

** On Howth   357.24   40.25 **

** Could you trust them?   357.31   7.16 **

She could see . . . that he was a FOREIGNER
   357.33   380.16   382.37   See also 118.30

The photo she had of MARTIN HARVEY, matinee idol
   357.33   767.08(G)   767.29

Because she wasn't stagestruck like WINNY RIPPINGHAM
   357.35   366.12

Whether he had an aquiline NOSE (BLOOM'S NOSE)
   357.37   369.33

** Reggy Wylie   358.04   333.28 **

** She felt instinctively   358.07   350.07 **

If he had suffered, MORE SINNED AGAINST THAN SINNING
   358.10   493.13

** She was a womanly woman   358.14   351.39 **

** Those cyclists   358.16   86.19 **

SHOWING OFF WHAT THEY HADN'T GOT
   358.16   746.10   750.22

** The memory of the past   358.18   86.32 **

** Refuge. . . . Comfortress   358.22   346.08 **

** <u>Ora</u> <u>pro</u> <u>nobis</u>   358.22+   205.24 **

** The <u>Tantum</u> <u>Ergo</u>	361.27	17.40	**
** Canon O'Hanlon	361.28+	358.30	**
** Father Conroy	361.29+	252.01	**

That thing must be coming on (MENSTRUATION)
  Gerty MacDowell
    361.39   366.13   368.07+   369.17
  Milly Bloom
    368.16   380.08
  Molly Bloom
    368.16   769.03++   770.16+   781.08
  Nurse Callan
    386.21
  Other references
    368.13   697.08

** Clipped her hair	361.40	349.12	**
** The moon	361.40	157.38	**
** Dark eyes fixed themselves on her	361.41	241.34	**
** Canon O'Hanlon	362.09	358.30	**
** Father Conroy	362.10	252.01	**
** About her best boy	362.15++	333.28	**
** Her throat, so slim, so flawless	362.21	348.14	**
** Loved him better than he knew	362.23	351.26	**
** Lighthearted deceiver	362.24	14.05	**
** It's leap year	362.32	171.21	**
** Baby Boardman	363.08+	346.16	**
** The ball	363.09	346.24	**

The slight <u>CONTRETEMPS</u> claimed her attention
    363.19   665.12

** Canon O'Hanlon	363.27	358.30	**
** Father Conroy	363.27	252.01	**
** The last glimpse of Erin	363.30	45.12	**
** Those evening bells	363.31	45.12	**

A BAT flew forth from the ivied belfry
    363.32   366.19   367.18+   377.29++   379.18   382.11+   382.20
    See also   48.02

      ** Reggy Wylie   363.39   333.28 **

      ** Bertha Supple   364.02   348.25 **

She laid it in the DRAWER [where] she kept her girlish treasures trove
    364.03   (442.18)   See also 543.08

      ** The eyebrowleine   364.07   349.06 **

      ** Hely's of Dame street   364.10   106.26 **

      ** The allimportant question   364.27   32.01 **

      ** Nature instinctively recoiled   364.33   350.07 **

      ** From days beyond recall   364.40   63.31 **

      ** Waiting, waiting   365.01   275.23 **

      ** She would follow her dream of love 365.02   45.12 **

      ** All in all   365.04   212.29 **

      ** Canon O'Hanlon   365.07   358.30 **

      ** Father Conroy   365.10   252.01 **

It's FIREWORKS, Cissy Caffrey said
    365.17++   371.18   372.22+   379.06   482.28   507.08   (413.36)

      ** It's the bazaar fireworks   365.22   183.05 **

      ** Trusted to the death   365.31   7.16 **

She leaned back . . . REVEALED ALL HER . . . LEGS
    365.36++   374.10   729.08   735.16

      ** Bertha Supple   365.40   348.25 **

Those SKIRTDANCERS and HIGHKICKERS
    366.02   366.35   545.12

      ** That dreamy kind of dreamy look 366.11   (166.08) **

      ** Winny Rippingham   366.12   357.35 **

      ** That other thing coming on   366.13   361.39 **

      ** Something queer was flying about 366.19   363.32 **

      ** To and fro   366.20   11.24 **

A divine, an entrancing BLUSH
    366.25   471.30

      ** Those skirtdancers   366.35   366.02 **

      ** Her snowy slender arms   366.38   348.14 **

      ** Dewy stars. . . . melted away dewily 367.05   (264.24) **

      ** Young guileless eyes   367.10   64.24 **

      ** Erred and . . . wandered   367.15   356.28 **

      ** The little bat that flew so softly   367.18+   363.32 **

      ** To and fro   367.18   11.24 **

Cissy Caffrey WHISTLED
    367.20   371.24

      ** Took out the wadding   367.25   350.13 **

She . . . WAVED in reply
    367.26   374.25

They would MEET AGAIN, there . . . tomorrow
    367.28   381.26   382.05

      ** Baby Boardman   367.37   346.16 **

Thought something was wrong by the CUT OF HER JIB
    368.02   636.04

CURIOSITY LIKE A NEGRESS
    368.05   See   443.17

      ** That squinty one   368.06   348.01 **

      ** Near her monthlies, I expect   368.07+   361.39 **

      ** Such a bad headache . . . letter?   368.08   72.30 **

      ** Tranquilla convent   368.09   155.03 **

      ** Sister?   368.11   155.05 **

      ** That's the moon   368.13+   157.38 **

      ** Why don't all women menstruate   368.13+   361.39 **

      ** Molly and Milly together   368.16   21.42   361.39 **

      ** Glad I didn't do it in the bath   368.17   85.08 **

** Her silly I will punish you letter	368.18	72.30	**
** That tramdriver this morning	368.19	74.29	**
** His wife engagement . . . valise	368.20	67.24	**
** Reserve better	368.24	73.40	**
** A dream of wellfilled hose	368.26	74.18	**
** In Capel street	368.27	300.28	**
** Peeping Tom	368.27	163.27	**
** Felt for the curves	368.29	236.05	**
** Milly delighted	368.32	21.42	**

PUT THEM ALL ON TO TAKE THEM ALL OFF. Molly
       368.32   742.06

** The violet garters	368.34	57.30	**
** The tie he wore	368.34	254.04	**
** His lovely socks	368.34	254.01	**
** Turnedup trousers	368.35	183.12	**
** The night that first we met	368.35+	69.27	**
** O Mairy lost the pin of her	368.38	78.38	**
** On the track of a secret	368.40	57.33	**
** The east	368.40	57.15	**
** Mary, Martha	368.41	79.06	**
** Barbed wire	369.07	155.16	**
** Josie Powell	369.09	156.32	**
** Tableau!	369.10	359.35	**
** Devils they are	369.17	157.33	**
** When that's coming on them	369.17	361.39	**
** Often meet what you feel	369.25	200.14	**
** Kiss in the dark and never tell	369.29	280.23	**
** To aid gentleman in literary	369.32	160.12	**

```
            ** See me in profile                    369.33    357.37   **

BEAUTY AND THE BEAST
     369.35      446.02

            ** Took off her hat to show her hair    369.36    356.19   **

            ** In Holles street                     369.40    268.40   **

SUPPOSE HE GAVE HER MONEY. . . . SHE'S WORTH TEN, FIFTEEN, MORE A POUND
     369.41      740.31

            ** Bold hand.  Mrs Marion                369.42     61.37   **

            ** On that letter                       370.01    182.11   **

            ** To Flynn                             370.01    171.25   **

            ** Drimmie's                            370.02    177.05   **

            ** Richie Goulding                      370.03     38.34   **

            ** Watch stopped . . . when he, she     370.04    361.21   **

            ** The name too                         370.15    209.10   **

            ** Nell Gwynn                           370.16    204.09   **

MRS BRACEGIRDLE
     370.16      382.13

MAUD BRANSCOMBE
     370.16      720.30

            ** Moonlight . . . pensive bosom        370.17     91.08   **

            ** I let off there behind               370.20    257.19   **

            ** Coming out of Dignam's               370.20     57.11   **

            ** Cider that was                       370.21    267.30   **

            ** Makes you want to sing after         370.21    274.12   **

            ** Lacaus esant taratara                370.22    168.20   **

            ** My arks she called it                370.30    123.23   **

            ** In the Burton . . . gumchewed gristle 370.38   161.19   **

            ** French letter                        370.39    214.41   **

            ** Come in. . . . . I dreamt            370.41    281.27   **

            ** Flatters them                        371.06    167.06   **
```

```
        ** First kiss                      371.09      67.13    **

LIEUTENANT MULVEY that kissed her
     371.12      382.17      693.08      731.25    756.09+    756.21      756.40+
     759.04++    782.25++      See also   67.13

Kissed her under the MOORISH WALL
     371.13      759.30      783.09

        ** Beside the gardens              371.13     319.39    **

        ** After Glencree dinner           371.15     155.23    **

        ** The featherbed mountain         371.15     234.25    **

        ** Gnashing her teeth in sleep     371.16     137.24    **

        ** Lord mayor. . . . Val Dillon    371.17     155.22    **

        ** The fireworks.  My fireworks    371.18     365.17    **

        ** The ways of the world           371.22     280.23    **

        ** The nigger mouth                371.23      80.19    **

        ** I knew she could whistle        371.24     367.20    **

High class whore in JAMMET'S
     371.25      606.07

        ** Say prunes and prisms           371.27      37.37    **

        ** Those lovely seaside girls      371.32      62.36    **

        ** Venus                           371.37     176.26    **

        ** All his belongings on show      371.37     270.36    **

        ** Call that innocence?            371.38      25.01    **

        ** Twigged at once he had a false arm  372.01  163.24   **

        ** Bred in the bone                372.05      19.18    **

        ** Milly for example               372.05++    21.42    **

        ** To Presscott's                  372.08      83.42    **

        ** That ad I must                  372.08     107.35    **

        ** Lombard street west             372.15     110.15    **

        ** Mullingar                       372.16      21.42    **
```

** Ways of the world   372.16   280.23   **

** Young student   372.17   21.41   **

** Straight on her pins   372.17   156.16   **

** Transparent stockings stretched 372.19   74.18   **

** That frump today   372.20   160.16   **

** A.E. (George Russell)   372.20   5.13   **

** Rumpled stockings   372.20   166.07   **

** The one in Grafton street. White 372.21   168.13   **

** In Grafton street   372.21   168.10   **

** Beef to the heel   372.21   66.08   **

** A monkey puzzle rocket burst   372.22+   365.17   **

** Kiernan's   372.29   280.29   **

** Dignam's   372.29   313.07   **

FOR THIS RELIEF MUCH THANKS
     372.30   412.35

** Your head it simply swirls   372.32   62.36   **

** Then I will tell you all   372.34   72.30   **

** It couldn't be   372.35   286.05   **

** False name like my   372.36   72.31   **

** Dolphin's barn   372.37   280.17   **

** Irishtown   372.39   87.40   **

** The ball   372.41   346.24   **

Only a few years till they SETTLE DOWN TO POTWALLOPING
     373.04   430.14

** Dignam   373.08   57.11   **

** Given that child an empty teat   373.10   357.16   **

** Mrs Beaufoy   373.11   67.39   **

** Mrs . . . Purefoy   373.11   158.36   **

** Must call to the hospital   373.12   97.29   **

Wonder is NURSE CALLAN there still
    373.12   385.12++   406.02+   410.08   423.06+   522.04   722.28

          ** In the Coffee Palace   373.14   268.37 **

That young DOCTOR O'HARE I noticed her brushing his coat
    373.14   385.32++   (41.36) (G)

          ** Mrs Breen   373.15   156.32 **

          ** Mrs Dignam   373.15   349.10 **

          ** The City Arms   373.17   35.27 **

STINK of pub off him LIKE A POLECAT
    373.17   453.03

It is the BLOOD of the south. MOORISH (MOLLY'S)
    373.23   377.26   439.30
    See also   28.14   84.40   285.38

          ** Hands felt for the opulent   373.24   236.05 **

          ** There's destiny in it   373.28   66.39 **

          ** Very strange about my watch   373.40+   361.21 **

Magnetic influence . . . that was the time he (HETEROSEXUAL MAGNETISM)
    373.41++   666.31   722.26

          ** In Pill lane   374.01   297.36 **

          ** The time the movement takes   374.04   (37.26) **

          ** Let you see more   374.10   365.36 **

About the FARMER in the ridingboots and spurs AT THE HORSE SHOW
    374.16   731.27

          ** In Lombard street west   374.17   110.15 **

          ** That's her perfume   374.25++   350.13 **

          ** Why she waved her hand   374.25   367.26 **

Molly likes OPOPONAX
    374.29   730.18   742.07   751.05   See also 78.12

Suits her with a little JESSAMINE mixed
    374.30   730.18   783.05

          ** Dance night she met him   374.31   69.27 **

          ** Dance of the hours   374.31   69.28 **

```
** Good conductor, is it?              374.33      57.10   **

** Cinghalese this morning             374.38      71.37   **
```

It's like a fine veil or web . . . GOSSAMER
    374.41   414.35

```
** Stays                               375.02     156.26   **

** Drawers                             375.02      63.40   **

** The shift                           375.03      92.33   **

** Or the armpits                      375.06     236.25   **

** Dogs at each other behind           375.09      89.08   **

** Long John (Fanning)                 375.17     119.20   **
```

THE TREE OF FORBIDDEN PRIEST
    375.21   408.06

```
** That's the soap                     375.27+     85.17   **

** That lotion                         375.28      84.03   **

** Like that hag this morning          375.30      61.15   **

** Hynes                               375.30      90.04   **

** That three shillings                375.30     119.33   **

** Meagher's                           375.31     119.33   **

** If he works that paragraph          375.32     117.05   **

** This nobleman passed before         375.38+    254.29   **

** Grace after meals                   375.41     155.26   **

** Like those newsboys me today        376.01     128.06   **

** See ourselves as others see us      376.02       6.28   **

** Still you learn something           376.02    (35.14)   **

** So long as women don't mock         376.03       3.37   **
```

THE MYSTERY MAN ON THE BEACH
    376.04   587.01   See also 354.29

```
** Prize titbit story                  376.05      67.39   **

** At the graveside                    376.06      57.11   **
```

```
   ** Fellow . . . in the brown macintosh    376.07      109.29   **

   ** On his kismet                          376.07     (66.39)   **

   ** In the Ormond                          376.09      230.02   **
```

MOTHER SHIPTON'S PROPHECY that is about ships around they fly
    376.11   377.02

And DISTANT HILLS seem coming nigh
    376.13   377.06

```
   ** Howth                                  376.14       40.25   **

   ** Bailey light                           376.14      357.24   **
```

GRACE DARLING
    376.15   382.14

```
   ** Also . . . cyclists                    376.16       86.19   **

   ** Vance taught us                        376.23       72.08   **
```

ROYGBIV . . . RED, ORANGE, YELLOW, GREEN, BLUE, INDIGO, VIOLET
    376.23   486.23

```
   ** A star I see.  Venus?                  376.24      210.08   **
```

Looks like a PHANTOM SHIP
    376.26   478.24   636.39   See also 297.12   478.24

```
   ** Homerule sun setting in the southeast 376.27       57.35   **

   ** My native land, goodnight              376.28      124.01   **

   ** Might get piles                        376.31       69.08   **

   ** Also the library today                 376.37       15.35   **

   ** Mat Dillon                             376.41+     106.19   **

   ** I wooed                                377.01      196.24   **
```

The YEAR RETURNS. History repeats itself
    377.01   377.20   382.17+   See also 200.14

```
   ** Ye crags and peaks                     377.01      297.08   **

   ** Voyage round your own little world     377.02      376.11   **

   ** And now?                               377.03      155.35   **

   ** Howth. . . . The rhododendrons         377.06      176.01   **
```

** The distant hills seem   377.06   376.13   **

** He gets the plums   377.07   95.10   **

** Names change: that's all   377.09   209.10   **

RETURNING NOT THE SAME
    377.13   382.11

** Are you not happy. . . . Naughty   377.15   72.30   **

** Charades in Luke Doyle's house   377.16   64.24   **

** Mat Dillon   377.17   106.19   **

Mat Dillon and his bevy of daughters: TINY
    377.17   422.15

Mat Dillon and his bevy of daughters: . . . ATTY
    377.17   422.15   758.38

** Floey   377.18   115.19   **

Mat Dillon and his bevy of daughters: . . . MAIMY
    377.18   780.12

** The old major   377.19   56.32   **

** So it returns   377.20   377.01   **

** Escaping and run into yourself   377.20   213.14   **

** Just when he and she   377.22   361.21   **

IRVING, WASHINGTON (Rip van Winkle we played)
  "Rip van Winkle"
    377.23++   495.15   527.20(T)   542.03+   624.27   728.08   (81.15)
  "The Legend of Sleepy Hollow"
    377.27   542.03+
  Knickerbocker's History of New York
    527.20(T)
  "The Broken Heart"—Possible parody of style
    (306.24++)(G)

TEAR IN Henny Doyle's OVERCOAT
    377.23   747.06   (463.01)   See also 584.07

HENNY DOYLE's overcoat
    377.24   747.05

** Moorish eyes   377.26   373.23   **

** Ba . . . Bat probably   377.29++   363.32   **

** Metempsychosis   377.30+   50.13   **

** Mass seems to be over   377.35   346.08   **

** Pray for us. And pray for us   377.35+   205.24   **

** When I was in Thom's   377.40   123.05   **

** Gabriel Conroy   377.40   125.18   **

** Gabriel Conroy's brother   377.40   252.01   **

** All instinct   378.02   92.16   **

** Like the bird in drouth   378.02   125.21   **

** Colours depend on the light   378.05   25.17   **

Stare in the sun for example like the EAGLE
    378.06   (480.07)

** In the City Arms   378.11   35.27   **

** Howth   378.12   40.25   **

** That wise man . . . Archimedes   378.13+   213.28   **

Or BROKEN BOTTLES in the furze
    378.16   758.06

** Might be the one bit me   378.21   68.18   **

** Like snuff at a wake   378.28   93.22   **

** Tail end   378.33   324.25   **

And the tephilim no what's this they call it (TEPHILIM--MEZUZAH) (G)
    378.36   487.08   777.23

** Poor papa   378.36   76.26   **

Poor papa's father (LIPOTI VIRAG)
    378.36   496.07   511.21++   552.03   723.26   766.12
    See also   337.37

** Out of the land of Egypt   378.37   122.15   122.20   **

** Into the house of bondage   378.38   122.23   **

DAVY JONES' locker
    379.04   624.25

** A lost long candle   379.06   365.17   **

** Mirus bazaar   379.06   183.05   **

```
    ** Mercer's hospital                      379.07      183.06   **

    ** The glowworm's lamp                    379.11       45.12   **

    ** Leahy's terrace                        379.14       37.33   **

    ** Evening Telegraph                      379.15       35.22   **

    ** The Gold Cup Race                      379.16       85.40   **

    ** A boy ran out and called               379.17      101.02   **

    ** Twittering the bat flew                379.18      363.32   **

    ** Howth                                  379.19      176.01   **

    ** Kish bank . . . lightship twinkled     379.23       44.13   **

    ** Penance for their sins                 379.26       83.02   **

    ** Cruise in the Erin's King              379.28       67.03   **

    ** Milly                                  379.31++     21.42   **

    ** No sign of funk.  Her blue scarf       379.32       67.04   **
```

When we hid behind the trees at CRUMLIN
    379.34   667.22

```
    ** Frightening them with masks            379.36        7.30   **

    ** Dearest Papli                          380.02       66.01   **

    ** Her first stays                        380.04      156.26   **

    ** When her nature came on her first      380.08      361.39   **

    ** Gibraltar                              380.10       56.29   **
```

O'HARA'S TOWER
    380.10   760.03

Old BARBARY APE that gobbled all his family
    380.11   760.05

GUNFIRE to the men to cross the lines
    380.12   757.18

LOOKING OUT OVER THE SEA she told me
    380.13   782.24

Buenas noches, SEÑORITA
    380.15   382.16   777.22   See also 476.13

```
      ** El hombre ama la muchacha             380.15      333.27   **
```

** So foreign from the others   380.16   357.33   **

** Too late for Leah   380.20   76.23   **

** Late for . . . Lily of Killarney   380.20   92.06   **

** Call to hospital to see   380.21   97.29   **

** Hope she's over   380.21   158.36   **

** Martha   380.22   72.31   **

** The bath   380.22   85.06   **

** Funeral   380.22   57.11   **

** House of keys   380.22   107.35   **

** Museum with those goddesses   380.22   80.10   **

** Dedalus' song   380.23   117.35   **

** That bawler   380.23   293.25   **

** Barney Kiernan's   380.23   280.29   **

** What I said about his god   380.25   342.26   **

** Three cheers for Israel   380.29   342.08   **

EVERYONE TO HIS TASTE
    380.34   453.03

** Dignam's   380.35++   57.11   **

** Poisoned by mussels here. The sewage 381.02+   174.42   **

** Love, lie and be handsome   381.07   172.04   **

** See him sometimes walking about   381.08   157.17   **

** U. p.: up   381.09   158.11   **

** Fate that is   381.09   66.39   **

** Dreamt last night?   381.11   281.27   **

She had RED SLIPPERS on.   TURKISH.
    381.12   397.28   439.09   780.03

WORE THE BREECHES. SUPPOSE SHE DOES
    381.12   527.20+   542.01

** Nannetti's gone   381.13   118.16   **

** That ad of Keyes's	381.15	107.35	**
** Hynes	381.15	90.04	**
** Crawford	381.15	125.07	**
** Petticoats for Molly	381.15	180.16	**
** Trust?	381.24	7.16	**
** Will she come here tomorrow?	381.26	367.28	**

Must COME BACK. MUDERERS do
    381.28   649.40

** Dark mirror	381.34	28.16	**
** Rocks with lines and scars	381.34	(37.02)	**
** That other world . . . not like	381.36	72.30	**
** Hopeless thing sand. Nothing grows	381.41	(61.09)	**
** Guinness's	382.01	81.39	**
** The Kish in eighty days 382.01	44.13	297.11	**

The STICK fell in SILTED SAND, stuck
    382.03   (440.13)

** We'll never meet again	382.05	367.28	**
** It was lovely. . . . Thanks	382.05	286.29	**
** Liverpool boat	382.07	97.41	**
** And Belfast. I won't go	382.09	75.11	**
** Back to Ennis	382.09	76.26	**
** It never comes the same	382.11	377.13	**
** Bat again	382.11+	363.32	**
** I saw dirty bracegirdle	382.13	370.16	**
** We two naughty	382.14	72.30	**
** Grace darling	382.14	376.15	**
** Half past	382.15	361.21	**
** Met him pike hoses	382.15	50.13	**

```
** Frillies for Raoul                        382.15      236.05    **

** To perfume your wife         382.16       72.30      350.13    **

** Black hair                                382.16      319.37    **

** Señorita                                  382.16      380.15    **

** Young eyes                                382.17       64.24    **

** Mulvey                                    382.17      371.12    **

** Years dreams return                       382.17+     377.01    **

** Tail end                                  382.17      324.25    **

** Agendath                                  382.17       60.16    **

** Next year                                 382.18      122.21    **

** Next year . . . return                    382.18      122.19    **

** A bat flew                                382.20      363.32    **

** Cuckoo                                    382.23++    212.36    **

** The clock on the mantelpiece              382.26+     359.04    **

** Canon O'Hanlon                            382.27      358.30    **

** Father Conroy                             382.27      252.01    **

** The reverend John Hughes S.J.             382.28      354.02    **

** Foreign gentleman                         382.37      357.33    **
```

OXEN OF THE SUN

    ** DESHIL HOLLES EAMUS   383.01   97.29 **

    ** Bright one   383.03+   (26.01) **

    ** Send us . . . Horhorn   383.03+   159.01 **

HOOPSA
     383.07+   501.26

    ** Of evils the original   383.19   212.14 **

    ** Absent . . . incorrupted benefaction 383.19+   142.21 **

    ** To consign that evangel . . . command 383.35   14.23 **

    ** By midwives attended   384.33   37.37 **

    ** Sunbright   384.41   26.01 **

    ** Of Israel's folk . . . wandering   385.04   34.05 **

    ** A. Horne   385.07++ 159.01 **

    ** God's angel   385.09   358.41 **

    ** To Mary   385.09   47.39 **

They twain are (NURSE QUIGLEY and Nurse Callan)
    385.12   392.08+   522.04+   (250.24)

    ** They twain (Nurse Callan)   385.12++ 373.12 **

    ** That God . . . for his evil sins   385.17+   84.06 **

** On her stow he ere was living   385.22+   268.40 **

** O'Hare Doctor   385.32++   373.14 **

** Holy housel   385.38   40.12 **

Therefore, EVERYMAN, look to that last end
     386.05   727.31+

** His mother's womb   386.07   38.09 **

** The woman that lay there in childbed   386.10++   158.36 **

** Had lived nigh that house   386.17   268.40 **

He felt with wonder WOMEN'S WOE
     386.18   388.16   403.37

** Nine twelve bloodflows   386.21   361.39 **

** A young learning knight yclept Dixon   386.26++   97.28 **

** In the house of misericord   386.28   8.27 **

** Sore wounded in his breast by a spear   386.30   68.18 **

** By magic of Mahound   387.09   77.26 **

** From Portugal   387.17   326.33 **

** Fecund wheat kidneys   387.20   40.07 **

** Did up his beaver   387.28   197.12 **

** A franklin that hight Lenehan   387.42#   125.10 **

** Knights . . . one emprise   388.02   57.35   128.02 **

** Expecting each moment to be her next   388.07   338.04 **

** Husbandly hand under hen   388.13   315.20 **

** Woman's woe   388.16   386.18 **

** Saint Mary Merciable's   388.20   8.27 **

** Lynch   388.20#   224.25 **

With other his fellows Lynch and MADDEN
     388.21#   493.19   509.10   See also 415.19

One from Alba Longa, one CROTTHERS
     388.22#   493.23+   509.10

Costello that men clepen PUNCH COSTELLO
    388.24#   493.26   506.14   509.10

       ** Young Malachi   388.28   3.01 **

       ** After longest wanderings   388.32   34.05 **

       ** Of Eblana   388.40   294.13 **

       ** In Horne's house   388.40   159.01 **

       ** Bring forth in pain   389.02   207.41 **

       ** Our Virgin Mother   389.10   47.39 **

       ** Limbo gloom   389.22   188.10 **

       ** The Holy Ghost   389.24   135.23 **

       ** Young Malachi's praise   389.33   3.01 **

That beast the UNICORN
    389.33   591.21

LILITH, patron of abortions
    390.01   497.12   (414.13)

       ** Wind of seeds of brightness   390.03   26.01 **

       ** Vampires mouth to mouth   390.03   48.01 **

       ** As Vergilius saith   390.04   88.15 **

       ** Averroes and Moses Maimonides 390.07   28.14 **

       ** Our holy mother   390.09   47.39 **

       ** To bring forth beastly   390.11   8.20 **

       ** That blessed Peter   390.12   109.10 **

       ** Who stealeth . . . to the Lord 390.24   23.07 **

       ** An only manchild   390.31   66.25 **

       ** So dark is destiny   390.33   66.39 **

For his burial did him on a FAIR CORSELET OF LAMB'S WOOL
    390.34   740..26   778.32   (609.30)

       ** Murdered his goods with whores 391.02   7.15 **

       ** Glistering coins of the tribute 391.13   29.25 **

       ** For a song which he writ   391.15   262.40 **

** Time . . . eternity 391.18	24.07	(9.22)	**
** Desire's wind (G) 391.19++ 9.22	20.20	339.20	**
** In the spirit . . . postcreation	391.22	145.10	**
** Omnis caro ad te veniet	391.23	48.01	**
** Her name	391.24+	47.39	**
** Agenbuyer	391.25	16.07	**
** Our mighty mother 391.26	5.06	5.13	**
** Mother most venerable (G)	391.26	346.08	**
** Saith Augustine	391.29	142.24	**
** That other, our grandam	391.30+	14.23	**
** Linked up with by . . . navelcords	391.30	38.09	**
** Vergine madre figlia di tuo figlio	391.34	20.20	**
** Peter Piscator	391.36	109.10	**
** The house that Jack built	391.36	279.38	**
** Joseph the Joiner	391.37	19.03	**
** M. Léo Taxil	391.38	41.14	**
** C'était le sacré pigeon	391.39	41.15	**
** Transubstantiality. . . .	391.40	21.09	**
** Birth without pangs	392.01	207.41	**
** Body without blemish	392.01	38.07	**

Sing a bawdy catch STABOO STABELLA
    392.05+   427.01

** Nurse Quigley	392.08	385.12	**
** Lord Andrew	392.11	159.01	**
** In Horne's house	392.25	159.01	**
** Mary in Eccles	392.28	8.27	**
** Womb . . . tomb	392.30	38.09	**

CORRUPTION OF MINORS
    392.34   733.12

As the priests use in MADAGASCAR island
    392.40   708.28

        ** Kyries   393.01   133.18 **

        ** Master John Fletcher . . . Beaumont 393.04++   188.29 **

        ** Life ran very high in those days   393.16   204.14 **

        ** Go thou and do likewise   393.19   80.24 **

        ** Thus . . . said Zarathustra   393.20   5.20 **

        ** French letters   393.21   214.41 **

        ** The university of Oxtail   393.21   4.19 **

        ** Stranger within thy tower 393.23   3.10   34.42 **

        ** The secondbest bed   393.24   203.06 **

        ** Remember, Erin . . .   393.25   40.07   45.12 **

KICK LIKE JESHURUM
    393.28   495.28

        ** Sinned against the light   393.29   34.03 **

        ** The slave of servants   393.30   6.41 **

        ** Forget me not, O Milesian   393.31   328.12 **

        ** A merchant of jalaps   393.33   4.13   7.11 **

        ** Didst deny me to the Roman   393.33   109.10 **

        ** With whom thy daughters. . . .   393.34   217.17 **

        ** From Pisgah   393.36   (149.25) **

Unto a land flowing with milk and money (MILK AND HONEY)
    393.37   424.14   734.29

        ** With a bitter milk   393.38+   (9.33) **

        ** A kiss of ashes   393.41   5.35 **

        ** Tenebrosity . . . illumined 393.41+   26.01   193.35 **

        ** Assuefaction minorates atrocities 394.03   193.35 **

        ** As Tully saith   394.03   124.20 **

** The adiaphane   394.05   25.17   **

** Ends . . . and originals   394.08   25.17   **

** The aged sisters draw us into life   394.14   37.37   **

** Wail, batten . . . dwindle, die   394.14+   86.32   **

** Clasp, sunder   394.15   38.12   **

** Saved from . . . old Nile   394.15   40.07   **

** Water of old Nile   394.16   (257.30)   **

** Among bulrushes   394.16   45.08   **

** To Edenville   394.20   38.04   **

** When we would backward see   394.21   51.04   **

** Whatness of our whoness   394.22   185.19   **

** The crystal palace   394.26   294.18   **

A penny for him who finds the pea (SHELL GAME)
     394.27   572.31

** Behold the mansion   394.29   279.38   **

** Dedal Jack   394.29   207.40   **

A black crack of noise (THUNDER CLAP)
     394.32++   397.09   741.34   See also   34.33

** Noise in the street   394.32   34.33   **

** He that had erst challenged   394.36+   242.17   **

** Mock   394.41   3.37   **

** Old Nobodaddy   395.04   24.07   **

** In Horne's hall   395.07   159.01   **

** A natural phenomenon   395.15++   304.35   **

** Land of promise   395.34   143.20   **

** No birth neither wiving nor mothering 395.36   213.26   **

** Patk. Dignam laid in clay   396.28   57.11   **

** After hard drought   396.29   56.09   **

** A bargeman   396.30   99.09   **

** The big wind of last February   396.38   13.02   **

** No more crack after that first   397.09   394.32   **

** Mr Justice Fitzgibbon   397.10   141.04   **

** Mr Healy the lawyer   397.10   141.11   **

** Mal. Mulligan   397.11+   3.01   **

** From Mr Moore's the writer's   397.12   191.32   **

** A good Williamite   397.13   31.23   **

** Alec. Bannon   397.14   21.41   **

** Mal M's brother   397.16   21.39   **

** To Andrew Horne's   397.19+   159.01   **

** A skittish heifer   397.20   21.42   **

** Beef to the heel   397.20   66.08   **

** Crawford's journal   397.22   35.22   125.07   **

** My lady of Mercy   397.24   8.27   **

** A racing horse he fancied   397.25   128.03   **

** Having dreamed tonight   397.27+   281.27   **

** Red slippers . . . Turkey trunks   397.28   381.12   **

** The midwives   397.32   37.37   **

** Her hub   397.39+   161.06   **

Off Bullock harbour DAPPING ON THE SOUND
     397.41+   491.24

Those in ken say after wind and water fire shall come (DESTRUCTION BY FIRE)
     398.04   428.10   433.26++   598.12+   See also 151.07   505.16

** Mr Russell   398.05   5.13   **

** A prophetical charm   398.05   140.30   **

** His farmer's gazette   398.06   35.22   **

** With this came up . . . (parody)   398.10   109.36   **

** The letter   398.11++   32.01   **

** A kind of sport gentleman   398.15   128.02   **

** He had it pat   398.17   83.17   **

** Burst their sides   398.28   103.30   **

** He had been off. . . .   399.09   7.15   **

** To the Liverpool boats   399.15   97.41   **

** Springers   399.17   97.40   **

** For Mr Joseph Cuffe   399.18   59.21   **

Hard by Mr GAVIN LOW's yard in Prussia street
     399.20   680.35

** The hoose   399.21   315.06   **

** The timber tongue   399.21   315.07   **

** Doctor Rinderpest   399.25+   32.01   **

** Take the bull by the horns   399.26   32.01   **

** Purling about   399.30   49.33   **

** An Irish bull. . . . (parody)   399.31   39.38   **

** That same bull   399.32++   199.19   **

Sent to our island by farmer Nicholas (ADRIAN IV, Pope)
     399.33+   400.35+

** An emerald ring in his nose   399.34   (186.35)   **

** Four fields of all Ireland 400.10   9.22   184.40   **

The WILDS OF CONNEMARA
     400.30   726.27

** In Sligo   400.30   332.11   **

** The lord Harry   400.35++   202.05   **

** Farmer Nicholas   400.35+   399.35+   **

The lord Harry was CLEANING HIS ROYAL PELT to go to dinner (G)
     400.40   565.21

** Champion bull of the Romans. . . . 401.04   109.10   **

** An arse and a shirt   401.17   123.23   **

    ** <u>Pope Peter</u>   401.29   109.10   **

    ** <u>A man's a man for a' that</u>   401.30   6.28   **

    ** Mr Malachi Mulligan   401.31#   3.01   **

    ** Alec Bannon   401.34#   21.41   **

    ** <u>Mulligan, Fertiliser and Incubator</u>   402.01   3.01   **

    ** Lord Talbot de Malahide   402.29   43.27   **

    ** <u>Omphalos</u>   402.31   7.33   **

His dutiful YEOMAN SERVICES
    402.33   613.23   651.34

    ** Of Mary's   403.11   8.27   **

<u>Testibus ponderosis atque excelsis erectionibus</u> CENTURIONUM ROMANORUM
    403.19   521.21

For whom there were LOAVES AND FISHES
    403.31   485.20

Was you in need of any PROFESSIONAL ASSISTANCE we could give
    403.32   494.11

    ** Of Horne's house   403.36   159.01   **

    ** Woman's woe   403.37   386.18   **

    ** Mother Grogan   404.04   12.33   **

    ** Her new coquette cap. . . .   404.36   62.35   **

    ** Artless disorder   404.37   (416.15)   **

    ** How great and universal. . . .   405.04   333.20   **

    ** A cloak of the French fashion   405.16+   214.41   **

    ** Monsieur Moore   405.18   191.32   **

    ** My dear Kitty told me today   405.28+   224.25   **

    ** Amid the general. . . . (parody)   406.01   191.16   **

    ** Miss Callan   406.02++   373.12   **

    ** The Mater hospice   406.13   8.27   **

    ** The young blood in the primrose vest   406.18   18.02   **

    ** In house of Horne   407.01   159.01   **

** Rolypoly   407.12   157.24   **

** To revert. . . . (parody)   407.15++   139.03   **

** Impudent mocks   407.16   3.37   **

** Like a crookback. . . .   407.27   209.22   **

That missing link . . . Mr [CHARLES] DARWIN
  General reference
     407.30   716.33
  Survival of the fittest
     419.42   657.18

** Eating of the tree forbid   408.06   14.23   375.21   **

** A frigid genius   408.18   (136.26)   **

** In such pain   408.20   207.41   **

** Old Glory Allelujerum   408.25+   161.06   **

** Dundrearies   408.26   139.05   **

** The event would burst anon   408.28   103.30   **

** The man in the gap   408.33   297.05   **

** Metempsychosis   408.36   50.13   **

** An art . . . esteemed the noblest   408.42   14.19   **

** The empire   409.11   73.02   **

The security of his FOUR PER CENTS
     409.13   723.12   See also 413.03

** A gallant major   409.18   56.32   **

With a female domestic (MARY DRISCOLL)
     409.26+   460.07++   739.25++   (163.30)

The hussy's SCOURINGBRUSH
     409.27   460.11   461.17

** Mr Cuffe   409.30   59.21   **

** Beauty may console   409.42   263.35   **

** The second female infirmarian   410.08   373.12   **

** The Childs murder   410.27   100.02   **

** Mr Advocate Bushe   410.28   100.04   **

The WRONGFULLY ACCUSED
    410.29   456.24   492.32

        ** Certain chinless Chinamen 410.33   96.40   215.31   **

        ** Twilight sleep   410.36   161.28   **

        ** Aristotle . . . in his masterpiece   411.06   235.19   **

        ** The navelcord   411.11   38.01   **

The case of MADAME GRISSEL STEEVENS
    411.19   569.10

        ** A plasmic memory   411.21   140.30   **

        ** Minotaur . . . Metamorphoses   411.29   207.40   **

        ** Genius   411.29   136.26   **

An INWARD VOICE
    412.01   653.24   See also 193.16

        ** To freeze them with horror   412.05+   10.22   **

        ** Haines   412.07++   4.13   **

        ** A portfolio full of Celtic literature 412.09   48.01   **

        ** History is to blame   412,13   20.39   **

        ** The murderer of Samuel Childs   412.14   100.02   **

        ** Tare and ages. . . . (parody)   412.16+   185.02   **

        ** Tramping Dublin   412.17   185.02   **

        ** The Erse language   412.21   141.07   **

        ** Laudanum   412.21   84.26   **

        ** His spectre stalks me   412.22   115.04   **

        ** The black panther!   412.23++   4.23   **

Meet me at WESTLAND ROW STATION at ten past eleven
    412.26   452.07+   619.40   620.11+

        ** The vendetta of Mananaan!   412.29   38.24   **

        ** Lex talionis   412.29   139.33   **

        ** The sentimentalist is he. . . .   412.29   199.21   **

** The mystery was unveiled   412.32   191.37 **

** The third brother   412.33   100.05   211.01 **

** His real name was Childs   412.33+   100.02 **

** The ghost of his own father   412.34   18.12 **

** He drank drugs to obliterate   412.34   81.12 **

** For this relief much thanks   412.35   372.30 **

** The nocturnal rat   412.37   (114.13) **

** Murderer's ground   412.38   100.10 **

** That staid agent of publicity   413.03   57.35 **

A modest substance in the funds (BLOOM'S INVESTMENTS)
     413.03   723.02++   725.15+   See also 409.13

** In a retrospective arrangement   413.04   91.07 **

CLANBRASSIL STREET
     413.08   615.09   723.18

** Fullfledged traveller   413.12   260.39 **

** The dark eyes   413.18   101.36 **

** The head of the firm   413.20   76.26 **

The head of the firm seated with JACOB'S PIPE
     413.20   517.18

Reading through round horned SPECTACLES (RUDOLPH BLOOM'S)
     413.23   437.14   723.29

** The wise father knows his own child   413.27   88.19 **

He thinks of a drizzling night in HATCH STREET. . . . Bridie! BRIDIE KELLY!
     413.28++   441.21+

The WATCH . . . two RAINCAPED shadows
     413.31   See   430.09

** Darkness . . . light   413.35   26.01 **

** Light shall flood the world   413.36   (365.17) **

She dare not bear the SUNNYGOLDEN BABE OF DAY
     413.40   414.24   See also 34.03

** None now to be for Leopold   414.01   66.25 **

** For Rudolph	414.02	76.26	**
** Agendath. . . . Netaim	414.12+	60.16	**
** A waste land	414.13++	61.09	**
** A home of screechowls (T)	414.13	(390.01)	**
** Huuh! Hark! Huuh!	414.16	97.38	**
** Parallax stalks behind	414.16	154.06	**

The LANCINATING lightnings of whose brow are SCORPIONS
   414.17   521.22

** Babylon	414.18	164.34	**
** To the sunken sea, Lacus Mortis	414.19+	61.13	**
** Murderers of the sun	414.24	413.40	**
** The equine portent	414.27	(3.16)	**
** Virgo . . . the everlasting bride	414.29	47.39	**
** Wonder of metempsychosis	414.29	50.13	**
** The daystar	414.30	210.07	**
** Martha, thou lost one 414.31	72.30	117.35	**
** Millicent	414.32	21.32	**
** What do you call it gossamer!	414.35	374.41	**

Sustained on currents of cold INTERSTELLAR wind
   414.37   704.28

** Simply swirling	414.38	62.36	**
** A ruby and triangled sign	414.40	154.19	**
** At school together	415.01	11.22	**
** In Conmee's time	415.01	80.03	**
** Bous Stephanoumenos	415.06	210.19	**
** Bullockbefriending bard	415.06	5.01	**
** Lord and giver of their life	415.07	145.10	**

Encircled his gadding hair with a CORONAL OF VINELEAVES
   415.08   427.10   (480.40)   See also 149.03

```
      ** Your genius                    415.11      136.26    **

      ** His mother                     415.15+       5.16    **
```

To be REMINDED OF HIS PROMISE
    415.17   645.33

MADDEN HAD LOST FIVE DRACHMAS
    415.19   426.27   See also 388.21

```
      ** Sceptre                        415.20++    128.03    **

      ** He told them of the race       415.21++    125.10    **

      ** Huuh                           415.21       97.38    **

      ** The dark horse Throwaway       415.26      325.31    **

      ** All was lost now               415.27      256.24    **

      ** Juno, she cried                415.28      176.26    **
```

A whacking fine whip . . . is W. LANE
    415.32   648.21

```
      ** You could have seen (Lynch's tryst)  415.39++   224.25  **

      ** In his booth near the bridge   416.04    (153.02)   **

      ** Mocked at peril                416.08       3.37    **

      ** Conmee himself!                416.11+      80.03    **
```

HERRICK, ROBERT (a slight disorder in her dress)
"Delight in Disorder"
    416.15
"To Anthea"
    661.14   (404.37)

```
      ** Bass's mare                    416.20      128.03    **

      ** Draught of his . . . scarlet label  416.20  154.19  **

      ** A druid silence                416.24       11.06    **

      ** Theosophos told me so          416.28      140.30    **

      ** Egyptian priests               416.29      142.11    **

      ** The mysteries of karmic law    416.30      182.30    **

      ** Assume the etheric doubles     416.32      301.16    **

      ** Number one Bass                417.03      154.19    **
```

** The turf   417.11   396.31   **

** An epitome of the course of life   417.23   86.32   **

** Horne's house   417.26   159.01   **

** The primrose elegance   417.39   18.02   **

** Socratic discussion   418.01   190.27   **

** The vigilant wanderer. . . .   418.03   34.05   **

Which the inspired pencil of LAFAYETTE has limned
    418.08   652.34

** With tangible phenomena   418.14   304.35   **

** To face hardheaded facts   418.15   184.11   **

** That cannot be blinked   418.15   325.02   **

** The future determination. . . . (G)   418.19+   25.17   **

** Hideous publicity posters   418.37   (92.05)   (229.23)   **

** Ministers of all denominations   418.37   (151.07)   **

** Mutilated soldiers and sailors   418.38   (219.08)   **

Exposed SCORBUTIC cardrivers
    418.39   472.14

** Venus   419.03   176.26   **

** Apollo   419.04   113.39   **

** All other phenomena   419.22   304.35   **

LUNAR PHASES
    419.22   702.06   727.18

** The survival of the fittest   419.42   407.30   **

** With pluterperfect imperturbability   420.03   32.01   **

** Staggering bob   420.07++   171.10   **

** Dr A. Horne   420.20   159.01   **

** Meanwhile the skill   420.30   37.37   **

** A weary weary while   420.31   3.41   **

She had FOUGHT THE GOOD FIGHT
    420.34   421.26

** The Universal Husband   420.41   140.30   **

** Her dear Doady   420.42++   37.37   161.06   **

Conscientious second accountant of the ULSTER BANK, COLLEGE GREEN BRANCH
    421.05   423.23   723.08   See also 161.06

** That faroff time of the roses   421.07   (293.38)   **

** With the old shake of her pretty head 421.08   37.37   **

** Victoria Frances   421.12   (43.13)   **

** Our famous hero   421.14   4.29   **

Our famous hero . . . lord Bobs (ROBERTS, LORD FREDERICK)
    421.14   748.30

** Dublin Castle   421.19   161.10   **

** Fought the good fight   421.26   420.34   **

** Harp   421.37   127.13   **

** A scene disengages itself. . . .   422.05   106.19   **

** The wellremembered grove of lilacs   422.09   106.19   **

** Floey   422.15   115.19   **

** Atty, Tiny   422.15   377.17   **

** His mother   422.25   5.16   **

** Alles Vergängliche   422.27   184.02   **

** The utterance of the Word   422.42   185.29   **

** Burke's!   423.01   137.11   **

** Ashplants   423.04   17.17   **

** Panama hats   423.04   19.01   **

** A dedale of lusty youth   423.05   207.40   **

** Nurse Callan   423.06+   373.12   **

** Burke's of Denzille and Holles   423.11   137.11   **

** In Horne's house   423.16   159.01   **

** Motherwit   423.17   348.04   **

**	The Allfather's air	423.22	185.29	**
**	Theodore Purefoy	423.23++	161.06	**
**	A Godframed . . . possibility	423.27	25.17	**
**	Thou art all their daddies	423.30	(145.10)	**
**	In the countinghouse	423.33	421.05	**
**	Slaughter of the innocents	423.39	172.03	**
**	Vegetables . . . beefsteaks	423.40	165.41	**
**	How saith Zarathustra?	424.08	5.20	**
**	The honeymilk of Canaan's land	424.14	393.37	**

BONAFIDES
    424.20   497.16

**	The drunken minister	424.24	4.09	**
**	The Denzille lane boys	424.26	(81.26)	**
**	Burke's!	424.30	137.11	**
**	Thence they advanced five parasangs	424.30	5.08	**
**	Slattery's mounted foot	424.31	42.18	**
**	Apostates' creed 424.32	20.42	(329.23)	**

BRITISH BEATITUDES!
    424.35+   509.09+

**	To be printed and bound. . . .	424.36	9.22	**
**	At the Druiddrum press	424.36	11.06	**

Calf covers of PISSEDON GREEN
    424.37   706.38   See also   5.02

**	Last word in art shades	424.38	5.01	**
**	Most beautiful book. . . .	424.38	9.22	**
**	Beer, beef, business . . . (G)	424.41+	304.33	**
**	Whether on the scaffold high. . . .	425.01+	163.16	**
**	Proud possessor of damnall	425.06	11.02	**
**	The Übermensch	425.09	5.20	**

```
        ** Five number ones                    425.09      154.19  **

CHASE ME
     425.10      515.33

        ** His ticker.  Stopped short          425.11      361.21+ **

        ** Absinthe                            425.12       42.38  **

        ** Got bet be a boomblebee    425.15    68.18      139.27  **

        ** Near the Mater                      425.16        8.27  **

        ** Two Ardilauns                       425.20       81.39  **

        ** Prime pair of mincepies             425.21      234.31  **

        ** Spud again the rheumatiz?           425.24       57.02  **

For the HOI POLLOI
     425.26      622.08

HARRIS, JOEL CHANDLER (Your corporosity sagaciating O K?)
  "The Wonderful Tar-Baby Story"
     425.27
  Parody
     508.26-30

        ** Stand and deliver                   425.29      295.22  **

        ** There's hair                        425.29      324.25  **

        ** The white death . . . ruddy birth   425.29        5.05  **

        ** Mummer's wire              425.31    5.26      185.05  **

        ** Cribbed out of Meredith!            425.31      199.21  **

        ** Jesified . . . jesuit!              425.31        3.08  **

        ** Aunty mine's                        425.32        5.16  **

        ** Writing Pa                          425.32       88.35  **

        ** Kinch                               425.32        3.08  **

        ** Your barleybree                     425.35        6.28  **

        ** Every cove to his gentry mort       425.39       47.13  **

        ** Venus Pandemos                      425.40      176.26  **

        ** Bold bad girl from . . . Mullingar  425.41       21.42  **

        ** Hauding Sara by the wame            425.42        6.28  **
```

** On the road to Malahide	425.42	43.27 **
** If she who seduced me. . . .	426.01	45.12 **
** Machree	426.02	186.35 **
** Macruiskeen	426.02	92.06 **

MOST DECIDUOUSLY
    426.04   553.12

** He've got the chink ad lib		426.06	11.02 **
** We are nae fou		426.11	6.28 **
** Bantam		426.14++	74.02 **
** Rose of Castille. Rows of cast		426.17	125.10 **
** The colleen bawn		426.19	92.06 **
** Had the winner today	426.21	74.02	325.31 **
** The ruffin cly the nab		426.21+	47.13 **
** I tipped him a dead cert	426.21	125.10	128.03 **
** Big bug Bass . . . Mare on form		426.23	325.33 **
** Madden back Madden's	426.27	128.03	415.19 **
** O, lust, our refuge		426.28++	82.37 **

You MOVE A MOTION?
    426.38   653.25

** You're going it some		426.38	11.02 **
** Largesize grandacious thirst		426.41	41.05 **
** Have you a good wine, staboo?		427.01	392.05 **
** Hoots, mon, wee drap to pree		427.01	6.28 **
** Absinthe the lot		427.02+	42.38 **
** Cadges ads		427.05	57.35 **
** Photo's papli	427.05	21.42	66.01 **
** By all that's gorgeous!		427.05	68.24 **
** And snares of the foxfiend		427.06+	83.22 **

```
        ** King to tower                      427.09        3.10   **

        ** Tuk bungalo kee                    427.10       11.35   **

        ** Will yu help . . . 2 night         427.10       23.20   **

        ** To lay crown off his head          427.10      415.08   **

        ** Licensed spirits                   427.15      173.39   **

DUSTY RHODES.   Peep at his wearables
    427.17      496.02

        ** Yon guy in the mackintosh?         427.17+     109.29   **

        ** D'ye ken bare socks?               427.19      289.38   **

        ** In the Richmond                    427.20        8.27   **

        ** Men all tattered and torn. . . .   427.23      279.38   **

        ** Lost love . . . lonely canyon      427.25       49.04   **

        ** At a runefal?                      427.26+      57.11   **

        ** Lay you two to one. . . .          427.33       97.15   **

        ** Jappies? . . . Rooshian            427.34       58.11   **

        ** We're nae tha fou                  427.39        6.28   **

        ** Mona, my thrue love                427.41      309.34   **

BLAZE ON
    428.01      434.27+      478.28      598.11++   (445.13)     See also 398.04

Brigade (DUBLIN METROPOLITAN FIRE BRIGADE)
    428.02      434.27      480.17      498.04+

        ** Tally ho                           428.03      254.27   **

        ** Sinned against the light           428.09       34.03   **

        ** Medical Dick                       428.12      184.24   **

YELLOW (Lynch's profanity)
    428.13      433.06

        ** Elijah . . . Blood of the Lamb     428.14      151.07   **

        ** You dog-gone, bullnecked           428.16+     296.06   **
```

CIRCE

** Will—o'—the—wisps   429.03   184.02 **

** Rabaiotti's halted ice gondola   429.05   225.16 **

** Whistles call and answer   429.10   3.26 **

** Wait, my love   429.12   (4.12) **

A gnome . . . crouches to shoulder a sack of RAGS AND BONES
   430.01   436.30

A DRUNKEN NAVVY grips with both hands the railings of an area
   430.07   433.19++   447.13+   450.31++   596.17+

Two NIGHT WATCH in shoulder capes
   430.09   453.17++   586.18   602.15++   See also 413.31

** Cissy Caffrey's voice   430.14++   346.15 **

** Still young   430.14   373.04 **

PRIVATE CARR AND PRIVATE COMPTON
   430.21++   450.31++   574.03+   587.16#

** Hairy arse   430.26   123.23 **

** I gave it to Nelly   430.29   (214.30) **

** Lynch   430.35#   224.25 **

** Way for the parson   431.02+   4.09 **

** Flourishing the ashplant   431.10   17.17 **

** His jockey cap low on his brow   431.11   224.25   **

** A latere dextro. Alleluia   431.15   (122.23) **

An ELDERLY BAWD
     431.16+   441.13++   448.07+   593.05   602.04

     ** Trinity medicals   431.24   163.04   **

     ** Edy Boardman   431.26+   346.14   **

     ** Bertha Supple   431.26   348.25   **

     ** Squarepusher   432.03   163.24   **

     ** Flourishes his ashplant   432.11   17.17   **

SHIVERING THE LAMP IMAGE, SHATTERING LIGHT over the world
     432.11   583.03

A liver and white spaniel (the DOG that changes its shape)
     432.12   437.11   441.13   448.08   449.29   452.02   452.34
     453.05   453.10   453.16   454.02   454.05   454.19   454.22
     472.14   472.17   560.21   See also 44.33   586.14   587.02

Gesture . . . a UNIVERSAL LANGUAGE
     432.19   436.19   490.01   600.22   (622.28)

     ** The first entelechy   432.20   189.39   **

     ** The structural rhythm   432.20   37.26   **

     ** Mecklenburg street   432.22   214.28   **

     ** Shrewridden Shakespeare   432.25   189.08++ **

HENPECKED Socrates
     432.25   563.04   See also 527.20

     ** Socrates   432.25   19.28   **

     ** The allwisest stagyrite   432.26   25.17   **

     ** A light of love   432.27   191.05   **

     ** My stick (ashplant)   433.04++   17.17   **

     ** Yellow   433.06   428.13   **

     ** Lecherous lynx   433.08   224.25   **

KEATS, JOHN (to la belle dame sans merci)
     "La Belle Dame sans Merci"
     433.08

Endymion
      509.28   546.10   771.06

         ** Georgina Johnson   433.08   189.26   **

         ** Ad deam qui laetificat   433.09   3.05   **

         ** It skills not   433.15   206.20   **

         ** The customhouse   433.15   227.09   **

         ** Tommy Caffrey   433.17   346.16   **

         ** Jacky Caffrey   433.19   346.17   **

         ** The navvy lurches   433.19++   430.07   **

         ** A glow leaps. . . .   433.26++   398.04   **

Cramming bread (SODA BREAD)
      433.30   711.30

CHOCOLATE
      433.31   525.15++   555.06+   711.28

         ** Gallant Nelson's image   433.32   148.09   **

         ** Longlost   434.01++   (272.32)   **

         ** Lugubru   434.01   283.14   **

BOOLOOHOOM
      434.01   538.06

         ** Grave Gladstone   434.01   80.07   **

         ** Truculent Wellington   434.03   297.16   **

         ** At Antonio Rabaiotti's door   434.06   225.16   **

A lukewarm pig's CRUBEEN . . . a cold sheep's TROTTER
      434.15   437.21   439.23   453.11++   463.34   472.11   711.26+

         ** Aurora borealis . . . London's burning434.27+   428.01   **

         ** The brigade   434.27   428.02   **

         ** Two cyclists   435.03   86.19   **

A dragon SANDSTREWER
      435.10   452.15   614.09+

BLOOM . . . STIFFLEGGED
      435.16   462.33   529.20

** The <u>motorman</u> . . . <u>pugnosed</u>   435.17   74.29   **

Doing THE HATTRICK?
    435.20   595.20

** Sandow's exercises   435.25   61.25   **

** Poor mama's panacea   435.27   57.02   111.13   **

** The fellow balked me this morning   436.02   74.29   **

** With that horsey woman   436.03   73.33   **

** True word spoken in jest   436.04   338.15   **

MARK OF THE BEAST
    436.06   459.23

** <u>Esperanto</u>   436.19   432.19   **

** <u>Slan leath</u>   436.19   314.32   **

** Gaelic League   436.19   141.07   **

** Sent by that fireeater   436.20   293.25   **

** Rags and bones   436.30   430.01   **

Wash off his sins of the world (<u>AGNUS DEI</u>)
    436.31   438.29   560.14+   See also 151.07

** <u>Jacky Caffrey</u>   437.01+   346.17   **

** <u>Tommy Caffrey</u>   437.01+   346.16   **

** <u>Sweets of sin</u>   437.07   236.08   **

** <u>Potato</u>   437.07   57.02   **

** <u>Soap</u>   437.07   85.17   **

** The <u>retriever</u> <u>approaches</u>   437.11   432.12   **

** <u>A stooped bearded figure appears</u>   437.12++   76.26   **

** <u>An elder of Zion</u>   437.13   44.09   **

** <u>Horned spectacles hang down</u>   437.14   413.23   **

** <u>Yellow poison streaks</u>   437.15   76.26   **

Second HALFCROWN
    437.18   453.14

WASTE MONEY today
     437.18   452.33

    ** The crubeen and trotter   437.21   434.15 **

    ** Vulture talons   437.25   47.03 **

    ** Are you not my dear son. . . ?   437.26   76.23 **

    ** Mosenthal   437.30+   76.29 **

ALPINE HAT
     438.06   531.17

    ** Keyless watch   438.07   11.35 **

    ** Your poor mother!   438.17++ 111.13 **

CAMEO BROOCH
     438.24   721.10

    ** An Agnus Dei   438.29   436.31 **

    ** A shrivelled potato   438.29   57.02 **

    ** Sacred Heart of Mary   438.30   47.39   113.34 **

    ** Handsome woman in Turkish costume 439.09++ 108.13 **
                                    281.27   381.12

    ** Opulent curves   439.09   236.05 **

    ** A white yashmak   439.11   281.27 **

    ** Raven hair   439.13   319.37 **

    ** Mrs Marion from this out   439.17   61.37 **

    ** Crubeens for her supper   439.23   434.15 **

    ** Scolding him in Moorish   439.30   373.23 **

    ** Nebrakada! Feminimum   440.02   242.41 **

    ** Mrs Marion . . .   440.09   61.37 **

    ** Mockery in her eyes   440.12   3.37 **

A poor old STICK IN THE MUD
     440.13   627.37   (382.03)

    ** That lotion   440.16   84.03 **

    ** Whitewax   440.16   84.38 **

** Orangeflower water   440.16   84.36   **

** A cake of new clean lemon soap   440.21+   85.17   **

** Sweny, the druggist   440.25+   84.04   **

** Mrs Marion   441.02   61.37   **

** Ti trema un poco il cuore?   441.08+   63.31   **

** About that pronunciati. . . .   441.12   64.04   **

** The sniffing terrier   441.13   432.12   **

** The elderly bawd   441.13++   431.16   **

** Her old father that's dead drunk   441.18   8.20   **

** Bridie Kelly. . . . Hatch street   441.21+   413.28   **

** She flaps her bat shawl   441.24   48.02   **

** Gerty MacDowell limps forward   442.06+   253.01   **

** Shows coyly her bloodied clout   442.07   361.39   **

** With all my worldly goods. . . .   442.09   352.04   **

** Secrets of my bottom drawer   442.18   (364.03) **

** Mrs Breen   442.21++   156.32   **

** Walls have ears   443.06   83.06   **

** Black refracts heat   443.08   57.10   **

The exotic . . . Negro servants (MOLLY'S SEXUAL INTEREST IN NEGROES)
    443.17   751.30   See also 368.05

** Eugene Stratton   443.18   92.05   **

** Flashing white Kaffir eyes   443.25   335.14   **

** Smackfatclacking nigger lips   443.27   80.19   **

** Masks   444.01   7.30   **

** The dear gazelle   444.14   45.12   **

** In a retrospective arrangement   444.22   91.07   **

Old Christmas night GEORGINA SIMPSON'S HOUSEWARMING
    444.23++   742.38

** Masonic badge in his buttonhole   445.03   73.05   **

** Ireland, home and beauty	445.05	15.32 **
** The dear dead days. . . .	445.07	63.31 **

I confess I'm TEAPOT with curiosity
    445.09+   541.05

** London's teapot	445.13	(434.29) **
** A Napoleon hat	445.19	297.06 **
** The witching hour	445.21	108.04 **
** A ruby ring	445.23	(64.25) **
** La ci darem. . . .	445.23+	63.31 **
** Beauty and the beast	446.02	369.35 **
** Dennis Breen	446.06+	157.17 **
** With Wisdom Hely's sandwichboard	446.06	154.25 **
** In carpet slippers	446.07	298.40 **
** Little Alf Bergan	446.08+	160.03 **
** The ace of spades	446.09	158.07 **
** U.p.: Up	446.12	158.11 **

The ANSWER IS A LEMON
    446.21   511.14

** Kosher	446.24	62.30 **
** Potted meat	446.25	75.02 **
** I was at Leah	446.25	76.23 **
** Mrs Bandman Palmer	446.25	76.23 **
** Trenchant exponent	446.26	91.04+ **
** Richie Goulding	446.29++	38.34 **
** Three ladies' hats	446.29	88.26 **
** Collis and Ward	446.30	88.23 **
** A skull and crossbones	446.31	272.15 **
** Best value in Dub	447.04	265.16 **

** Bald Pat, bothered beetle   447.05+   256.32   **

** Steak and kidney. Bottle of lager   447.08   269.11   **

** Hee hee hee   447.09   257.01   **

** Wait till I wait   447.09   257.01   **

** Good god Inev erate inall   447.11   256.31   **

** The navvy lurching by   447.13+   430.07   **

GORES HIM WITH HIS FLAMING PRONGHORN
     447.13   See   256.25

** Cry of pain . . . to his back   447.15   39.26   **

** Bright's!   447.15   272.14   **

** Your cock and bull story   447.21   119.05   **

** The bawd   448.07+   431.16   **

** The terrier follows   448.08   432.12   **

** Just after Milly   448.18   21.42   **

MRS JOE GALLAHER's lunch basket
     449.15   586.32   768.02

** Her advisers or admirers   449.16   313.12   **

MAGGOT O'REILLY
     449.21   731.28

** Marcus Tertius Moses   449.23   233.14   **

** Yes, yes, yes, yes, yes, yes, yes   449.28   61.31   **

** The whining dog   449.29   425.12   **

The SCAFFOLDING
     450.08   587.07

In BEAVER STREET
     450.08   462.31   587.07   613.25   729.12

DOING IT . . . INTO THE BUCKET OF PORTER that was there waiting
     450.09+   462.30+   590.23+

Waiting on the shavings for DERWAN'S PLASTERERS
     450.10   484.25

** Their lodges   450.14   (73.05)   **

** Coincidence too	450.16	68.24	**
** The navvy	450.31++	430.07	**
** The two redcoats	450.31++	430.21	**
** We are the boys. Of Wexford	451.17++	129.13	**
** Bennett?	451.21	250.33	**
** The dog approaches	452.02	432.12	**
** Wildgoose chase	452.05	(41.17)	**
** Scene at Westland row	452.07+	412.26	**
** Jump in first class	452.07	294.04	**
** To Malahide	452.09	43.27	**
** Mrs Beaufoy Purefoy 452.12	67.39	158.36	**
** Kismet	452.13	66.39	**
** That cash	452.13	11.02	**
** That . . . juggernaut	452.15	435.10	**
** Kildare street club	452.20	86.29	**
** Sweet are the sweets. Sweets of sin	452.30	236.05	**
** Waste of money	452.33	437.18	**
** One and eightpence too much	452.33	93.41	**
** Retriever. . . . wolfdog . . . mastiff	452.34++	432.12	**
** Stinks like a polecat	453.03	373.17	**
** Chacun son goût	453.03	380.34	**
** Garryowen!	453.05	295.13	**
** Provided nobody	453.08	242.18	**
** Crubeen . . . trotter	453.11++	434.15	**
** Two and six	453.14	437.18	**
** Two raincaped watch	453.17++	430.09	**
** Of Bloom. For Bloom. Bloom	453.20	(276.09)	**
** A covey of gulls	453.26+	152.22	**

** With Banbury cakes   453.27+   153.07   **

** Friend of man   453.31+   295.13   **

** Trained by kindness   453.31   311.19   **

** Bob Doran   454.01+   74.01+   **

** Munching spaniel . . . greyhound   454.02++   432.12   **

** Give us the paw   454.04   305.22   **

** Tales of circus life   454.14+   64.25   **

** The glint of my eye   454.29   40.04   **

** His high grade hat   455.05   56.40   **

** Dr Bloom . . . dental surgeon   455.05   250.14   **

Von BLOOM PASHA
     455.06   719.31

** A card falls   455.10+   56.41   **

** Messrs John Henry Menton . . .   455.16   102.38   **

** Henry Flower   455.19++   72.31   **

NO FIXED ABODE
     455.19   470.20   (735.26)   See also 23.20

** A crumpled yellow flower   455.24   73.11   **

** That old joke . . . Rose of Castille 455.26   125.10   **

** The change of name Virag   455.27   76.26   **

** Uniform that does it   456.01   72.39   **

** Your Waterloo   456.02   297.06   **

** A glass of old Burgundy   456.03   171.28   **

** A dark mercurialized face   456.06   8.06   **

** The Castle   456.08   161.10   **

MARTHA
     456.10+   See 72.30   73.11   117.35

** A crimson halter   456.11   80.26   **

** Irish Times   456.12   160.07   **

** Lionel, thou lost one!   456.13   117.35   **

** Sign and dueguard of fellowcraft   456.19   73.05   **

** Light of love   456.20   191.04   **

** The Childs fratricide case   456.22   100.02   **

** I am wrongfully accused   456.24   410.29   **

** Better one guilty escape. . . .   456.25   100.08   **

** He was miserable   456.28   49.04   243.32   **

** Majorgeneral Brian Tweedy   457.13   56.32   **

** Heroic defense   457.15   4.29   **

The heroic defense of RORKE'S DRIFT
    457.15   596.27   757.20

** The royal Dublins   457.19   47.18   **

** Salt of the earth   457.19   217.36   **

** Up the Boers!   457.26+   163.10   **

** Who booed Joe Chamberlain?   457.26   162.40   **

** As staunch a Britisher as you are   457.29   (118.30)   **

** The absentminded war   457.30   187.22   **

Disabled at . . . BLOEMFONTEIN
    458.01   748.43

** A collection of prize stories   458.08   67.39   **

** Myles Crawford   458.12+   125.07   **

** His scarlet beak blazes   458.13+   125.07   **

** The aureole of his straw hat   458.13   146.07   **

** A hank of Spanish onions   458.14   172.13   **

** Freeman's Urinal 458.19   57.35   70.01   123.23   **

** Paralyse Europe   458.19   135.31   **

** Mr Philip Beaufoy. . . .   458.21+   67.39   **

A PLAGIARIST
    458.31   491.16

** Masquerading   458.31   7.30   **

** The laughing witch. . . .   459.06   67.39   **

UNIVERSITY OF LIFE
    459.18   682.34

** The hallmark of the beast 459.23+   70.01   436.06   **

** Moses, Moses   459.25   40.07   **

** Wiped his arse   459.26   123.23   **

** The woman Driscoll   460.07++   409.26   **

** A scouringbrush in her hand   460.11   409.27   **

SMART EMERALD GARTERS (Mary Driscoll's)
    460.28   739.40   See also 57.30

ACCUSED OF PILFERING (oysters)
    461.01+   739.33+

** The scouringbrush   461.17   409.27   **

** GEORGES FOTTRELL   461.21+   344.20   **

** The memory of the past   461.28   86.32   **

** Heaving bosom   462.07   236.05   **

** Dockrell's wallpaper   462.13   155.36   **

** The family rosary   462.18   354.03   **

** PROFESSOR MACHUGH   462.27+   123.18   **

** The bucket   462.30   450.09   **

** In Beaver street   462.31+   450.08   **

** By walking stifflegged   462.33   435.16   **

** Untold misery   462.33   243.32   **

** Burgundy   462.34   171.28   **

** Some spinach   462.34   179.22   **

** A Titbits back number   462.36   67.39   **

** In a torn frockcoat   463.01   (377.23)   **

** J.J. O'MOLLOY   463.04++   124.32   **

** We are not in a beargarden   463.08   188.16   **

** An Oxford rag   463.08   4.19   7.19   **

** Poor foreign immigrant . . . Pharaoh   463.09+   (40.07)   **

There have been cases of . . . SOMNAMBULISM in my client's family
    463.19   692.26++   695.02   (608.18)

** He could a tale unfold   463.20   162.36   **

** Tiny mole's eyes   463.28   101.36   **

** Blingee pigfoot evly night   463.34   434.15   **

** The Mosaic code   464.04   139.32   **

** The hidden hand   464.12   139.05   **

** Agendath Netaim   464.20   60.16   **

** The lake of Kinnereth   464.25   59.16   **

** With blurred cattle   464.25   59.18   **

** Moses Dlugacz . . . ferreteyed   464.26+   56.11   **

** A pork kidney   464.29   55.04   **

** Bleibtreustrasse, Berlin, W. 13   464.31   60.26   **

** Blotches of phthisis   464.34   162.02   **

** Hectic cheekbones   464.35   125.03   **

** John F. Taylor   464.35   141.03   **

** Recently come from a sickbed   465.03   141.27   **

** A few wellchosen words   465.03   140.01   **

** Seymour Bushe   465.05   100.04   **

** The pensive bosom   465.06   91.08   **

** Soultransfigured and. . . .   465.07   140.15   **

** Messrs Callan, Coleman   465.12   91.16   **

** Mr Wisodom Hely J.P.   465.13   106.26   **

** My old chief Joe Cuffe   465.13   59.21   **

** Mr V.B. Dillon   465.13   155.22   **

** Sir Robert and lady Ball   465.17   154.05 **

MRS YELVERTON BARRY . . . MRS BELLINGHAM
    465.19++   594.08

An anonymous letter in PRENTICE BACKHAND
    465.23   563.22   684.30

** James Lovebirch   465.25   235.37 **

** Seen from the gods . . . box   465.26   (284.38) **

** The _Theatre_ _Royal_   465.26   271.13   272.25 **

** Half past four p.m. . . . Thursday   465.29   361.21 **

** Dunsink time   465.30   154.05 **

** Monsieur Paul de Kock   465.31   64.39 **

** _The_ _Girl_ _with_ _the_ . . . _Stays_   465.32   156.26 **

** The homegrown potato plant   466.09   57.02 **

** The model farm   466.10   (59.16) **

** Ikey Mo!   466.16   57.38 **

** Venus in furs   466.21   235.25 (176.26) **

** In silk hose   466.28   74.18 **

** THE HONOURABLE MRS   467.01++   73.40 **

** The Phoenix park   467.06   170.41 **

ALL IRELAND versus the Rest of Ireland
    467.06   543.25

** This plebeian Don Juan   467.10   63.31 **

AS ARE SOLD after dark ON PARIS BOULEVARDS
    467.12   529.28   See also   12.18

OBSCENE PHOTOGRAPH . . . [of] a partially NUDE SEÑORITA
    467.13   721.26   753.24   See also 380.15

** To do likewise   467.16   80.24 **

He implored me to . . . BESTRIDE AND RIDE HIM
    467.19   (534.20)

** Refined birching   468.11   235.37 **

FORGET, FORGIVE
        468.25   541.30

** Kismet	468.26	66.39 **
** He offers the other cheek	468.26	217.36 **
** Davy Stephens	469.12+	116.30 **
** A bevy of barefoot newsboys	469.13	128.06 **
** The Sacred Heart	469.15	113.34 **
** Evening Telegraph	469.15	35.22 **
** Canon O'Hanlon	469.18	358.30 **
** A marble timepiece	469.19	359.04 **
** Father Conroy	469.19	252.01 **
** The reverend John Hughes S.J.	469.20	354.02 **
** Cuckoo	469.23+	212.36 **
** The brass quoits of a bed	469.26+	56.27 **
** Martin Cunnigham	469.30	80.13 **
** Jack Power	470.01	87.03 **
** Tom Kernan	470.01	71.24 **
** Ned Lambert	470.01	90.03 **
** John Henry Menton	470.02	102.38 **
** Myles Crawford	470.02	125.07 **
** Lenehan	470.02	125.10 **
** Paddy Leonard	470.03	90.39 **
** Nosey Flynn	470.03	171.25 **
** M'Coy	470.03	67.24 **
** A Nameless One	470.04+	292.01 **
** He organised her	470.06	173.09 **
** Arse over tip	470.10	123.23 **
** Hundred shillings to five	470.10	325.31+ **

** No fixed abode		470.20	455.19 **
** Bawd and cuckold		470.21	212.31 **
** His Honour, sir Frederick Falkiner		470.24++	138.02 **
** Ramshorns		470.25	139.33 **
** Mosaic		470.27	40.07 **
** Scandalous!		471.03	322.29 **
** Long John Fanning		471.10+	119.20 **
** A pungent Henry Clay		471.11	247.11 **
** Hang Judas Iscariot?	471.14	14.05	103.24 **
** H. Rumbold, master barber		471.15	303.35 **
** George's church		471.24	57.09 **
** Gulls		471.28	152.22 **
** Innocence		471.28	25.01 **

PELVIC BASIN
    471.30   710.28

** Her artless blush	471.30	253.01	366.25 **
** Hynes		472.01+	90.04 **
** That three shillings		472.02	119.33 **
** Pig's feet		472.11	434.15 **
** I was at a funeral		472.11	57.11 **
** Beagle lifts . . . dachshund coat		472.14+	432.12 **
** Scorbutic face		472.14	418.39 **
** He has gnawed all	472.15	114.21	(17.13) **
** Ghouleaten		472.19	10.25 **
** I am Paddy Dignam's spirit		473.02	152.39 **
** List, list, O list!		473.02	188.03 **
** The voice of Esau	473.04	76.23	211.25 **
** By metempsychosis		473.10	50.13 **

```
    **  O rocks                                 473.12        64.22   **

    **  Mr J.H. Menton                          473.14       102.38   **

    **  Keep her off that bottle of sherry      473.18       250.26   **

    **  John O'Connell                          473.21++     106.37   **

    **  A bunch of keys                         473.22        11.35   **

    **  Father Coffey                           473.23       103.25   **

    **  Toadbellied                             473.23       103.23   **

    **  A staff of twisted poppies              473.25        80.06   **

    **  A hoarse croak                          473.27       103.25   **

    **  Namine                                  473.27       103.27   **

    **  Jacobs Vobiscuits         473.27        305.29     (130.24)   **

    **  Overtones                               474.05        70.14   **

    **  My master's voice!                      474.06       (6.41)   **

    **  U.P.                                    474.08       158.11   **

    **  House of Keys             474.09         11.35       107.35   **

    **  An obese grandfather rat                474.16       114.13   **

    **  Tom Rochford                            474.18+      178.20   **

    **  Robinredbreasted                        474.19       178.21   **

    **  Reuben J.                               474.22        93.41   **

    **  A daredevil salmon leap                 474.25     (332.22)   **

    **  Two discs on the columns wobble         464.26       229.15   **

    **  Giddy flecks, silvery sequins           475.06        36.22   **
```

THREE BRONZE BUCKLES
    475.11   501.03+

A slim BLACK VELVET FILLET round her throat
    475.11   499.23

Mrs [BELLA] COHEN'S
    475.18++   729.10

```
    **  Mother Slipperslapper                   475.19        87.18   **
```

Her SON IN OXFORD
        475.21   585.14   See also   4.19

            ** My tailor, Mesias   476.05   110.17   **

            ** A hard black shrivelled potato   476.13+   57.02   **

YOU'LL KNOW ME NEXT TIME
        476.25   554.09   See also 527.25

            ** I never loved a dear gazelle   477.02   45.12   **

            ** Fascinated   477.16   92.25   **

            ** Breath of stale garlic   477.20   171.06   **

Make a STUMP SPEECH out of it
        478.06   499.09

            ** Sir Walter Raleigh   478.09   201.26   **

            ** That potato   478.10   57.02   **

            ** Rotunda   478.21   95.42   **

            ** Better run a tramline. . . .   478.21   58.03   **

Our buccaneering Vanderdeckens in their phantom ship of finance (THE FLYING
    DUTCHMAN)
        478.24   479.19   (139.05)   (297.12)   See also 376.26

            ** The aurora borealis   478.28   428.01   **

            ** Councillor Lorcan Sherlock   479.07+   247.21   **

            ** These flying Dutchmen   479.19   478.24   **

            ** Rover for rever and ever   479.28   97.21   **

            ** Royal Dublin Fusiliers   479.33   47.18   **

The CAMERON HIGHLANDERS
        479.34   727.06   753.26++   See also 228.30

            ** The pillar of the cloud   480.05   143.11   **

            ** Imperial eagles hoisted   480.07   (378.06) **

            ** John Howard Parnell   480.10   165.02   **

ULSTER KING OF ARMS
        480.12   572.17

            ** Joseph Hutchinson   480.13   247.21   **

** <u>Sligo</u>   480.15   332.11   **

** <u>Dublin Metropolitan Fire Brigade</u>   480.17   428.02   **

<u>HIS EMINENCE MICHAEL CARDINAL LOGUE ARCHBISHOP OF ARMAGH</u>
   480.19   482.20

<u>HIS GRACE, THE MOST REVEREND DR WILLIAM ALEXANDER</u>
   480.21   482.13

** <u>Newspaper canvassers</u>   480.27   57.35   **

** <u>Poplin weavers</u>   480.29   168.19   **

** <u>Gold Stick</u>   480.33   334.13   **

** <u>Saint Stephen's iron crown</u>   480.40   (415.08)   **

** <u>A sunburst appears</u>   482.03   57.35   **

** WILLIAM, ARCHBISHOP OF ARMAGH   482.13   480.21   **

** MICHAEL, ARCHBISHOP OF ARMAGH   482.20   480.19   **

** <u>Ruby ring</u>   482.25   (64.25)   **

** <u>Destiny</u>   482.25   66.3   **

** <u>Joybells ring in</u> . . . <u>Malahide</u>   482.27   43.27   **

** <u>George's</u>   482.28   57.09   **

** <u>Mirus bazaar fireworks</u>   482.28   183.05   365.17   **

** <u>We hereby nominate</u>   483.09   117.06+   **

** JOHN HOWARD PARNELL   483.17+   165.02   **

** My famous brother!   483.19   35.02   **

** The promised land   483.23   143.20   **

** <u>The keys of Dublin</u>   483.25   11.35   107.35   **

** TOM KERNAN   483.28+   71.24   **

** We overcame the hereditary enemy   484.02   163.10   **

At LADYSMITH
   484.02   748.43

** Half a league onward!   484.04   50.31   **

** All is lost now!   484.05   256.24   **

** Across the heights of Plevna	484.07	56.32	**
** FREEMAN TYPESETTERS	484.09	57.36	**
** JOHN WYSE NOLAN	484.11+	177.18	**
** James Stephens	484.12	43.25	**
** A BLUECOAT SCHOOLBOY	484.13	182.37	**
** The new Bloomusalem	484.23+	(122.21)	**
** Thirtytwo . . . counties	484.24	308.13	**
** Derwan the builder	484.25	450.10	**
** With crystal roof	484.26	294.18	**
** A huge pork kidney	484.27	55.04	**
** All marked . . . L.B.	485.02	116.18	**
** Man in a brown macintosh	485.08+	109.29	**
** His real name is Higgins	485.12	(126.26)	**
** Strikes down poppies	485.16	80.06	**
** Loaves and fishes	485.20	403.31	**
** Henry Clay cigars	485.21	247.11	**
** Pineapple rock	485.23	151.01	**
** Hungarian lottery	485.28	156.11	**
** Penny dinner counters	485.28	157.29	**
** Canvasser's Vade Mecum	485.34	57.35	**
** The lady Gwendolen Dubedat	486.04	175.30	**
** Baby Boardman	486.13+	346.16	**
** Hajajaja	486.16	357.05	**
** A blind stripling	486.18	180.31	**
** My more than Brother! (G)	486.18	50.31	**
** Peep! Bopeep! 486.21	256.10	(39.38)	**
** Red, orange . . . Roygbiv	486.23	376.23	**
** 32 feet per second	486.24	72.10	**

** U.p.:up. U.p.:up	486.28	158.11 **
** Maurice Butterly, farmer	486.31	17.16 **
** Three shillings offered him	486.32	119.33 **
** Joseph Hynes, journalist	486.32	90.04 **
** THE CITIZEN	487.01+	293.25 **
** The standard of Zion	487.04	44.09 **

ALEPH BETH CHIMEL DALETH. . . .
     487.08   688.15

** Hagadah	487.08	122.20 **
** Tephilim	487.08	378.36 **
** Kosher	487.09	62.30 **
** Yom Kippur	487.09	152.01 **
** Meshuggah	487.10	159.38 **
** Jimmy Henry	487.11+	246.30 **
** Free medical and legal advice	487.15	119.07 **
** Solution of doubles	487.16	301.16 **
** PADDY LEONARD	487.19+	90.39 **
** NOSEY FLYNN	487.25+	171.25 **
** J.J. O'MOLLOY	488.05	124.32 **
** A Peter O'Brien!	488.06	297.09 **
** PISSER BURKE	488.09	305.40 **
** For bladder trouble?	488.10	119.07 **
** Acid. nit. hydrochlor dil.	488.12+	(84.20) **
** CHRIS CALLINAN	488.16+	137.31 **
** What is the parallax	488.17	154.06 **

K II
    488.19   523.02   683.32

** JOE HYNES	488.20+	90.04 **

```
  ** My progenitor . . . a dank prison      488.23      36.10   **

  ** BEN DOLLARD                            488.25+     91.01   **

  ** LARRY O'ROURKE                         489.07      57.40   **
```

I'm SENDING AROUND a dozen of stout FOR THE MISSUS
    489.09   750.33+

```
  ** CROFTON                                489.14     336.16   **

  ** ALEXANDER KEYES. . . .                 489.18     107.35   **

  ** Universal brotherhood                  489.22+    333.20   **

  ** Saloon motor hearses                   489.24      98.13   **

  ** With masked licence                    489.27       7.30   **

  ** Esperanto                              490.01     432.19   **

  ** Dropsical impostors         490.02     45.25     293.25   **

  ** Patriotism of barspongers              490.02     293.25   **

  ** O'MADDEN BURKE                         490.04     131.30   **

  ** Free fox in a free henroost            490.05     160.29   **

  ** DAVY BYRNE                             490.06     170.19   **

  ** Iiiiiiiiiaaaaaaach!                    490.07     177.39   **

  ** LENEHAN                                490.10+    125.10   **

  ** Museum . . . goddesses                 490.14      80.10   **

  ** Venus Callipyge, Venus Pandemos        490.15     176.26   **

  ** Venus Metempsychosis                   490.16      50.13   **

  ** FATHER FARLEY                          490.22+     80.15   **

  ** MRS RIORDAN                            490.25+     97.25   **

  ** MOTHER GROGAN                          490.27+     12.33   **

  ** NOSEY FLYNN                            491.01+    171.25   **

  ** One of the old sweet songs             491.02      63.31   **

  ** A cruel deceiver                       491.06      14.05   **

  ** With my tooraloom. . . .               491.07      71.18   **
```

** HOPPY HOLOHAN   491.08   73.29   **

** PADDY LEONARD   491.10   90.39   **

** What railway opera. . . .   491.13   125.10   130.28   **

** LENEHAN   491.15+   125.10   **

** Plagiarist!   491.16   458.31   **

** THEODORE PUREFOY   491.23+   161.06   **

** In fishing cap and oilskin jacket   491.24   397.41   **

** My hero god!   492.02   4.29   **

** Suicide by . . . drowning   492.04   4.28   **

** Drinking prussic acid   492.04   336.08   **

Drinking . . . ACONITE
    492.04   499.19   514.28   684.36   724.04   724.37

** Nelson's Pillar   492.06   95.09   **

** The great vat of Guinness's   492.07   81.39   **

** ALEXANDER J. DOWIE   492.11   151.07   **

** The cities of the plain   492.16   61.12   **

Mentioned in the APOCALYPSE
    492.18   520.26

** Caliban!   492.20   6.37   **

** Parnell   492.22   35.02   **

MR   FOX! (Parnell's pseudonym)
    492.22   649.30   See also   26.33

** Mother Grogan   492.23   12.33   **

THROW OBJECTS OF LITTLE OR NO COMMERCIAL VALUE . . .
    492.24   544.25   726.03

** My brother Henry   492.31   72.31   **

** Dolphin's Barn   492.32   280.17   **

** Wrongfully accused   492.32   410.29   **

** Dr Malachi Mulligan   493.01++   3.01   **

** To give medical testimony   493.02   403.32   **

** More sinned against than sinning	493.14	358.10 **
** His high grade hat	493.18	56.40 **
** DR MADDEN	493.19	388.21 **
** DR CROTTHERS	493.23+	388.22 **
** DR PUNCH COSTELLO	493.26	388.24 **
** DR DIXON	493.28	97.28 **
** The new womanly man	493.30	321.09 **
** Glencree reformatory	494.08	(155.23) **
** He is about to have a baby	494.11	403.32 **
** MRS THORNTON	494.21	66.23 **
** Chrysostomos	494.31	3.28 **
** Silversmile, Silberselber. . . .	494.31	8.06 **
** The Messiah	495.02	337.39 **
*% Joseph	495.02	82.04 **
** BROTHER BUZZ	495.05	83.30 **
** BANTAM LYONS	495.07	74.02 **
** Climbs Nelson's Pillar	495.10	95.09 **
** Lord Byron	495.14	124.01 **
** Moses of Egypt	495.14	40.07 **
** Moses Maimonides	495.15	28.14 **

MOSES MENDELSSOHN
495.15   687.23+

** Rip van Winkle	495.15	377.23 **
** Baron Leopold Rothschild	495.16	174.11 **
** Robinson Crusoe	495.17	109.36 **

SHERLOCK HOLMES
495.17   636.01   708.30   (495.25)

** Bloom . . . eclipses the sun	495.19	16.36 **

```
    ** BRINI, PAPAL NUNCIO                    495.21+    321.24    **

    ** Moses                                  495.24     40.07    **

Moses begat NOAH and NOAH begat Eunuch
    495.25      569.11      688.29

O'Halloran begat GUGGENHEIM and GUGGENHEIM begat Agendath
    495.26      719.31

    ** Agendath begat Netaim                  495.27     60.16    **

LE HIRSCH
    495.27      719.31

    ** Begat Jesurum                          495.28    393.28    **

    ** Begat O'Donnell Magnus                 495.33    296.38    **

    ** Begat Maimun                           496.02   (29.13)    **

    ** Dusty Rhodes                           496.02    427.17    **

SZOMBATHELY and SZOMBATHELY begat Virag
    496.06      511.30      682.10      723.19    724.26

    ** Begat Virag                            496.07    378.36    **

    ** Virag begat Bloom                      496.07     76.26    **

A DEADHAND
    496.09      514.23

    ** A CRAB.  (In bushranger's kit)         496.11+    217.06    **

    ** A HOLLYBUSH                            496.16     26.33    **

THE IRISH EVICTED TENANTS (land troubles)
    496.21      629.26      651.33      656.42    661.02    771.18
    See also    599.03

    ** Donnybrook fair                        496.22     86.30    **

    ** Don Giovanni, a cenar teco             496.25     63.31    **

    ** Artane orphans                         496.26+   101.41    **

    ** HORNBLOWER                             497.09+    86.23    **

    ** Lilith, the nighthag                   497.12    390.01    **

    ** Agendath Netaim                        497.13     60.16    **

    ** The land of Ham                        497.14    171.31    **
```

**	Bonafide travellers	497.16	424.20 **
**	Ownerless dogs	497.16	44.33 **
**	Mastiansky and Citron	497.17+	60.33 **
**	The false Messiah!	497.20	337.39 **
**	George S. Mesias	497.21+	110.17 **
**	Reuben J. Dodd	497.27+	93.41 **
**	Balackbearded Iscariot	497.27	14.05 **
**	The drowned corpse of his son	497.28	4.28 **
**	THE FIRE BRIGADE	498.04+	428.02 **
**	BROTHER BUZZ	498.06	83.30 **
**	Forgive him his trespasses	498.10	6.33 **
**	THE CITIZEN	498.13+	293.25 **
**	Marked I.H.S.	498.16	81.20 **
**	O daughters of Erin	498.17+	217.17 **
**	Kidney of Bloom	498.23	55.04 **

**	Pray for us	498.23++	205.24	346.08 **
**	Flower of the Bath	498.24	72.31	86.40 **

**	Mentor of Menton	498.25	102.38 **
**	Canvasser for the Freeman	498.26	57.36 **
**	Charitable Mason	498.27	73.05 **

**	Wandering Soap	498.28	85.17	(34.05) **

**	Sweets of Sin	498.29	236.05 **
**	Music without Words	498.30	285.37 **
**	Reprover of the Citizen	498.31	293.25 **
**	Friend of all Frillies	499.01	236.05 **
**	Midwife Most Merciful	499.02	37.37 **
**	Potato Preservative. . . .	499.03	57.02 **
**	The Alleluia chorus	499.05	97.21 **

```
    ** Joseph Glynn                            499.06        82.06    **

    ** Talk away till. . . .        499.09     352.09       478.06    **

    ** In caubeen with clay pipe               499.11       192.15    **

    ** With a smile in his eye                 499.13+       45.12    **

    ** To be or not to be                      499.17       280.25    **

    ** A few pastilles of aconite              499.19       492.04    **

    ** In her neckfillet                       499.23       475.11    **

    ** A necessary evil                        500.02       207.10    **

    ** I'm Yorkshire born                      500.06      (254.01)   **

    ** Unparalleled . . . pears                500.17       121.15    **

    ** The greeneyed monster                   500.19        42.38    **

    ** Laughing witch?                         500.25        67.39    **

    ** The hand that rocks the cradle          500.25       288.13    **

    ** Its bronze buckles                      501.03       475.11    **

    ** Passtouch of secret          501.10      73.05       167.23    **

    ** The odour of her armpits                501.13       236.25    **

    ** The lion reek                           501.15        28.03    **

    ** Swaying to and fro                      501.19        11.24    **

He TRIPS awkwardly
   501.23      764.11

    ** Hoopsa!                                 501.26       383.07    **

On the ANTLERED RACK of the hall
   502.04    565.14      567.19

    ** A man's . . . waterproof               502.05        56.37    **

The spaniel eyes of a running fox  (BELLA COHEN'S STUFFED FOX)
   502.12      554.15         See also   26.33

A shade of MAUVE TISSUEPAPER dims the light
   502.14     510.25     515.08     517.13    526.28      584.19
   See also    96.04
```

Round and round a MOTH flies
      502.15   515.08++   516.34++

            ** A morris of shuffling feet   502.19   28.11   **

Tapestried with a paper of YEWFRONDS and clear glades
      502.21   545.02++

            ** Cap back to the front   502.23   224.25   **

            ** Indicates mockingly   502.30   3.37   **

Enter a ghost and HOBGOBLINS
      503.07   506.13++

            ** His hat   503.11   17.08   **

            ** And ashplant   503.11   17.17   **

            ** Her boa uncoils   503.23   (156.20) **

            ** Cap back to the front   503.27   224.25   **

            ** David's altar and David's tip   504.04+   292.27   **

            ** Jetez la gourme   504.07   192.29   **

            ** Jewgreek is greekjew   504.12   3.38   **

            ** Disloyalty   504.16   14.05   **

            ** Whetstone!   504.16   211.21   **

            ** The dominant . . . return   504.22+   275.31   **

            ** The Holy City   504.31++   122.21   **

            ** Went forth . . . become   505.01+   25.17   213.14   **

            ** God, the sun, Shakespeare   505.03   212.40   **

A COMMERCIAL TRAVELLER
      505.03   560.09   585.29+   606.06   606.30   (213.01)
      See also   204.30   260.39

            ** Noise in the street   505.05   34.33   **

            ** A mocking whinny   505.09   3.37   **

They say the last day is coming this summer (END OF THE WORLD)
      505.16   506.31++   738.10   741.35   See also 151.07   398.04

O, my FOOT'S TICKLING
      505.23   557.04

```
   ** Ragged barefoot newsboys          505.24+    128.06   **

   ** Reuben J. Antichrist              506.07+     93.41   **

   ** Wandering jew                     506.07      34.05   **

   ** A pilgrim's wallet                506.09      29.40   **

   ** His only son, saved from Liffey   506.12       4.28   **

   ** A hobgoblin                       506.13++   503.07   **

   ** Punch Costello                    506.14     388.24   **

   ** To and fro                        506.20      11.24   **

   ** C'est moi.  L'homme qui rit!      506.23     195.37   **

   ** He springs off into vacuum        506.29     164.42   **

   ** The end of the world!             506.31++   505.16   **

   ** A rocket rushes up                507.08     365.17   **

   ** Second coming of Elijah           507.10++   150.07   **

   ** From zenith to nadir              507.11      24.07   **

   ** Twoheaded octopus                 507.11     165.25   **

   ** End of the World . . . accent     507.11+    165.26   **

   ** Tartan filibegs                   507.12      31.15   **

   ** Three Legs of Man                            507.14   **
                                        See         38.24

   ** A corncrake's                     507.19    (103.25)  **

   ** Just one word more                507.30     (43.27)  **

A GOD or a DOGgone clod
     507.30     599.30+     See also    6.02

   ** The higher self                   508.01    (140.30)  **

   ** A Gautama                         508.02      80.10   **

   ** Jeru. . . . hohhhh                508.14+    122.21   **

   ** Black in the face                 508.21     352.09   **

   ** I don't never . . . seed you      508.26+    425.27   **

   ** World without end                 509.08      29.24   **
```

```
**  The eight beatitudes              509.09+     424.35   **

**  Dixon                             509.10       97.28   **

**  Madden                            509.10      388.21   **

**  Crotthers                         509.10      388.22   **

**  Costello                          509.10      388.24   **

**  Lenehan                           509.10      125.10   **

**  Bannon                            509.11       21.41   **

**  Mulligan                          509.11        3.01   **

**  LYSTER                            509.17      184.01   **

**  Seek thou the light               509.19      193.16   **

**  He corantos by                    509.21      184.14   **

**  Best enters                       509.21      186.02   **

**  John Eglinton                     509.22+     184.20   **

**  Mandarin's kinmono       509.23+   96.40      215.31   **

**  An orange topknot                 509.27      206.38   **

**  A thing of beauty. . . .          509.28      433.08   **

**  Don't you know                    509.29      186.25   **

**  Yeats says                        509.29        9.22   **

**  Greencapped dark lantern          510.02      184.31   **

**  Tanderagee wants the facts 510.05  (44.03)   (184.11)  **

**  Ollave holyeyed                   510.06      184.33   **

**  Mananaan MacLir          510.07++   5.13       38.24   **

**  His druid mantle                  510.09       11.06   **

**  Bicycle pump                      510.11+     165.29   **

**  Aum! Hek! Wal! . . .              510.14+     140.30   **

HEK!
      510.14      521.25

**  Hermes Trismegistos               510.15      193.38   **
```

```
           ** Cooperative dial                    510..20    191.28  **

           ** Light of the homestead              510.23      35.22  **

           ** Dreamery creamery butter   510.23   166.08     185.32  **

           ** A skeleton judashand               510.24      14.05  **

           ** Light wanes to mauve               510.25     502.14  **

           ** Her armpits                        511.07     236.25  **

Makes SHEEP'S EYES
       511.14    773.19

           ** Would you suck a lemon?            511.15     446.21  **

           ** Lipoti Virag                       511.21++   378.36  **

           ** Brown macintosh                    511.24     109.29  **

           ** Cashel Boyle . . . Farrell         511.26     159.15  **

           ** Szombathely                        511.30     496.06  **

           ** Tightly staysed                    512.08     156.26  **

           ** Parallax!                          512.21     154.06  **

           ** Tumble her                         512.31     191.17  **

           ** Two protuberances                  513.18    (234.31) **

           ** Pincushions                        513.26    (168.23) **

           ** Fleshpots of Egypt                 513.28      41.32  **

           ** Eve's sovereign remedy             514.05      14.23  **

           ** Huguenot                           514.06      84.06  **

Exercise your MNEMOTECHNIC
       514.18+     526.25     544.11     689.09     710.08+

           ** La causa e santa                   514.18     168.20  **

           ** Touch of a deadhand                514.23     496.09  **

           ** Aconite                            514.28     402.04  **

And the summer months of 1882 to SQUARE THE CIRCLE
       515.01     699.20     718.12     737.24
```

POMEGRANATE!
    515.02   688.07

    ** The sublime to the ridiculous   515.02   297.06 **

    ** <u>Mauve</u> <u>light</u>   515.08   502.14 **

    ** <u>The</u> <u>everflying</u> <u>moth</u>   515.08++   502.15 **

    ** Tomorrow is . . . past yester   515.11   186.19 **

    ** Insects . . . reiterated coition   515.15   175.39 **

    ** Chase me, Charley   515.33   425.10 **

    ** Buzz! . . . Bee. . . .   515.33+   (68.18) **

    ** Open Sesame!   516.05+   47.05 **

    ** Cometh forth!   516.05   105.42 **

    ** Redbank oysters   516.08   175.02 **

    ** Truffles of Perigord   516.10   171.07 **

DISLODGED THROUGH MISTER OMNIVOROUS PORKER
    516.10   531.10+

    ** Jocular . . . in my ocular   516.13   38.35 **

    ** Eve and the serpent   516.18   14.23 **

    ** Instinct rules the world   516.31   92.16 (288.13) **

    ** <u>Peers</u> <u>at</u> <u>the</u> <u>moth</u>   516.34++   502.15 **

Who's Ger Ger? Who's DEAR GERALD?
    516.35   536.32+   (586.39)

    ** The <u>mauve</u> <u>shade</u>   517.13   502.14 **

    ** <u>Henry</u> <u>Flower</u>   517.15++   72.31 **

    ** <u>A</u> <u>dark</u> <u>mantle</u> . . . <u>plumed</u> <u>sombrero</u>   517.16++   63.31 **

    ** <u>Dulcimer</u>   517.18   57.32 **

    ** <u>Jacob's</u> <u>pipe</u>   517.18   413.20 **

    ** <u>The</u> <u>romantic</u> <u>Saviour's</u> <u>face</u>   517.21   117.23 **

    ** <u>The</u> <u>tenor</u> <u>Mario</u>   517.23   117.30 **

    ** There is a flower that bloometh   517.28   86.32 **

```
** Filling my belly. . . .          517.33+      7.15  **

** Must visit Old Deasy            518.01+     27.25  **

** Minor chord comes now           518.04     280.09  **

** Almidano Artifoni               518.06+    228.13  **

** Ci rifletta                     518.09     228.28  **

** Love's old sweet song           518.11      63.31  **
```

Did I show you the letter about the LUTE
    518.14   661.40

The BIRD that can SING and won't sing
    518.16   541.06

```
** Philip Drunk and Philip Sober   518.17++ (311.13)  **

** Two Oxford dons                 518.18       4.19  **

** Masked with Matthew Arnold's face  518.19    7.30  **

** Like a good young idiot         518.22      38.27  **

** Three pounds twelve you got     518.22      11.02  **

** If youth but knew               518.23      30.24  **

** Mooney's . . . Mooney's         518.24     144.04  **

** The Moira                       518.24      93.38  **

** Holles street hospital          518.25      97.29  **

** Burke's                         518.25     137.11  **

** I paid my way                   518.28      30.39  **

** Reduplication of personality    518.29     301.16  **

** Zoe mou sas agapo               519.01     124.01  **

** Atkinson                        519.02     216.02+ **

** Swinburne                       519.04       5.05  **

** Are you out of Maynooth?        519.10     212.16  **

** A rigadoon of grasshalms        519.14       7.32  **

** The ashplant                    519.16      17.17  **
```

There was a PRIEST DOWN HERE
     519.19++   526.29

          ** Fall of man   519.23   14.23   **

          ** Why I left the Church of Rome   519.26   180.26   **

          ** Penrose   519.27   156.02   **

          ** Coactus volui   520.01   250.12   **

He had TWO LEFT FEET (BOOK OF KELLS)
     520.22   599.15   688.35

          ** Judas Iacchias   520.22   14.05   **

          ** Apocalypse   520.26   492.18   **

In the lock (WESTMORELAND NATIONAL LOCK HOSPITAL)
     520.28   633.02

          ** Mary Shortall   520.28   47.39   **

          ** Jimmy Pidgeon . . . sacré pigeon   520.29+   41.14   **

          ** A daintier head of winsome curls   521.06   348.11   **

          ** Three wise virgins   521.17++   145.18   **

          ** Lovephiltres   521.20   84.26   **

          ** Whitewax   521.20   84.38   **

          ** Orange flower   521.20   84.36   **

          ** Panther, the Roman centurion   521.21   403.19   **

          ** Her   521.21   47.39   **

          ** Flickering phosphorescent scorpion   521.22   414.17   **

          ** Messiah!   521.23   337.39   **

          ** Burst her tympanum   521.23   256.22   **

          ** Hik! Hek! Hak!   521.25   140.30   **

          ** Hek!   521.25   510.14   **

          ** Ben Jumbo Dollard   521.26++   91.01   **

          ** Rubicund, musclebound   521.26   287.26   296.06   **

          ** Genitals tightened into a pair   521.28   268.22   **

** Nakkering castanet bones		522.02	257.13 **
** Base barreltone		522.03	91.01 **
** When love absorbs my ardent soul		522.03	256.21 **
** Nurse Callan		522.04	373.12 **
** Nurse Quigley		522.04+	385.12 **
** Big Ben! . . . Ben MacChree		522.08+	91.01 **
** Hold that fellow with. . . .		522.10+	244.19 **
** HENRY (FLOWER)		522.13++	72.31 **
** When first I saw. . . .		522.15	117.35 **
** Farewell. Fare thee well		522.21	(124.01) **
** Steered by his rapier		522.24	117.18 **
** His wild harp	522.25	45.12	127.13 **
** K. II		523.02	488.19 **
** Post no bills		523.02	153.37 **
** Dr Hy Franks		523.02	153.33 **
** All is lost now		523.04	256.24 **
** Quack!		523.08	153.31 **
** Antisthenes, the dog sage		523.13	148.30 **
** Arius Heresiarchus	523.13	21.06	21.08 **
** The agony in the closet		523.14	38.18 **
** Monks of the screw (G)		523.24	139.13 **
** A rosary of corks		524.05	354.03 **
** To and fro		524.16	11.24 **
** Shall carry my heart		525.03+	156.08 **
** The waterproof		525.13	56.37 **
** Chocolate from his pocket		525.15++	433.31 **
** At the bazaar . . . The viceroy		526.04+	183.05 **
** With his lady		526.06	138.03 **

The gas we had on the TOFT'S HOBBYHORSES
     526.06   578.06   578.22

In Svengali's fur overcoat (TRILBY)
     526.09   767.14+

** Napoleonic forelock		526.09	456.09 **
** Then, rigid . . . past master		526.11	73.05 **
** Aphrodisiac?		526.24+	(175.02) **
** Mnemo		526.25	514.18 **
** Eat and be merry for tomorrow		526.27	172.04 **
** Mauve		526.28	502.14 **
** That priest		526.29	519.19 **
** Truffles at Andrews	526.30	60.30	171.07 **
** A black horn fan		527.04++	69.30 **
** In Carmen		527.04	212.33 **
** Embonpoint		527.13	236.05 **

PETTICOAT GOVERNMENT
     527.20+   See   377.25   381.12   432.25

** Have you forgotten me?	527.25	476.25 **
** It is fate	528.10	66.39 **
** The too late box	528.15	72.21 **
** Thirtytwo feet per second	528.17	72.10 **
** Poor dear papa	528.20+	76.26 **
** King David	528.22	292.27 **
** Athos	528.23	90.20 **
** RICHIE GOULDING	528.25+	38.34 **
** Mocking is catch	528.26	3.37 **
** Best value in Dub	528.26	265.16 **
** Fit for a prince	528.27	265.18 **
** Liver and kidney	528.27	55.03 **

** All things end	528.29	50.29	**
** My talisman	529.03	57.02	**
** Phenomenon . . . natural	529.04	304.35	**
** I knelt once before	529.17	103.17	**
** Bloom, stifflegged	529.20	435.16	**
** My love's young dream	529.23	45.12	**
** Her cobweb hose	529.27	74.18	**
** In Paris	529.28	467.12	**

FEEL MY royal WEIGHT
    529.30   531.19

** Handy Andy	530.04	63.01	**
** Night of the bazaar dance	530.06	69.27	**
** A hard basilisk stare	530.17	40.04	**

ADORER OF THE ADULTEROUS RUMP
    530.22   734.38

** On the hands down	531.06	61.25	**
** Truffles!	531.09	171.07	**
** Grunting, snuffling, rooting	531.10+	516.10	**
** Alpine hat	531.17	438.06	**
** Feel my entire weight	531.19	529.30	**
** My thumping good breakfast	532.27	55.07	**
** Bottle of Guinness's porter	532.28	81.39	**

The brothel cook, MRS KEOGH
    533.25+   539.08

** Richmond Asylum	534.08	6.20	**

GUINNESS'S PREFERENCE SHARES ARE AT SIXTEEN THREE QUARTERS
    534.08   535.07

** Guinness's preference shares	534.08	81.39	**
** Throwaway	534.11	86.07	**

** Twenty to one   534.11   325.31 **

Gee up! A CO'CKHORSE TO BANBURY CROSS
    534.20+   566.26   (467.19)

** The lady goes a pace a pace   534.25   50.08 **

** By Jingo   535.07   111.16 **

** Sixteen three quarters   535.07   534.08 **

** Blow hot and cold   535.12   125.21 **

** Your punishment frock   535.14   72.30 **

** Ruby Cohen   535.16   64.25 **

** As they are now. . . .   535.22   113.42 **

** With smoothshaven armpits   535.24   236.25 **

** Martha and Mary   535.31   79.06 **

** A charming soubrette   536.05   229.23 **

** In Holles street   536.07   268.40 **

** Mrs Miriam Dandrade   536.16+   160.39 **

** The Shelbourne Hotel   536.17   160.40 **

DEMIMONDAINE
    536.19   570.21   615.20

** Signor Laci Daremo   536.25   63.31 **

** Henry Fleury   536.26   72.31 **

** Gordon Bennett fame   536.26   97.15 **

** Gerald converted me . . . dear Gerald 536.32+   516.35 **

** Impersonator   536.33   76.24 **

** Fascinated by . . . stays 537.01   92.25   156.26 **

** A postal order   537.33   182.11 **

** Booloohoom   538.06   434.01 **

** Poldy Kock   538.06   64.39 **

** Bootlaces a penny   538.06   93.17 **

** Cassidy's hag   538.07   61.15 **

** Blind stripling		538.07	180.31 **
** Larry Rhinocerous		538.07	57.40 **
** The [nextdoor] girl		538.07	59.04 **
** The woman		538.08	73.33 **
** The whore		538.08	290.06 **
** Pleasants street		538.10	60.38 **
** Rererepugnosed		538.19	74.29 **
** With this ring I thee own		539.02	352.04 **
** Mrs Keogh's the cook's		539.08	533.25 **
** Lap it up		539.10	41.18 **

Drink me PIPING HOT
      539.10   551.28

** Miss Ruby		539.12	64.25 **
** Dillon's lacquey	539.32	128.30	226.31 **
** One and eightpence too much		539.34	93.41 **
** Caliph Haroun Al Raschid		540.19	47.05 **
** Transparent stockings		540.23	74.18 **
** Power of fascination		540.28	92.25 **
** Gomorrhan vices		540.29	61.12 **
** Into his armpit		540.31	236.25 **

An IMPOTENT THING LIKE YOU
      541.02   725.33

** His fan		541.03	69.30 **
** Manx cat		541.04	(94.21) **
** Your curly teapot		541.05	445.09 **
** Sing, birdy, sing		541.06	518.16 **
** Boy of six doing his pooly		541.07	(346.16) **
** I forget! Forgive!		541.30	468.25 **

** Changed by woman's will	542.02	381.12 **
** Rip Van Winkle!	542.07	377.23 **
** The diamond panes	542.11	202.08 **
** The first night at Mat Dillon's	542.11	106.19 **

But that dress, the GREEN
    542.12+   (691.10++)

** Laughs mockingly	542.15	3.37 **
** Mullingar student	542.16	21.41 **
** Milly Bloom	542.17	21.42 **
** Slimsandalled	542.17	61.32 **
** Blue scarf in the seawind	542.18	67.04 **
** Simply swirling	542.18	62.36 **
** The arms of her lover	542.18	67.18 **
** Young eyes	542.19	64.24 **
** It's Papli!	542.21	66.01 **
** Our writing table	542.23	55.20 **

AUNT HEGARTY's armchair
    542.24   682.13

** The Cuckoo's Rest!	542.26	212.36 **
** Sauce for the goose, my gander	542.29	279.31 **
** Wren's auction	543.05	99.17 **

The little statue you carried home in the rain (STATUE OF NARCISSUS)
    543.07   710.15   728.23   766.22   775.41+   See also 99.17

The SECRETS OF YOUR BOTTOM DRAWER
    543.08   720.24++   See also 364.03++

** Your handbook of astronomy	543.09	233.34 **
** Your secondbest bed	543.21	203.06 **
** Your epitaph is written	543.21	114.18 **
** You are down and out	543.22	93.21 **
** All Ireland versus one!	543.25	467.06 **

```
     ** We'll bury you. . . .            544.03     108.31   **

     ** Mr Flower!                       544.09      72.31   **

     ** Byby, Papli!                     544.09      66.01   **

     ** Memory!                          544.11     514.18   **

     ** I have sinned!                   544.11      81.20   **

     ** Broken                           544.16    (95.22)   **
```

The CIRCUMCISED . . . stand by the wailing wall
    544.18+   703.15   724.15

```
     ** Moses Herzog                     544.19     292.20   **

     ** M. Moisel                        544.20      60.38   **

     ** J. Citron . . . O. Mastiansky    544.20      60.33   **

     ** With swaying arms                544.22      49.36   **

     ** Dead sea fruit          544.25    61.13     492.24   **

     ** Shema Israel Adonai Elohenu      544.26     122.23   **

     ** The suttee pyre                  544.31     102.11   **

     ** A nymph                        544.33++      65.11   **

     ** With hair unbound              544.33++     (3.17)   **

     ** Interlacing yews               545.02++     502.21   **

     ** Highkickers                      545.12     366.02   **

     ** You mean Photo Bits?             546.02      65.12   **

     ** Your classic curves              546.09     173.36   **

     ** A thing of beauty                546.10     433.08   **

     ** For the rest                     546.18      51.02   **

     ** That English invention           546.18     289.16   **

     ** Frailty, thy name is marriage    546.21     325.40   **

     ** Soiled personal linen            547.05      62.17   **

     ** The quoits are loose             547.06      56.27   **

     ** Gibraltar by long sea            547.06      56.28   **
```

** The antiquated commode   547.11   65.27   **

** That absurd orangekeyed utensil   547.14   64.07   **

POULAPHOUCA POULAPHOUCA
    547.18++   552.14   628.03   718.31

WHISPER.   She is right, our sister
    547.21   549.02   564.10

** JOHN WYSE NOLAN   547.24+   177.18   **

** Trees of Ireland   547.26   326.34   **

** The old Royal stairs   548.12   272.25   **

** Sunspots that summer   548.14   166.39   **

** Halcyon days   548.15+   355.21   **

Master Donald TURNBULL
    548.18   667.17

** Master Owen Goldberg   548.19   162.17   **

** Master Percy Apjohn   548.20   162.16   **

** Mackerel!   548.23   162.18   **

** Live us again   548.23   (145.10) **

** Hobbledehoy   548.26   94.23   **

** Mammamufflered   548.26   111.13   **

** Whisper   549.02   547.21   **

** The flowers that bloom in the spring 549.17   38.35   **

** It was pairing time   549.17   199.07   **

** A natural phenomenon   549.18   304.35   **

** Poor papa   549.20   76.20   **

** Staggering Bob   549.25+   171.10   **

** High on Ben Howth   550.04   176.01   **

** A nannygoat   550.04+   176.14   **

** Thirtytwo . . . per second   550.11+   72.10   **

** Giddy Elijah   550.12   151.07   **

```
**  Fall from cliff                    550.12+     37.16   **

**  Government printer's clerk         550.13     123.05   **

**  Lion's Head                        550.15     176.03   **

**  Purple waiting waters              550.15       5.07   **

**  Bailey . . . light                 550.19     357.24   **

**  Kish light                         550.19      44.13   **

**  Erin's King                        550.19      67.03   **

**  COUNCILLOR NANNETTI                550.22     118.16   **

**  Hand in his waistcoat opening      550.23     297.06   **

**  When my country . . . done         550.24+    114.18   **

**  As you saw today                   551.02      80.10   **

**  We eat electric light              551.04     176.34   **

**  Lascivious crispation              551.04      43.20   **

**  Hamilton Long's                    551.11      84.05   **

**  Peccave!                           551.16      81.20   **

**  The hand that rules                551.18     288.13   **

**  Figures wind serpenting            551.20      46.16   **

**  Cooeeing                           551.21     185.02   **

**  Piping hot!                        551.28     539.10   **

**  VIRAG                              552.03     378.36   **

**  Phillaphulla . . . Poulaphouca     552.14+    547.18   **

**  Tranquilla convent                 552.20     155.03   **

**  Sister Agatha                      552.20     155.05   **

**  Mount Carmel                       552.21     155.09   **

**  The apparition of Knock            552.21      81.12   **

**  The apparition of . . . Lourdes    552.21      81.12   **

**  Only the ethereal                  552.23     166.08   **
```

** Dreamy creamy gull. . . .   552.23   152.34   166.08 **

His back TROUSERS' BUTTON snaps
    552.24+   613.43   710.35

    ** Two sluts of the Coombe   552.27   78.37 **

    ** O Leopold . . . To keep it up   553.02+   78.38 **

    ** If there were only ethereal   553.08   166.08 **

    ** Arms . . . swaying   553.11   49.36 **

    ** Deciduously!   553.12   426.04 **

    ** Sully my innocence!   553.15   25.01 **

    ** Satan   553.17   50.25 **

    ** Nebrakada   553.21   242.41 **

    ** The fox and the grapes   553.22   125.21 **

    ** Your barbed wire   553.23   155.16 **

The SPOUTLESS STATUE OF THE WATERCARRIER (Aquarius)
    553.25   671.27

    ** Unveiled   553.28   191.37 **

I have SIXTEEN YEARS OF BLACK SLAVE LABOUR behind me (the Blooms' marriage)
    554.03   772.09   782.16   See also 560.03

    ** You'll know me the next time   554.09   476.25 **

    ** Your stuffed fox   554.15   502.12 **

    ** Canvasser   554.25   72.16 **

    ** Dead march from Saul?   555.02   97.21 **

    ** My sweeties   555.06+   433.31 **

    ** That potato   555.12++   57.02 **

    ** Poor mama   555.16   111.13 **

    ** To have or not to have   555.25   280.25 **

    ** Taking out a banknote   556.09++   11.02 **

    ** Kinch   556.14   3.08 **

It's TEN SHILLINGS here
    556.23   584.16

** My foot's asleep 557.04 505.23 **

** What, eleven? A riddle 557.16+ 26.33 **

Such a SLYBOOTS
     558.12   (739.12)

** Le distrait 558.21 49.12 187.17 **

** Absentminded beggar 558.21 187.22 **

** A handful of coins 558.22++ 11.02 29.25 **

LUCIFER. Thanks
     558.27   669.08   670.03

** Be just before you are generous 559.05 31.11 **

** Why striking eleven? 559.10+ 26.33 **

** Lessing says 559.11 37.14 **

** Thirsty fox 559.11 41.05 **

** Georgina Johnson 559.21 189.26 **

** Lynx eye 560.02 224.25 **

SIXTEEN YEARS AGO (Stephen fell and broke glasses at Clongowes)
     560.03   561.19   563.17   679.22   See also 11.22   554.03

** Ineluctable modality 560.05 25.17 **

** Sphinx 560.06 77.25 (6.37) **

** Beast that has two backs 560.06 139.28 **

** A commercial traveller 560.09 505.03 **

** Who takest away. . . . 560.14 436.31 **

** The sins of our world 560.14+ 151.07 **

** Cursed dog I met 560.21 432.12 453.16 **

** Dusk of the gods 560.26 297.12 **

** Fragende Frau 560.29 297.12 **

** Hamlet, I am they father's gimlet 561.02 152.39 **

** The youth who could not. . . . 561.07 210.42 **

** See it in your face 561.11++ 135.18 **

** Broke his glasses		561.19	560.03 **
** Don John Conmee	561.21+	63.31	80.03 **
** Read His handwriting		562.02	37.02 **
** Thumbprint on the haddock		562.03	109.10 **
** Line of fate		562.11	66.39 **
** Henpecked husband		563.04	432.25 **
** Black Liz		563.06+	315.21 **
** Moves to one great goal		563.17	34.27 **
** Sixteen years ago I . . . tumbled		563.17	560.03 **
** Must see a dentist		563.20	50.35 **
** In backhand		563.22	465.23 **
** A hackneycar		563.26+	279.32 **
** Lenehan		564.01++	125.10 **
** The Ormond boots	564.02 230.02		258.12 **
** Over the crossblind		564.03	246.08 **
** Lydia Douce and Mina Kennedy		564.03+	246.07 **
** Mocks them with thumb		564.06	3.37 **
** Haw, have you the horn?		564.07	256.25 **
** Bronze by gold		564.08	246.07 **
** Whisper		564.10	547.21 **
** Red flower in his mouth		564.13	228.02 **
** In a yachtsman's cap		564.14	125.10 **
** Bloom's antlered head		565.14	502.04 **
** Raoul, darling		565.21	236.05 **
** I'm in my pelt	565.21	235.25	400.40 **
** The pishogue!		566.02	321.14 **
** Orangeflower?		566.15	84.36 **

** MINA KENNEDY . . . LYDIA DOUCE	566.20+	246.07	**
** Ride a cock horse	566.26	534.20	**
** Hee hee hee	567.02	257.01	**
** The reindeer antlered hatrack	567.19	502.04	**
** 'Tis the loud laugh. . . .	567.22	191.16	**
** His Thursdaymomun	567.25	(109.37)	**
** The great Napoleon	568.06	297.06	**
** Mrs Dignam	568.08	349.10	**
** Tunny's tawny sherry	568.09	250.26	**
** A pen chivvying her	568.11	188.23	**
** Her late husband's . . . boots	568.12	57.11	**
** Scottish widow's insurance policy	568.14	57.11	**
** Patsy (Dignam)	568.15	101.02	**
** A hank of porksteaks	568.16	234.02	**
** Freddy (Dignam)	568.17+	355.02	**
** Weda seca whokilla farst	568.25	203.01	**
** The face of Martin Cunningham	568.26+	80.13	**
** Shakespeare's beardless face	568.26	96.27	**
** Mrs Cunningham	568.29+	96.33	**
** And they call me the jewel of Asia	569.03	96.40	**
** Immense!	569.05	90.39	**
** Queens lay with prize bulls	569.08	207.40	**
** My grandoldgrossfather	569.09	210.35	**
** Madame Grissel Stevens	569.10	411.19	**
** And Noah was drunk	569.11	495.25	**
** Back from Paris	569.16++	12.18++	**
** Claps hat on head	569.20	17.08	**
** Mocker	570.09	3.37	**

**	Vampire		570.11+	48.01	**
**	Demimondaines		570.21	536.19	**
**	Pièce de Shakespeare	570.30	49.12	187.18	**
**	Double entente cordiale		571.03	330.22	**
**	Waterloo		571.04	297.06	**
**	Watercloset		571.04	38.18	**
**	I dreamt		571.11	47.05	**
**	Serpentine avenue . . . fubsy widow		571.19	40.22	**
**	The red carpet		571.21	47.05	**
**	I flew . . . Pater! Free!		572.02	207.40	**
**	World without end		572.02	29.24	**
**	His vulture talons		572.07	47.03	**
**	Ulster king at arms!		572.16	480.12	**
**	A stout fox. . . .		572.21	26.33	**
**	Ward Union huntsmen		572.25	160.28	**
**	Thimbleriggers		572.31	394.27	**
**	A dark horse. . . .		573.11	39.38	**
**	Sceptre		573.14	128.03	**
**	Maximum the Second		573.14	85.34	**
**	Zinfandel		573.14	174.02	**
**	Duke of Westminster's Shotover		573.14	32.15	**
**	Dwarfs ride them		573.16	32.17	**
**	Leaping, leaping in their saddles		573.16	233.22	**
**	Garrett Deasy		573.19++	27.25	**
**	Whitegaitered feet		573.21	29.08	**
**	The rocky road		573.21	31.35	**
**	THE ORANGE LODGES		573.22	31.19	**

** His nailscraped face	573.26	132.22+	**
** Per vias rectas!	573.30	31.32	**
** His rearing nag	573.31	(49.31)	**
** Dancing coins	573.32	29.25	**
** Soft day, sir John!	574.02	31.38	**
** Private Carr, Private Compton	574.03+	430.21	**
** Cissy Caffrey	574.03+	346.15	**
** Noise in the street!	574.06	34.33	**
** Yet I've a sort of Yorkshire relish	574.10++	254.01	**

** My augur's rod	574.21	17.17	48.19	**
** In tripudium		574.22	49.20	**

** Professor Goodwin	575.01+	63.05	**
** His ashplant	575.12	17.17	**
** Professor Maginni	575.17++	153.34	**
** Deportment	575.30	37.37	**

The KATTY LANNER STEPS
    575.30   745.26

** Two young fellows	576.02++	254.01	**
** The morning hours	576.04++	69.28	**
** Slim . . . waspwaisted	576.04	61.32	**

** In mocking mirrors	576.08	3.37	28.16	**

** Their curves	576.14	173.36	**
** Languideyed	576.29	49.36	**
** With dark bat sleeves	576.30	48.02	**
** They are masked	577.04	7.30	**
** Weary	577.05+	3.41	**
** Heigho! Heigho!	577.08	57.09	**
** Weaving, unweaving	577.14	21.14	**

** Simply swirling	577.14	62.36	**
** The Mirus bazaar!	578.03	183.05	**
** Toft's cumbersome whirligig	578.06	526.06	**
** His ashplant	578.16+	17.17	**
** Jujuby women	578.18	151.05	**
** Stephen with hat	578.19	17.08	**
** Tallyho hornblower 578.21	86.23	254.27	**
** Toft's . . . hobbyhorse riders	578.22	526.06	**
** Think of your mother's people!	579.04	38.33	**
** Lacquey's bell	579.07	226.31	**
** Conmee	579.08	8.03	**
** Lame crutch and leg sailor	579.08	219.08	**
** Corny in coffin	579.11	71.15	**
** Onehandled Nelson	579.12	148.09	**
** Two trickies Frauenzimmer	579.12	37.34	**
** Plumstained	579.12	145.03	**
** Fuseblue	579.13	43.22	**
** Rev. evensong Love	579.14	225.24	**
** Jaunt Blazes	579.14	253.42	**
** Blind coddoubled bicyclers	579.15	86.19	**
** Dilly with snowcake	579.15	151.33	**
** Bump mashtub	579.17	310.37	**
** Viceroy and reine 579.17	138.03	183.05	**
** Stephen's mother	579.25++	5.32	**
** Faded orange blossoms . . . veil	579.26	43.26	**
** Her hair is . . . lank	579.28	423.09	**
** Her toothless mouth	579.29	(3.08)	**
** Liliata rutilantium. . . .	580.02	10.23	**

**	<u>From</u> <u>the</u> <u>top</u> <u>of</u> <u>a</u> <u>tower</u>	580.04	3.10	**
**	<u>Buck Mulligan</u>	580.04++	3.01	**
**	<u>Particoloured jester's dress</u>	580.05	25.09	**
**	<u>A smoking buttered split scone</u>	580.06	249.23	**
**	She's beastly dead	580.09+	8.20	**
**	Mercurial Malachi	580.10	8.06	**
**	Lemur, who are you?	580.15	(25.25)	**
**	The mockery of it!	580.18	3.37	**
**	Kinch killed her	580.18	3.08	**
**	Her dogsbody bitchbody	580.19	6.02	**
**	She kicked the bucket	580.19	113.14	**
**	Our great sweet mother!	580.20	5.05	**
**	<u>Epi</u> <u>oinopa</u> <u>ponton</u>	580.21	5.07	**
**	<u>Breath</u> <u>of</u> <u>wetted</u> <u>ashes</u>	580.24	5.35	**
**	More women than men in the world	580.24	102.10	**
**	<u>Horror</u>	580.27	10.22	**
**	He offended your memory	580.28	8.42	**
**	Destiny	580.29	66.39	**
**	<u>Love's</u> <u>bitter</u> <u>mystery</u>	581.03	9.22	**
**	The word known to all men	581.05	10.17	**
**	Sad among the strangers	581.09	7.15	**
**	The ghoul! Hyena!	581.14	10.25	**
**	In my other world	581.16	72.30	**
**	Dilly	581.16	151.33	**
**	The corpsechewer 581.28	213.23	10.25	**
**	Raw head and bloody bones	581.28	171.12	**
**	<u>An</u> <u>ashen</u> <u>breath</u>	582.02	5.35	**

** All or not at all   582.14   20.20   **

** O Sacred Heart of Jesus   582.18+   113.34   **

** Inexpressible was my anguish   582.26   91.20   **

** Nothung!   583.02   297.12   **

** He lifts the ashplant   583.03   17.17   **

** Smashes the chandelier   583.03+   242.15   432.11   **

** Time's livid final flame   583.04   24.07   **

** Flame . . . darkness   583.05   26.01   **

** Ruin of all space. . . .   583.05   24.07   **

** His ashplant   583.16++   17.17   **

HE TORE HIS COAT
    584.07   677.15   See also 377.23

** A ten shilling house   584.16   556.23   **

** Mauve purple shade   584.19   502.14   **

** He makes a masonic sign   585.06   73.05   **

** The vicechancellor   585.07   124.11   **

** Your son in Oxford!   585.14   475.21   **

** Corny Kelleher   585.28+   71.15   **

** Two silent lechers   585.29+   505.03   **

** Haroun al Raschid   586.06   47.05   **

** Step of a pard   586.07   4.23   **

** Torn envelopes   586.08   72.30   **

** The ashplant   586.09   17.17   **

** A pack of bloodhounds . . . follows   586.09++   128.06   **

** Hornblower of Trinty   586.10   86.23   **

** In tallyho cap   586.10   254.27   **

** Lug's laid back   586.14   345.19   **

** Biscuitboxes   586.15   305.29   **

** Woman's slipperslappers	586.16	87.18	**
** The hue and cry	586.17	129.34	**
** 65 C 66 C night watch	586.18	430.09	**
** John Henry Menton	586.18	102.38	**
** Wisdom Hely	586.19	106.26	**
** V. B. Dillon	586.19	155.22	**
** Councillor Nannetti	586.19	118.16	**
** Alexander Keyes	586.20	107.35	**
** Larry O'Rourke	586.20	57.40	**
** Joe Cuffe	586.20	59.21	**
** Mrs O'Dowd	586.20	306.09	**
** Pisser Burke	586.20	305.40	**
** The Nameless One	586.21	292.01	**
** Mrs Riordan	586.21	97.25	**
** The Citizen	586.21	293.25	**
** Garryowen	586.22	295.13	**
** Whatdoyoucallhim	586.22	61.02	**
** Chris Callinan	586.23	137.31	**
** Sir Charles Cameron	586.23	234.05	**
** Benjamin Dollard	586.24	91.01	**
** Lenehan	586.24	125.10	**
** Bartell d'Arcy	586.24	156.06	**
** Joe Hynes	586.24	90.04	**
** Red Murray	586.25	116.27	**
** Editor Brayden	586.25	117.09	**
** T. M. Healy	586.25	141.11	**
** Mr Justice Fitzgibbon	586.25	141.04	**
** John Howard Parnell	586.26	165.02	**

** The reverend Tinned Salmon   586.26   164.40   **

** Professor Joly   586.27   167.04   **

** Mrs Breen (Josie Breen)   586.27+   156.32   **

** Denis Breen   586.27   157.17   **

** Theodore Purefoy   586.27   161.06   **

** Mina Purefoy   586.28   158.36   **

** The Westland Row Postmistress   586.28   72.24   **

** C. P. M'Coy   586.29   67.24   **

** Friend of Lyons   586.29   74.02   **

** Hoppy Holohan   586.29   73.29   **

MAN IN THE STREET
     586.29   619.07   627.33   See also 154.42

** Pugnosed driver   586.30   74.29   **

** Rich protestant lady   586.31   73.33   **

** Davy Byrne   586.31   170.19   **

** Mrs Ellen M'Guinness   586.31   220.30   **

** Mrs Joe Gallaher   586.32   449.15   **

** George Lidwell   586.32   256.40   **

** Jimmy Henry on corns   586.32   246.30   **

** Father Cowley   586.33   76.07   **

** Crofton   586.33   336.16   **

** Dan Dawson   586.34   91.08   **

** Dental surgeon Bloom   586.34   250.14   **

** Mrs Bob Doran   586.35   303.03   **

** John Wyse Nolan   586.36   177.18   **

** Clonskeatram   586.37   116.04   **

** The bookseller of Sweets of Sin   586.38   236.05   **

** Miss Dubedatandshedidbedad   586.38   175.30   **

** Gerald	586.39	516.35	**
** The managing clerk of Drimmie's	586.40	177.05	**
** Colonel Hayes	586.40	(297.08)	**
** Mastiansky	586.40	60.33	**
** Citron	586.40	60.33	**
** Penrose	586.40	156.02	**
** Aaron Figatner	586.41	259.37	**
** Moses Herzog	586.41	292.20	**
** Michael E. Geraghty	586.41	292.24	**
** Inspector Troy	586.42	292.01	**

Mrs Galbraith
    586.42   751.21+

** The mystery man on the beach	587.01	376.04	**

Old DOCTOR BRADY with stethoscope
    587.01   731.33   754.13

A RETRIEVER
    587.02   601.20++

** Mrs Miriam Dandrade	587.02	160.39	**
** THE HUE AND CRY	587.04	129.34	**
** Beaver Street . . . scaffolding	587.07	450.08	**
** Seventh of Edward	587.14	31.15	**
** History to blame	587.14	20.39	**
** Fabled by mothers of memory	587.14	24.07	**
** PRIVATE CARR	587.16#	430.21	**
** Cissy Caffrey	587.17#	346.15	**
** Hail, Sisyphus	587.30	(96.36)	**
** LORD TENNYSON	588.11	50.31	**

In UNION JACK blazer
    588.12   705.33   759.13

** Their's not to reason why   588.13   50.31   **

** Doctor Swift says   588.18   39.38   **

** The bold soldier boy   588.24   63.01   **

** Rahab (G)   589.08   (24.07)   **

** Cook's son, goodbye   589.08   187.22   **

** The girl you left behind   589.09   191.01   **

** The king of England   589.27   31.15   **

** I must kill the priest and the king 589.29   20.34   **

** Such apposite trenchancy   590.10   91.03   **

** Edward the Seventh   590.15+   31.15   **

** Image of the Sacred Heart   590.16   113.34   **

** A red jujube   590.20   151.05   **

** Perfect and sublime mason   590.21+   73.05   **

** Made in Germany   590.22   330.26   **

** Plasterer's bucket   590.23+   450.09   **

** Peace, perfect peace   590.26   330.37   **

I say: LET MY COUNTRY DIE FOR ME
     591.12   645.09   647.10   See also 118.30

** Joking Jesus   591.17+   19.03   **

** A white jujube   591.17   151.05   **

** Kings and unicorns!   591.21   389.33   **

** Absinthe, the greeneyed monster   591.28   42.38   **

** Judge of impostors   592.03   45.25   **

Green rag to a bull ("JOHN BULL")
     592.09   662.04+   See also 151.04

** Kevin Egan of Paris   592.10+   41.17   **

** Spanish tasselled shirt   592.10   43.11   **

** Peep-o'-day boy's hat   592.11   43.24   **

** The vieille ogresse   592.13   43.13   **

**	Patrice Egan	592.14+	41.16	**
**	His rabbit face	592.14	41.19	**
**	Socialiste!	592.17	41.23	**
**	Two wild geese volant	592.19	41.17	**
**	Johnyellows	592.21	326.29	**
**	Green above the red	593.04	316.33	**
**	Wolfe Tone	593.04	229.20	**
**	THE BAWD	593.05	431.16	**
**	Up King Edward!	593.07	31.15	**
**	Hands up to De Wet	593.09	163.11	**
**	THE CITIZEN	593.10+	293.25	**
**	THE CROPPY BOY	593.18++	91.01	**
**	RUMBOLD, DEMON BARBER	593.23+	303.35	**
**	Drag him downward	594.02	304.11	**
**	A violent erection	594.06	304.32	**
**	Mrs Bellingham, Mrs Yelverton Barry	594.08	465.19	**
**	The Honourable Mrs Mervyn Talboys	594.09	73.38	**
**	EDWARD THE SEVENTH	594.18+	31.15	**
**	On coronation day. . . .	594.21	11.10	**
**	Some brutish empire	594.29	73.02	**
**	Gave it to someone	594.30	11.02	**
**	These necessary evils	595.05	207.10	**
**	Ça se voit aussi à Paris	595.05	208.03	**
**	By Saint Patrick!	595.06	198.28	**
**	Old Gummy Granny. . . .	595.07+	13.41	**
**	Rocking to and fro	595.14	11.24	**

The KING OF SPAIN'S DAUGHTER
    595.14   652.12

```
** Strangers in my house            595.15        9.22    **

** Silk of the kine!                595.16       14.02    **

** You met with poor old Ireland    595.17       44.05    **

** The hat trick                    595.20      435.20    **

** The reverend Carrion Crow        595.21      135.23    **

** THE CITIZEN                      596.04+     293.25    **

** Major Tweedy                     596.06       56.32    **

** He's a proboer                   596.10+     163.10    **

We FOUGHT FOR [ENGLAND] in South Africa
      596.14       641.38

** Royal Dublin Fusiliers           596.15       47.18    **

** Honoured by our monarch (G)      596.16       43.13    **

** THE NAVVY                        596.17+     430.07    **

** Gutted spear points. . . .       596.21       32.36    **

** Major Tweedy                     596.21++     56.32    **

** Turko the terrible               596.21       10.02    **

** The pilgrim warrior's sign. . . .  596.24     73.05    **

** Rorke's Drift                    596.27      457.15    **

** Up, guards, and at them!         596.27      297.16    **

** Garryowen                        597.06      295.13    **

** God save the king                597.06      151.04    **

** The harlot's cry. . . .          597.17       24.07    **

** Weave                            597.18       21.14    **

** White thy fambles. . . .         598.06       47.13    **

** Dublin's burning!                598.11++    428.01    **

** Pandemonium                      598.13      (25.25)   **

** Vultures                         598.19       47.03    **

** Gulls                            598.20      152.22    **
```

** Barnacle geese		598.21	50.13 **
** From Prospect		598.22	100.22 **
** Mount Jerome		598.23	100.01 **
** Tom Rochford		598.25	178.20 **
** Leaps into the void		598.27	21.13 **
** Factory lasses. . . .		598.29	254.01 **
** Laughing witches	598.32	6.28	67.39 **
** Quakerlyster		598.33	184.01 **
** It rains dragon's teeth. . . .		598.33	(26.02) **
** They exchange in amity. . . .		599.01	73.05 **
** Wolfe Tone		599.02	229.20 **
** Henry Grattan		599.02	139.03 **
** Smith O'Brien		599.03	93.11 **
** Daniel O'Connell		599.03	31.18 **

MICHAEL DAVITT against Isaac Butt
599.03   657.07   681.17   716.38   See also 496.21

** Isaac Butt		599.04	138.11 **
** Parnell		599.04	35.02 **
** Arthur Griffith		599.04	43.08 **
** Lord Edward Fitzgerald		599.06	45.26 **
** Saint Barbara		599.09	359.39 **
** High barbicans	599.11+	11.18	3.10 **
** The smokepalled altarstone		599.11	218.11 **
** Mrs Mina Purefoy		599.12	158.36 **
** A chalice. . . .		599.13++	(81.37) **
** Father Malachi O'Flynn	599.14+	3.01	170.30 **
** Two left feet back to the front		599.15	520.22 **
** Hugh C. Haines Love	599.16+	4.13	225.24 **

** Introibo ad altare diaboli	599.21	3.05	**
** To the devil which hath made. . . .	599.23	433.09	**
** Elevates a blooddripping host	599.25+	3.23	**
** Corpus Meum	599.26	80.34	**
** The celebrant's petticoats	599.28	3.02	**
** Grey bare hairy buttocks	599.29	191.32	**
** My body . . . Dooooooooooog!	599.30+	6.02	**
	44.33	507.30	
** Htengier . . . Aiulella 599.32+	97.21	428.10	**
** Sing to Mary	600.10	47.39	**
** OLD GUMMY GRANNY	600.15+	13.41	**
** Acushla	600.17	186.35	**
** You will be in heaven	600.17	26.33	**
** Ireland will be free	600.17	17.37	**
** Dialectic, the universal language	600.22	432.19	**
** Exit Judas. . . .	600.26	14.05	**
** Here's your stick	601.03	17.17	**
** This feast of pure reason (G)	601.05	304.33	**

STEPHEN . . . FALLS stunned
    601.15   735.23+

** His hat	601.16	17.08	**
** MAJOR TWEEDY	601.18+	56.32	**
** THE RETRIEVER	601.20++	587.02	**
** Let them . . . fight the Boers!	602.03	163.10	**
** THE BAWD	602.04	431.16	**
** Two raincaped watch	602.15++	430.09	**
** Bennett	603.13+	250.33	**
** Corny Kelleher	603.25#	71.15	**

** <u>Weepers round his hat</u>   603.25   103.36 **

** <u>A death wreath in his hand</u>   603.25   103.13 **

** Gold Cup   604.09   85.40 **

** Throwaway . . . Twenty to one   604.09+   325.31 **

** Do you follow me?   604.10   89.27 **

** What are you all gaping at?   604.12   74.33 **

** Wipe your name off the slate (T)   604.22   (187.22) **

** With my tooraloom   604.23   71.18 **

** Do you follow me?   604.24   89.27 **

** Just a little wild oats   605.09   192.29 **

** <u>The scaffolding</u>   606.06   450.08 **

** Two commercials   606.06   505.03 **

** In Jammet's   606.07   371.25 **

** Like princes   606.07   265.18 **

** Drowning his grief   606.08   4.28 **

** With the mots   606.15   251.06 **

** Do you follow me?   606.18   89.27 **

** He, he, he!   606.21   257.01 **

** Virag   606.22   76.26 **

** The two commercials   606.30   505.03 **

Somewhere in CABRA
     607.02   670.20

** In Sandycove   607.04+   12.19 **

** I have his money   607.12   11.02 **

** His hat   607.12+   17.08 **

** His . . . stick   607.12++   17.17 **

** <u>The horse harness jingles</u>   607.22++   168.11 **

** I'll shove along   607.14   (83.30) **

```
**  To and fro                          608.01+    11.24   **

**  The car jingles tooraloom. . . .    608.08+    71.18   **

**  Somnambulist                        608.18   (463.19)  **

**  Black panther vampire     608.23     4.23     48.01    **

**  Who . . . drive. . . .    608.26++   5.16      9.22    **

**  One pound seven                     608.34    11.02    **

**  His poor mother                     609.11     5.16    **

**  In the shady wood. . . .            609.11     9.22    **
```

FERGUSON, I think I caught
     609.11   656.11   See also   9.22

```
**  Swear that I will. . . .            609.13+    73.05    **

**  A fairy boy of eleven               609.20++   66.25    **

**  In an Eton suitt                    609.21     89.05    **

**  Reads from left to right            609.22    122.20    **

**  A delicate mauve face               609.28     96.04    **
                                        See also  502.14

**  A white lambkin                     609.30   (390.35)   **
```

EUMAEUS

** The hat	613.02	17.08	**
** Ashplant	613.02	17.17	**
** In orthodox Samaritan fashion	613.03	80.24	**
** No pumps of Vartry water	613.07	272.20	**
** The cabman's shelter	613.09	136.15	**

THE RUB
    613.13   627.22

FOR THE NONCE
    613.13   648.16   657.42

** Soapsuddy handkerchief	613.23	85.17	**
** Yeoman service	613.23	402.33	**
** Along Beaver street	613.25	450.08	**
** Dan Bergin's	613.29	221.24	**
** Buttons of his trousers	613.43	552.24+	**
** Sandstrewer	614.09	435.10	**
** His _fidus_ _Achates_	614.22	88.15	**
** Our daily bread	614.25	6.33	**
** Corny Kelleher	614.41	71.15	**

** That man in the gap	614.42	297.05	**
** The Bridewell	615.02	162.38	**
** Old Wall	615.03	162.07	**
** Clanbrassil street	615.09	413.08	**
** Fast women of the demimonde	615.20	536.19	**
** A good burgundy	615.25	171.28	**
** All his pubhunting confrères but one	615.30+	224.25	**
** And that one was Judas	615.33	14.05	**
** The Customhouse	615.36	227.09	**
** Gumley	616.04	136.18	**

TO POINT A MORAL
     616.22   639.19   649.38

** The Lords Talbot de Malahide	616.34	43.27	**
** Lenehan	617.02	125.10	**
** Boys' school . . . Deasy 617.15+	11.02	27.25	**
** The Christian Brothers	617.19	151.02	**

At THE FIRST GO—OFF
     617.22   661.07

The BRAZEN HEAD
     617.27   658.35   See also 187.27

** Friar Bacon	617.29	187.27	**
** Haud ignarus malorum. . . .	617.35	88.15	**
** He got paid his screw	617.37	11.02	**

With Boylan THE BILLSTICKER
     618.20   619.19   732.02   741.26

** Carry a sandwichboard	618.21	154.30	**
** In Nagle's back	618.30	297.19	**
** The corporation watchman's sentrybox	618.36+	136.18	**
** Shrewd observation	619.01	(495.25)	**
** One preying on his nextdoor neighbour	619.05	122.29	**

** In every deep . . . a deeper depth	619.06	(25.25)	**
** The man in the street	619.07	586.29	**
** Boylan, a billsticker	619.19	618.20	**
** Eblana	619.24	294.13	**
** Alongside Customhouse Quay	619.24	227.09	**
** Sandycove	619.38	12.19	**
** Westland Row station	619.40	412.26	**
** Why . . . father's house? 619.42	76.23	76.35	**
** Westland Row terminus	620.11+	412.26	**
** Mulligan	620.12++	3.01	**
** That English tourist friend	620.13	4.13	**
** Dilly	620.20	151.33	**
** Maggy	620.25	226.10	**
** Boody	620.25	225.20	**
** Katey	620.25	225.20	**
** Trust in that boon companion	620.32	7.16	**
** If I were in your shoes	620.34	(3.01)	**
** Rescue . . . artificial respiration	621.03	4.28	**
** Malahide	621.05	43.27	**
** An icecream car	621.23	(225.16)	**
** The cabman's shelter	621.33#	136.15	**
** Skin-the-goat, Fitzharris	621.37	136.12	**
** The invincible	621.37	81.27	**
** The actual facts	621.38	(184.11)	**

Something in the shape of SOLID FOOD
    622.05+   635.19   656.22

** The hoi polloi	622.08	425.26	**
** Voglio	622.16+ 63.31	64.04	**

** More languages . . . necessary   622.28   (432.19) **

** Sounds are impostures   622.40   45.25   **

** Like names, Cicero, Podmore   622.41   124.20   **

** Napoleon   622.41   297.06   **

** What's in a name?   622.43   209.10   **

** Our name was changed too (Virag)   623.02   76.26   **

** I've heard of him   623.16   88.19   **

** All Irish. . . . All too Irish   623.21   119.11   **

** Hengler's Royal Circus   624.11   64.30   **

** Curious coincidence   624.13   68.24   **

** Queenstown Harbour   624.17   278.40   **

FORT CAMDEN and FORT CARLISLE
     624.18   726.29

** For England, home and beauty   624.20   15.32   **

** Diddled Davy Jones   624.25   379.04   **

** Enoch Arden   624.27   50.31   **

** Rip van Winkle   624.27   377.23   **

** Anybody . . . remember Caoc O'Leary   624.28   97.20   **

** A grass widow   624.36   132.29   **

** Rocked in the cradle of the deep   624.37   (288.13) **

** Brokenhearted   625.02   95.22   **

** The threemaster Rosevean   625.14   51.05   **

** From Bridgwater with bricks   625.14   249.36   **

** The best bloody man   625.26   124.01   **

Under CAPTAIN DALTON
     625.26   631.26

** The Russians   625.28   58.11   **

CHOZA DE INDIOS
     625.41   629.22

A. BOUDIN
    626.15   647.12

    ** William Tell   626.19   297.08 **

    ** Maritana   626.20   86.32 **

    ** A trick of fate   626.32   66.39 **

    ** Martin Cunningham   626.33   80.13 **

    ** Work a pass   626.34   67.24 **

    ** The fare to Mullingar   626.39   67.22 **

    ** Our modern Babylon   627.03   164.34 **

    ** A concert tour   627.07+   (75.23) **

    ** Mrs C.P. M'Coy . . . valise   627.14   67.24 **

    ** Tweedy-Flower grand opera company   627.16   72.31 **

    ** The Elster Grimes   627.18   92.07 **

    ** That was the rub   627.22   613.13 **

    ** Brown, Robinson and Co.   627.31   154.42 **

    ** The man in the street   627.33   586.29 **

    ** My old stick-in-the-mud   627.37   440.37 **

    ** New lease of life   627.41   109.19 **

    ** Poulaphouca   628.03   547.18 **

    ** Further away from the madding crowd   628.04   46.39 **

    ** Rhododendrons   628.11   176.01 **

    ** Silken Thomas   628.12   45.26 **

    ** Grace O'Malley   628.12   330.07 **

    ** When young men's fancy   628.15   50.31 **

    ** Deaths by falling off the clifs   628.16   37.16 **

    ** From the pillar   628.18   95.09 **

KNIFE IN HIS BACK
    628.34   636.07   636.42

```
   ** The park murders of the invincibles    629.09++     81.27   **

   ** Where ignorance is bliss               629.11       46.39   **

   ** Choza de                               629.22      625.41   **

   ** The land of troubles                   629.26      496.21   **

   ** The Rock of Gibraltar                  629.33       56.29   **
```

EUROPA POINT
    629.36   761.40   775.26

WATER ABOUT THE GLOBE . . . COVERED FULLY THREE FOURTHS OF IT
    630.08   671.38

```
   ** Rule the waves                         630.11       18.33   **

   ** Dollymount                             630.12      297.15   **

   ** Fresh woods and pastures new           630.15       25.25   **

   ** Odds were twenty to nil                630.20     (325.31)  **

   ** The lottery                            630.27      156.11   **

   ** Ireland expects that every man         630.35       15.32   **

   ** The Irish lights, Kish                 630.37       44.13   **

   ** Rounding which . . . stormy weather    630.38       67.03   **
```

Bore a distant RESEMBLANCE TO HENRY CAMPBELL, the townclerk
    631.06   638.07   641.10   650.26   659.22

```
   ** The old stager                         631.13      114.14   **

   ** Bridgwater                             631.16      249.36   **
```

The FIGURE 16 (tattoo)
    631.23   646.06+

```
   ** Under Captain Dalton                   631.26      625.26   **
```

Fellow the name of ANTONIO (sailor)
    631.27+   636.10   646.07

```
   ** As bad as old Antonio. . . .           632.10       97.20   **

   ** A streetwalker . . . a black staw hat 632.12++     290.07   **

   ** Grist to her mill                      632.15      204.39   **

   ** The Abbey Street organ                 632.18++      35.22   **
```

```
        ** In Holles Street              632.28     268.40   **

        ** The Lock Hospital             633.02      52.28   **

        ** Bad merchant. . . buys dear . . .  633.12   34.01   **

        ** A necessary evil              633.18     207.10   **

        ** Ventilated the matter         633.22    (32.01)   **
```

The SOUL. . . . Intelligence . . . CONVOLUTIONS OF THE GREY MATTER
    633.29   720.17   742.01

```
        ** As X rays                     633.31++    179.22   **

        ** On the best authority         633.35+      17.40   **

        ** It is . . . incorruptible     633.35      142.21   **
```

A SIMPLE SOUL
    634.06   636.32

GALILEO was the man I mean
    634.09   700.25

```
        ** A farreaching natural phenomenon  634.10  304.35   **

        ** Who precisely wrote them . . . Bacon  634.27  195.20  **

        ** The Coffee Palace             634.38+     268.37   **
```

BEYOND YEA OR NAY
    634.39   664.11

```
        ** His good genius               635.19    (136.26)   **

        ** Solid food                    635.19     622.05   **
```

SINE QUA NON
    635.21   656.09

```
        ** Knife . . . Roman history     635.25      25.14   **
```

OUR MUTUAL FRIEND's
    635.32   655.14   (37.37)

```
        ** Like old boots                635.35     305.30   **

        ** Sherlockholmesing him up      636.01     495.17   **

        ** The cut of his jib            636.04     368.20   **

        ** Done for his man              636.07     628.34   **

        ** The Antonio personage         636.10     631.27   **
```

** Any ancient mariner   636.17   57.18   **

** About the schooner Hesperus   636.18   296.41   **

Those WAXWORKS IN HENRY STREET
    636.25   683.24

** Simple souls   636.32   634.06   **

** Friend Sinbad   636.33   47.05   **

** The Gaiety   636.35   92.09   **

** Michael Gunn   636.35   284.26   **

** The Flying Dutchman   636.36   (139.05)   (297.12)   **

** Ships . . . phantom or the reverse   636.39   376,26   **

** That stab in the back touch   636.42   628.34   **

** With garlic . . . off him or her   637.06   171.06   **

** Impetuous as Old Nick   637.09   50.25   **

** My wife . . . Spanish, half, that is   637.13   285.38   **

** Gibraltar   637.15   56.29   **

** Dante   637.25   20.20   **

** San Tomasso Mastino   637.26   17.40   **

** Washed in the blood of the sun   637.28   151.07   **

** Coincidence   637.28   68.24   **

** Kildare street Museum   637.29   80.10   **

** Rumpled stockings   637.37   160.16   166.07   **

** A look of Henry Campbell   638.07   631.06   **

** The Irish Times   638.10   160.07   **

** Petrified with horror   638.12   10.22   **

** Lady Cairns . . . Mona   638.13   236.33   **

** Harness jingled   639.04   168.11   **

** The Gumley aforesaid   639.07   136.18   **

In the arms of MORPHEUS
    639.11   660.38

    ** Decent home comforts   639.14   301.31 **

    ** At the end of his tether   639.17   122.11 **

    ** Pointed . . . a moral   639.19   616.22 **

    ** The falling off in Irish shipping   639.23+   328.01 **

A PALGRVE MURPHY boat
    639.25   719.20

    ** The Galway Harbour scheme   639.31   32.01 **

    ** Palmoil   639.34   239.29 **

Captain JOHN LEVER of the Lever Line
    639.35++   642.36

    ** <u>Lot's wife's arse</u>   640.07   123.23 **

    ** Richest country . . . on . . . earth 640.16+   326.11 **

    ** The Boers   640.33   163.10 **

    ** Her Achilles heel   640.35+   193.35 **

    ** The Greek hero   640.37   4.29 **

    ** Parnell   640.41   35.02 **

    ** The cabby like Campbell   641.10   631.06 **

    ** Peasant . . . backbone of our empire 641.13+   73.02 **

    ** To be or not to be   641.25   280.25 **

    ** Fought for England   641.38   596.14 **

    ** Fitzharris . . . invincible 641.41++ 81.27   136.12 **

    ** A golden rule   642.06   347.07 **

    ** A Dannyman   642.08   92.06 **

    ** Like Denis or Peter Carey   642.09   81.26 **

    ** Legal luminary (Richard Adams)   642.27   137.18 **

    ** Or on the scaffold high   642.31   163.16 **

    ** Positively last performance   642.32   63.05 **

** Snapping at the bone for the shadow   642.35   125.21   **

** Mr Johnny Lever   642.36   639.35   **

** Come back to Erin   642.38   343.11   **

** Silenced the offender   642.41+   293.25   **

** I . . . told him   643.02+   342.24+   **

** Plain facts   643.02   (184.11)   **

** His God, I mean Christ, was a jew   643.03   342.25   **

** Our own distressful [country]   643.18   44.05   **

** Jews . . . are accused of ruining   643.43++   21.21   **

** Cromwell   644.04   334.03   **

GOAHEAD America
    644.11   664.28

** Turks   644.11   108.13   **

** That rude person   644.16   293.25   **

** Words changing colour   644.28+   37.04   **

** About Ringsend   644.29   41.09   **

Not merely for the KUDOS OF THE THING
    644.40   655.06

** Faubourg Saint Patrice   645.06   80.12   **

** Ireland . . . belongs to me   645.09   591.12   **

** From Paris   645.30   12.18   **

** Fellows that promised so brilliantly   645.33   415.17   **

** The case of O'Callaghan   645.36+   93.22   **

** Lower Castle Yard   646.01   161.10   **

** The Criminal Law Amendment Act (T)   646.02   (6.37)   **

** Six sixteen   646.06   631.23   **

** Antonio and so forth   646.07+   631.27   **

** Then heir apparent   646.09   31.15   **

** The cannibal islands   646.25   80.37   **

** Sheer force of natural genius	646.29	136.26 **
** The coincidence of meeting	646.39	68.24 **
** Philip Beaufoy	647.03	67.39 **
** The Telegraph	647.08++	35.22 **
** A country belonging to him	647.10	591.12 **
** THe vessel (Rosevean)	647.11	51.05 **
** From Bridgwater	647.11	249.36 **
** A. Boudin	647.12	626.15 **
** Give us this day our daily press	647.15	6.33 **
** Turned out to be . . . H. du Boyes	647.16	151.10 **
** Great battle Tokio	647.18	58.11 **
** Lovemaking in Irish £200 damages (G)	647.18	141.07 **
** Gordon Bennett	647.19	97.15 **
** Emigration swindle	647.19	027.28 **
** Letter from His Grace William	647.19	121.30 **
** Ascot	647.20	85.40 **
** Throwaway	647.20	325.31 **
** New York disaster	647.22	4.28 **
** Foot and mouth	647.23	32.01 **
** Funeral of the late Mr Patrick Dignam	647.23++	57.11 **
** Hynes put it in	647.26	90.04 **
** Sandymount	647.28	37.01 **
** Glasnevin	647.29	100.22 **
** A nudge from Corny	647.34+	71.15 **
** Patk. Dignam (son)	647.35	101.02 **
** Bernard Corrigan	647.36	101.25 **
** John Henry Menton, solr.	647.36	102.38 **

```
** Martin Cunningham                    647.37      80.13   **

** John Power                           647.37      87.03   **

** Monks the dayfather                  647.38     121.33   **

** Keyes's ad                           647.39     197.35   **

** Thomas Kernan                        647.39      71.24   **

** Edward J. Lambert                    647.40      90.03   **

** Joseph M'C. Hynes                    647.41      90.04   **

** C. P. M'Coy                          647.41+     67.24   **

** M'Intosh                             647.41+    109.29   **

** Put thy foot in                      648.09      16.22   **

** The archbishop                       648.11     121.30   **

** Foot and mouth                       648.11      32.01   **

** Myles Crawford                       648.13     125.07   **

** For the nonce                        648.16     613.13   **

** Ascot                                648.18+     85.40   **

** Alexander's Throwaway                648.20+    325.31   **

** W. Lane                              648.21     415.32   **

** De Walden's Zinfandel                648.21+    174.02   **

** Bass's Sceptre           648.22+     128.03     325.33   **

** 20 to 1 Throwaway                    648.23     325.31   **

** The rank outsider drew to the fore   648.24     325.31   **

** Lenehan's version                    648.27     125.10   **

** French horse . . . Maximum II        648.30      85.40   **

** Bantam Lyons                         648.30+     74.02   **

** Not yet in but expected any minute   648.32     325.34   **

** Lovemaking damages                   648.33     141.07   **
```

Whose HAND by the way was HURT
  648.41   657.27   (608.34)

** <u>Return of Parnell</u>   648.43++   35.02 **

** A Dubin fusilier   649.01   47.18 **

The COFFIN they brought over was FULL OF STONES
    649.08   660.40

       ** De Wet, the Boer general   649.09   163.11 **

       ** Under several aliases such as Fox   649.30   492.22 **

The IDOL WITH FEET OF CLAY
    649.38   654.35   (6.37)

       ** It certainly pointed a moral   649.38   616.22 **

And then SEVENTYTWO of his trusty henchmen rounding on him
    649.39   660.41

       ** Murderers . . . had to come back   649.40   381.28 **

THE <u>INSUPPRESSIBLE</u> . . . <u>UNITED</u> <u>IRELAND</u>
    650.01   654.26

Handed him his silk hat when it was knocked off (PARNELL'S HAT)
    650.03   654.43

       ** Bred in the bone   650.06   19.03 **

       ** Tom for and Dick and Harry against   650.09   19.03 **

       ** That bitch, that English whore   650.23+   35.02 **

       ** Henry Campbell   650.26   631.06 **

       ** A cottonball one   650.28   329.17 **

To PROCLAIM it to the rank and file FROM THE HOUSETOPS
    651.03   658.43

Falling a victim to her SIREN CHARMS
    651.17   663.16   665.23

       ** <u>Farewell, my gallant captain</u>   651.26   86.32 **

       ** His beloved evicted tenants   651.33   496.21 **

       ** Yeoman service   651.34   402.33 **

       ** The fabled ass's kick   651.38   125.21 **

       ** Retrospective kind of arrangement   651.39   91.07 **

       ** Coming back was the worst thing   651.40   (377.23) **

** Irishtown Strand   651.43   87.40   **

** She also was Spanish or half so   652.06   285.38   **

** The king of Spain's daughter   652.12   595.14   **

** Spanish onions   652.14   172.13   **

** Book in his pocket Sweets of   652.19   236.05   **

** Capel street library book   652.20   64.42   **

Do you consider . . . (MOLLY'S PHOTOGRAPH)
    652.23++   774.29+

** In old Madrid   652.32   275.27   **

** Lafayette . . . photographic artist   652.34   418.08   **

** Major Brian Tweedy   652.42   56.32   **

** Numbered barely sweet sixteen (T)   653.01   (185.09)   **

** Certain opulent curves of the . . .   653.06   236.05   **

** A bit of an artist   653.07   235.17   **

** Those Grecian statues   653.11   80.10   **

** The original   653.11   5.08   **

** St. Joseph's sovereign   653.13   41.15   **

** Inward voice   653.24   412.01   **

** By moving a motion   653.25   426.38   **

** Creased by opulent curves   653.27   236.05   **

** Gauging her symmetry   653.29   121.15   **

** Heaving embonpoint   653.30   236.05   **

** Good as new   653.31   121.20   **

** I looked for the lamp   653.33   45.12   **

** Met him pike hoses (sic)   653.36   50.13   **

** The book about Ruby   653.35   64.25   **

** Which must have fell down   653.37   64.07   **

** The domestic chamberpot   653.38   64.07   **

** Fated to meet   654.06++   35.02   66.39   **

** Then the decree nisi   654.15+   324.06   **

** Erin's uncrowned king   654.20   (67.03) **

** Insuppressible . . . United Ireland   654.26   650.01   **

The facile pens of the O'Brienite scribes (WILLIAM O'BRIEN)
    654.29   708.24

** Erstwhile tribune's private morals   654.31+   31.18   **

** Their idol had feet of clay   654.35   649.38   **

** Bloom was the man who picked it up   654.43   650.03   **

** More for the kudos of the thing   655.06   644.40   **

** What's bred in the bone   655.06   19.03   **

** The ornament of the legal profession 655.11   102.38   **

** Headgear Bloom also set to rights   655.12   115.22+   **

** Burial of a mutual friend   655.14   57.11   635.32   **

** The why and the wherefore   655.20   304.20   **

** Not knowing their own minds   655.20   (50.31) **

** The usual boy Jones (G)   655.24   114.18   **

Always hanging around on the WAITING LIST about a lady
    655.36   731.24+

** Conditio sine qua non   656.09   635.21   **

** About Miss Ferguson   656.11   609.11   **

** The particular lodestar   656.12   319.25   **

** Irishtown   656.13   87.40   **

** Something substantial . . . to eat   656.22   622.05   **

** Recollected in retrospect   (656.39)   91.07   **

** The evicted tenants' question   656.42   496.21   **

** Michael Davitt   657.07   599.03   **

** Barney Kiernan's   657.11   280.29   **

** Give him . . . one in the gizzard   657.13   293.25   **

```
        ** Destruction of the fittest              657.18        407.30    **

ONTARIO TERRACE
     657.27       692.32       739.25       772.10

        ** Sandymount                              657.30         37.01    **

        ** Sandycove                               657.30         12.19    **

        ** For the nonce                           657.42        613.13    **

A cup of EPPS'S COCOA
     657.43       675.16       676.33       677.11     775.18

        ** That merry old soul                     658.08        162.04    **

        ** His dearly beloved Queenstown           658.08        278.40    **

        ** The mermaids                            658.12       (261.35)   **

        ** Blood and ouns champion     658.19        3.23        293.25    **

        ** His God being a jew                     658.20+       342.25    **

        ** Tender Achilles                         658.23        193.35    **

        ** County Sligo                            658.25        332.11    **

        ** Our hero                                658.26          4.29    **

        ** Matter of that Brazen Head 658.35       187.27        617.27    **

All kinds of UTOPIAN PLANS
     658.37       701.19       712.26++

        ** Prize titbits                           658.39         67.39    **

        ** Concert tours . . . watering resorts    658.40+      (75.23)    **

        ** Italian . . . accent perfectly true     658.41         64.04    **

        ** To tell . . . from the housetops        658.43        651.03    **

        ** His father's voice                      659.02         38.11    **

        ** That particular red herring             659.05        321.13    **

        ** Echo answered why                       659.14        124.01    **

        ** Give us a squint                        659.15        324.15    **

        ** The ancient mariner                     659.15         57.18    **

        ** Personage like the town clerk           659.22        631.06    **
```

** The <u>Arabian Nights'</u> <u>Entertainment</u>	659.28	47.05 **
** Found drowned	659.31	4.28 **

The amount due was FOURPENCE
    660.04   711.31

** The last of the Mohicans	660.05	297.03 **
** As Wetherup used to remark	660.09	126.14 **
** Seeing . . . the coast was clear	660.11	127.18 **
** The elite society	660.12	175.17 **
** <u>Dolce</u> <u>far</u> <u>niente</u>	660.14	71.38 **
** His tender Achilles	660.26	193.35 **
** Weak on his pins	660.27	156.16 **
** His left arm in Stephen's right	660.31	7.01 **
** Ex-Gumley	660.37	136.18 **
** Wrapped in the arms of Murphy	660.38	639.11 **
** Fresh fields and pastures new	660.39	25.25 **
** Coffin of stones. . . . 660.40+	35.02	649.08 **
** Seventytwo out of eighty	660.41	649.39 **
** The selfsame evicted tenants	661.02	496.21 **
** Wagnerian music	661.05	297.12 **
** At the first go-off	661.07	617.22 **
** Mercadante's <u>Huguenots</u>	661.08	82.16 **
** Meyerbeer's <u>Seven</u> <u>Last</u> <u>Words</u>	661.08	168.20 **
** Mozart's <u>Twelfth</u> <u>Mass</u>	661.09	63.31 **
** The acme of first class music	661.11	·294.04 **
** <u>Bid</u> <u>me</u> <u>to</u> <u>live</u>. . . .	661.14	416.15 **
** Rossini's <u>Stabat</u> <u>Mater</u>	661.16	82.09 **
** The jesuit fathers' church	661.20	82.08 **
** <u>Don</u> <u>Giovanni</u>	661.21	63.31 **

** <u>Martha</u>   661.27+   117.35   **

** Mendelssohn   661.29   285.37   **

** <u>M'appari</u>   661.31   117.35   **

** Lips of Stephen's respected father   661.34   271.25   **

** Near Gerard, the herbalist   661.39   202.09   **

** An instrument he was contemplating 661.40   518.14   **

** John Bull   662.04+   592.09   **

** A striking coincidence   662.12   68.24   **

** The lord of his creation   662.23   (145.10) **

** Mongrel in . . . Kiernan's   662.28   295.13   **

A HOLY HORROR to face
   662.29   769.41   (10.22)

** Image of his mother   663.04   5.16   **

An old German song of JOHANNES JEEP
   663.15+   665.17

** Voices of sirens   663.16   651.17   **

** Barraclough   663.26   277.17   **

** Beyond yea or nay   664.11   634.39   **

** Original music   664.16   (5.08)   **

** The King street house   664.25   92.09   **

** Impetus of the goahead sort   664.28   644.11   **

** <u>Fools</u> <u>step</u> <u>in</u> <u>where</u> <u>angels</u>   664.40   304.33   **

** A certain budding practitioner   664.41+   3.01   **

** The end of his tether   665.05   122.11   **

** Profiting by the <u>contretemps</u>   665.12   363.19   **

** <u>Und</u> <u>alle</u> <u>Sciffe</u> <u>brücken</u>   665.17   663.15   **

** Sat on his lowbacked chair   665.19   63.01   **

** About sirens   665.23   651.17   **

** Usurpers   665.25   23.23 **

ITHACA

** George's church	666.11	57.09	**
** Paris	666.15	12.18	**

The MALEFICENT INFLUENCE OF THE PRESABBATH
    666.21   781.29

** Influence of heterosexual magnetism	666.31	373.41	**
** Stephen's views on . . . literature	666.35	145.10	**
** From druidism	666.39	11.06	**
** Patrick son of Calpornus	666.39	80.12	**
** Pope Celestine I	666.40	339.25	**
** The reign of Cormac MacArt	667.02	169.24	**
** Reapparition of a matutinal cloud	667.08	9.32	**
** Sandycove	667.10	12.19	**
** Owen Goldberg	667.17	162.17	**
** Cecil Turnbull	667.17	548.18	**
** Percy Apjohn	667.20	162.16	**
** Gibraltar villa	667.21	(56.29)	**
** Crumlin	667.22	379.34	**
** Prospective purchasers on doorsteps	667.23	260.39	**

```
** Major Brian Tweedy                    667.26      56.32   **

** Matthew Dillon's house               667.27     106.19   **

** Julius Mastiansky                    667.28      60.33   **

** Lombard street, west                 667.30     110.15   **

** To obtain his latchkey               668.09      11.35   **

** Premeditatedly . . . keyless         668.16      23.20   **
```

A STRATAGEM. . . .
    668.20+   735.27   768.30   772.31

His body . . . by its LENGTH OF FIVE FEET NINE INCHES AND A HALF
    668.23   727.25

```
** A lucifer match                      669.09     558.27   **

** Messrs Flower and M'Donald           670.01    (72.31)   **

** One ignited lucifer match            670.03     558.27   **

** Kindled fires . . . sister Dilly     670.09     243.10   **

** Clongowes Wood                       670.10      11.22   **

** Miss Julia Morkan                    670.15     162.33   **

** His mother Mary                      670.15       5.16   **

** Of his sister Dilly                  670.20     151.33   **

** His father's house in Cabra          670.20     607.02   **
```

Four smallsized square HANDKERCHIEFS
    670.25   677.17   751.08

```
** Prolonged summer drouth              671.11      56.09   **

** Bloom, waterlover . . . watercarrier 671.27     553.25   **

** Preponderance . . . over the dry land 671.38    630.08   **

** Its . . . volume and density         672.04      72.05   **

** Hole in the wall at Ashtown gate     672.16      79.15   **

** Barrington's lemonflavoured soap     672.42+     85.17   **

** His last bath . . . preceding year   673.07      15.38   **

** The erratic orginality of genius     673.19     136.26   **
```

** What concomitant phenomenon   673.29+   304.35   **

** In part reflected, in part absorbed   674.05   57.10   **

** A moustachecup   675.07   62.37   **

** A phial of aromatic violet comfits   675.09   274.18   **

** A chipped eggcup   675.10   62.33   **

** Black olives   675.11   60.29   **

** Empty pot of Plumtree's potted meat   675.12   75.02   **

** An oval wicker basket   675.13   227.11   **

** One Jersey pear   675.14   227.17   **

** Invalid port . . . coralpink tissue   675.15   227.12   **
                                              227.35

** Epps's soluble cocoa   675.16   657.43   **

** Two onions, one the larger, Spanish   675.19   172.13   **

** A jar of Irish Model Dairy's cream   675.21   63.13   **

** Mrs Fleming   675.25   87.20   **

** Two lacerated scarlet betting tickets   675.32+   265.35   **

** Coincidences   675.35+   68.24   **

** Truth stranger than fiction (T)   675.35   (124.10)   **

** The result of the Gold Cup   675.36   85.40   **

** The Evening Telegraph   675.38   35.22   **

** In the cabman's shelter   675.38   136.15   **

** Bernard Kiernan's licensed premises   676.03   280.29   **

** David Byrne's licensed premises   676.04   170.19   **

** A throwaway   676.06   151.07   **

** Elijah . . . the church in Zion   676.07   150.07   **

** Zion   676.08   44.09   **

** F. W. Sweny and Co (Limited)   676.08   84.08   **

** Frederick M. (Bantam) Lyons   676.10   74.02   **

** The <u>Freeman's</u> <u>Journal</u>   676.12   57.36   **

** About to throw away   676.13   85.42   **

** The Turkish and Warm Baths   676.14   85.06   **

**   The light of inspiration shining . . . the language of   **
      prediction   676.15(G)   40.07   143.14

** Light to the gentiles   676.30   29.27   **

** Epps's soluble cocoa   676.33   657.43   **

** The moustache cup   677.01   62.37   **

** Millicent (Milly)   677.03   21.42   **

** Cream . . . reserved for ... Molly   677.05   63.13   **

** The breakfast of his wife   677.06   55.07   **

** Epps's massproduct . . . cocoa   677.11   657.43   **

** A fissure . . . in . . . jacket   677.15   584.07   **

** The four lady's handkerchiefs   677.17   670.25   **

** His first piece of original verse   677.35   5.08   **

** If <u>Brian</u> <u>Boru</u> <u>could</u> <u>but</u> <u>come</u>   678.28   99.25   **

** Michael Gunn . . . Gaiety 678.29   92.07   284.26   **

Christmas pantomime <u>SINBAD</u> <u>THE</u> <u>SAILOR</u>
     678.33   737.17+   See also   47.05

** Mrs Michael Gunn   678.37   (284.26)   **

Sung by NELLY BOUVERIST principal girl
     678.38   679.10+

** Queen Victoria   678.40   43.13   **

** The new municipal fish market   679.02   294.18   **

** His majesty Brian Boru   679.05   99.25   **

** The Theatre Royal (G)   679.08   (272.25)   **

** Nelly Bouverist   679.10+   678.38   **

** Daniel Tallon   679.18   58.24   **

** Dunbar Plunket Barton   679.20   198.27   **

** 16 years before. . . .	679.22	560.03 **

The maximum postdeluvian AGE OF 70
    679.33   698.36   720.07

** Methusalah	679.35	336.06 **
** Lilacgarden . . . Matthew Dillon	680.06	106.19 **
** In the company of Stephen's mother	680.08	5.16 **
** Mrs Riordan	680.20++	97.25 **
** The City Arms Hotel	680.23	35.27 **
** Elizabeth O'Dowd	680.23	306.09 **
** Joseph Cuffe	680.27	59.21 **
** Mr Gavin Low's place of business	680.35	399.20 **
** The Phoenix Park	681.02	170.41 **
** Her bézique cards	681.13	306.01 **
** Her Skye terrier	681.13	174.23 **
** Statue of the Immaculate Conception	681.16	47.39 **
** Charles Stewart Parnell	681.17	35.02 **
** Michael Davitt	681.17	599.03 **
** Strength and How to Obtain It	681.23	61.25 **
** Only born male transubstantial heir	682.09	21.09 **
** Rudolf Virag . . . Bloom	682.09+	76.26 **

SZOMBATHELY, VIENNA, BUDAPEST, MILAN, LONDON AND DUBLIN
    682.10   724.25

** Szombathely	682.10	496.06 **
** Milan	682.11	98.13 **
** Ellen Higgins	682.11	111.13 **
** Born Hegarty	682.13	542.24 **
** Male consubstantial heir	682.13	21.09 **
** Mary . . . Goulding	682.14	5.16 **

IN THE PROTESTANT CHURCH
    682.19   716.23+

    ** Philip Gilligan   682.20   155.19 **

In the CHURCH OF THE THREE PATRONS
    682.22+   716.27

** A dame's school	682.28	77.28 **
** The university of life	682.34	459.18 **
** Waxwork exhibition	683.24	636.25 **
** K. II	683.32	488.19 **
** Kino's 11/- Trousers	683.32	153.25 **
** House of Keys. Alexander J. Keyes	683.33	107.35 **
** Plumtree's Potted Meat	684.05+	75.02 **
** Concillor Joseph P. Nannetti	684.09	118.16 **
** Rotunda Ward	684.10	(95.42) **
** Beware of imitations	684.13	50.21 **
** Illuminated showcart	684.19	154.31 **
** In sloping, upright and backhands	684.30	465.23 **
** Queen's hotel	684.30++	76.26 **
** An overdose of monkshood	684.36+	492.04 **
** Coincidence	685.09+	68.24 **
** A Pisgah Sight of Palestine	685.17	149.25 **
** The Parable of the Plums?	685.18	145.03 **
** Precedent of Philip Beaufoy	685.28	67.39 **
** S. Aloysius Gonzaga	685.36	339.30 **
** Beggar my neighbour	686.04	333.24 **
** Metempsychosis (met him pike hoses)	686.31	50.13 **
** Alias	686.32	334.18 **
** Moses of Egypt	687.21	40.07 **
** Moses Maimonides	687.21+	28.14 **

** Moses Mendelssohn   687.23+   495.15   **

** Aristotle   687.27+   25.17   **

** Felix Bartholdy Mendelssohn   687.33   285.37   **

** Baruch Spinoza (Philosopher)   687.33   284.36   **

** Walk, walk, walk your way   688.04   286.31   **

** A slice of pomegranate   688.07   515.02   **

** Sweets of Sin   688.11   236.05   **

** Hebrew characters ghimel. . . .   688.15   487.08   **

** The revived [Irish language]   688.20++   141.07   **

** Noah, progenitor of Israel   688.29   495.25   **

TORAH
    688.33   729.03

TALMUD
    688.33   708.37

** Book of Ballymote   688.34   531.40   **

** Book of Kells   688.35   520.22   **

** Garland of Howth   688.35   (40.25)   **

** Their . . . persecution   688.36   36.10   **

** S. Mary's Abbey   688.37   230.15   **

** Masshouse (Adam and Eve's tavern)   688.38   (148.01)   **

** The restoration . . . of Zion   689.01   44.09   **

** Defective mnemotechnic   689.09   514.18   **

** Figure of hypostasis   689.29   40.14   **

** Winedark hair   689.32   5.07   **

** The very reverend John Conmee S.J.   690.04   80.03   **

** The reverend T Salmon, D.D.   690.04   164.40   **

** Dr Alexander J. Dowie   690.05   151.07   **

** Seymour Bushe, K.C.   690.06   100.04   **

```
**  Little Harry Hughes                      690.17++    108.31  **

**  Son of Rudolph                           691.05       76.26  **

**  The second part (minor)                  691.08      275.32  **

**  All dressed in green                     691.10++   (542.12) **

**  He challenges his destiny                692.03       66.39  **

**  From somnambulism                        692.26++    463.19  **

**  Any cognate phenomenon                   692.30      304.35  **

**  Holles street                            692.32      268.40  **

**  Ontario terrace                          692.32      657.27  **

**  His daughter Millicent                   692.32++     21.42  **

**  Lieutenant Mulvey, British navy          693.08      371.12  **

**  A letter from Mullingar                  693.21+      21.42  **

**  Brief allusion to a local student        693.22+      21.41  **

**  Instinct of tradition                    693.36       92.16  **

**  Silly Milly                              694.10       62.38  **

**  Instinct of tradition                    694.14       92.16  **

**  An owl                                   694.16      113.29  **

**  A clock                                  694.16      106.19  **

**  Moustachecup of imitation crown Derby    694.31       62.37  **

**  A natural phenonmenon                    694.35      304.35  **

**  Bloom, diambulist                        695.01      (34.05) **

**  Somnambulist                             695.02      463.19  **

**  Correct Italian pronunciation            695.12       64.04  **

**  Eventuality of reconciliatory union      695.15       38.12  **

**  A schoolfellow and a jew's daughter      695.16      108.31  **

**  A schoolfellow                           695.16      (21.41) **

**  A jew's daughter                         695.16       21.42  **

**  The late Mrs Emily Sinico                695.21      114.41  **
```

```
** The interment of Mrs May Dedalus      695.26        5.16  **

** Decease of Rudolph Bloom (born Virag) 695.27       76.26  **

** Italian instruction                   696.04       64.04  **

** The Ship hotel and tavern             696.09        6.19  **

** The National Library of Ireland       696.11       15.35  **

** The National Maternity Hospital       696.12       97.29  **

** Albert Hengler's circus               696.20       64.30  **

** The Rotunda                           696.20       95.42  **

** Menstruation of . . . human females   697.08      361.39  **

** Other more acceptable phenomena       697.20+     304.35  **
```

FROM THE KNOWN TO THE UNKNOWN . . . FROM THE UNKNOWN TO THE KNOWN
    697.24+   701.20

```
** Ineluctable constructed               697.26       25.17  **

** Incertitude of the void    697.26+    21.13      207.26  **

** A competent keyless citizen           697.30       11.35  **

** The exodus from the house of bondage  697.34      122.23  **

** Diaconal hat                          698.03+      17.08  **

** An ashplant                           698.03       17.17  **

** What spectacle . . . nightblue fruit  698.14+      20.20  **
```

The HEAVENTREE OF STARS
    698.18   701.18

```
** Nova in 1901                          698.32      210.07  **

** Parallax                              698.33      154.06  **
```

Socalled FIXED STARS
    698.34   727.37

```
** The years . . . allotted human life   698.36      679.33  **

** Millions of imperceptible molecules   699.08     (11.22)  **

** Void space                            699.11       21.13  **

** The quadrature of the circle          699.20      515.01  **
```

** Vanities . . . all that is vanity   700.12   188.31   **

** Discoveries of Galileo   700.25   634.09   **

** The appearance of a star. . . .   700.36+   210.07   **

** The . . . constellation of Cassiopeia 700.41   48.18   **

THE CONSTELLATION OF THE CORONA SEPTENTRIONALIS
     701.02   728.04

** Rudolph Bloom, junior   701.08   66.25   **

** The attendant phenomena   701.11+   304.35   **

** It was not a heaventree   701.18   698.18   **

** It was a Utopia   701.19   658.37   **

** From the known to the unknown   701.20   697.24   **

** A past . . . actual present existence 701.24++   186.19   **

** The moon and women   702.01   47.39   **

** Her constancy under all her phases   702.06   419.22   **

** To render insane   702.10   157.38   **

The light of a paraffin oil LAMP
     702.20   736.32   742.02   781.25

** Jesus circumcised   703.15   544.18   **

** The church of Saint George   704.07+   57.09   **

** Liliata rutilantium. . . .   704.10   10.23   **

** From Sandymount . . . to Glasnevin   704.17+   37.01   **
                                           57.11   100.22

** Martin Cunningham   704.18   80.13   **

** Jack Power   704.18   87.03   **

** Tom Kernan   704.19   71.24   **

** Ned Lambert   704.19   90.03   **

** Joe Hynes   704.20   90.04   **

** John Henry Menton   704.20   102.38   **

** Bernard Corrigan   704.20   101.25   **

```
** Patsy Dignam                              704.21    101.02  **

** A jew's harp                              704.25    127.13  **

** Interstellar space                        704.28    414.37  **

** Lonechill                                 704.32     49.04  **

** Percy Apjohn                              704.34    162.16  **

** Philip Gilligan                           704.35    155.19  **

** Phthisis                                  704.35+   162.02  **

** Accidental drowning                       705.01      4.28  **

** Philip Moisel                             705.01     60.38  **

** Mater Misericordiae Hospital              705.02      8.27  **

** Patrick Dignam                            705.03     57.11  **

** Sandymount                                705.03     37.01  **

** What phenomena                            705.04+   304.35  **

** Charades in the house of Luke Doyle       705.08     64.24  **

** The east                                  705.11     57.15  **
```

What suddenly arrested his ingress? (CHANGE IN POSITION OF ROOM FURNITURE)
    705.23++   779.31

```
** The compactly furled Union Jack           705.33    588.12  **

** Love's Old Sweet Song                     706.26     63.31  **

** Colour containing the gradation green 706.38   424.37  **

** Agendath Netaim                           707.09     60.16  **

** Timepiece of striated Connemara marble          707.22  **
                                     326.25    694.16

** Matthew Dillon                            707.24    106.19  **

** Luke and Caroline Doyle                   707.25+    64.24  **

** An embalmed owl                           707.26+   113.29  **

** Brothers and sisters had he none          708.04   (18.10)  **

** Thom's Dublin Post Office Directory       708.16    123.05  **
```

** William O'Brien M.P.	708.24	654.29 **
** Thoughts from Spinoza	708.26	284.36 **
** The Story of the Heavens	708.27	154.05 **
** Ellis's Three Trips to Madagascar	708.28	392.40 **
** Stark-Munro Letters 708.30	64.42	495.17 **
** Public Library, 106 Capel Street	708.31	64.42 **
** Voyages in China	708.35	114.24 **
** Philosophy of the Talmud	708.37	688.33 **
** Lockhart's Life of Napoleon	708.38	297.06 **

HOZIER'S HISTORY OF THE RUSSO-TURKISH WAR
     709.05   709.41   See also 56.32

** Gibraltar	709.07	56.29 **
** A Handbook of Astronomy	709.11+	233.34 **
** In the Track of the Sun	709.16	57.33 **
** Physical Strength. . . .	709.18	61.25 **
** Hozier's History	709.41	709.05 **
** Major Brian Cooper Tweedy	710.04	56.32 **
** To exercise mnemotechnic	710.08+	514.18 **
** Plevna	710.11	56.32 **
** A statue . . . image of Narcissus	710.14	543.07 **
** P. A Wren	710.15	99.17 **
** From the pelvic basin	710.28	471.30 **
** Trouser buttons . . . one incomplete	710.35	552.24 **
** A sting	711.01	68.18 **
** The interment of Mrs Emily Sinico	711.08	114.41 **
** 16 June 1904	711.09	229.18 **
** Pork kidney	711.12	55.04 **
** Freeman's Journal	711.13	57.36 **

** Bath	711.14	85.06 **
** Loan (Stephen Dedalus)	711.15	11.02 **
** In Memoriam Patrick Dignam	711.16	57.11 **
** Banbury cakes	711.18	153.07 **
** Lunch	711.19	171.20 **
** Renewal fee for book	711.20	64.42 **
** Packet notepaper and envelopes	711.21	264.04 **
** Postal order and stamps	711.24	182.11 **
** Pig's Foot . . . Sheep's Trotter	711.26+	434.15 **
** Cake Fry's plain chocolate	711.28	433.31 **
** Square soda bread	711.30	433.30 **
** Coffee and bun	711.31	660.04 **
** Loan (Stephen Dedalus)	711.32	11.02 **
** Mrs Ellis's juvenile school	712.13	77.28 **
** What ultimate ambition	712.16++	658.37 **

EMBOSSED MURAL PAPER at 10/- per dozen
   713.21   See   155.36

** A glass summerhouse	713.41	68.09 **
** Lilac trees	714.18	106.19 **
** Flowerville	714.32+	72.31 **
** Erotic masterpieces	715.18	(235.19) **
** Family crest and coat of arms	715.31	210.02 **
** Fashionable intelligence	715.35	351.23 **
** Homogeneous indisputable justice	716.05	122.29 **
** Instigators 716.17	36.10	293.25 **
** Master Percy Apjohn	716.22	162.16 **
** Disbelief in . . . Irish church	716.23	682.19 **
** Rudolf Virag, later Rudolph Bloom	716.24	76.26 **

```
** Abjured by him . . .                716.27      682.22   **

** Theories of Charles Darwin          716.33      407.30   **

** J.F.X. O'Brien                      716.37     (68.27)   **

** Michael Davitt                      716.38      599.03   **

** Charles Stewart Parnell             716.39       35.02   **

** William Ewart Gladstone             716.41       80.07   **

** Equine handicap . . . at Ascot      717.28+      85.40   **

** Won by an outsider                  717.30      325.31   **

** 2.59 p.m. (Dunsink time)            717.32      154.05   **

** To break the bank at Monte Carlo    718.11      297.04   **

** The quadrature of the circle        718.12      515.01   **

** Agendath Netaim                     718.16       60.16   **

** Bleibtreustrasse, Berlin, W. 15     718.16       60.26   **

** Head of water at Poulaphouca        718.31      628.03   **

** Dollymount                          718.35      297.15   **

** Ringsend                            719.01       41.09   **

** Connect . . . with the quays        719.06       58.03   **

** Palgrave, Murphy and Company        719.20      639.25   **

** Portugal                            719.22      326.33   **

** Blum Pasha                          719.31      455.06   **

** Rothschild                          719.31      174.11   **

** Guggenheim                          719.31      495.26   **

** Hirsh                               719.31      495.27   **

** Montefiore                          719.31       59.17   **

** 70 years of complete human life     720.07      679.33   **

** The cerebral convolutions           720.17      633.29   **

** The first drawer unlocked  720.24++ 364.03      543.08   **

** Milly (Millicent) Bloom             720.25       21.42   **
```

```
        ** Papli                              720.27      66.01   **

        ** Maude Branscombe, actress          720.30     370.16   **

A Yuletide card . . . from MR AND MRS M. COMERFORD
      720.34      753.36

        ** Messrs Hely's, Ltd.                720.37+    106.26   **

        ** William Ewart Gladstone            721.03      80.07   **

        ** An infantile epistle               721.06      21.42   **

        ** Capital pee Papli                  721.07      66.01   **

        ** A cameo brooch, property of Ellen Bloom        721.10   **
                                              111.13     438.24

        ** Henry Flower                       721.11      72.31   **

        ** Letters . . . Martha Clifford      721.11+     72.30   **

        ** Two . . . rubber preservatives     721.20     214.41   **

        ** The . . . Hungarian Lottery        721.24     156.11   **

        ** Nude señorita                      721.26     467.13   **

Anal violation by male religious . . . of FEMALE RELIGIOUS (NUN)
      721.28      738.26

        ** Queen Victoria                     721.33      43.13   **

        ** Sandow-Whiteley's pulley exerciser 721.35+     61.25   **

        ** The Wonderworker                   721.38++   289.16   **

        ** Absentminded beggar                722.15+    187.22   **

        ** The South African campaign         722.19     163.10   **

        ** Letter . . . from Martha Clifford  722.22      72.30   **

        ** Henry Flower                       721.22      72.31   **

        ** His magnetic, face, form and address 722.26   373.41   **

        ** Josephine Breen, born Josie Powell 722.27     156.32   **

        ** Miss Callan                        722.28     373.12   **

        ** Gertrude (Gerty, family name unknown) 722.29  253.01   **

        ** The virile power of fascination    722.32      92.25   **
```

** An endowment assurance policy. . . . 723.02++   413.03 **

** Scottish Widows' Assurance Society   723.03   57.11   **

** Millicent (Milly) Bloom   723.03   21.42   **

** Ulster Bank, College Green branch   723.08   421.05 **

** Canadian . . . government stock   723.12   409.13 **

** Cemeteries' (Glasnevin) Committee   723.14   100.22 **

** I, Rudolph Virag   723.18++   76.26   **

** 52 Clanbrassil street   723.18   413.08 **

** Formerly of Szombathely   723.19   496.06 **

** Leopold Virag (Lipoti Virag)   723.26   378.36 **

** The portrait atelier   723.26   155.39 **

** An ancient hagadah book   723.28   122.20 **

** Hornrimmed convex spectacles   723.29   413.23 **

** The ritual prayers for Pessach   723.30   122.15 **

** To my Dear Son Leopold   723.32   76.26   **

** Your dear mother   723.37   111.13 **

** Be kind to Athos   723.39+   90.20   **

** Aconite, resorted to   724.04++   492.04 **

** Circumcision of male infants   724.15   544.18 **

** A retrospective arrangement   724.24   91.07   **

** Dublin, London, Florence, Milan . . . 724.25   682.10 **

** Milan   724.25   98.13   **

** Szombathely   724.26   496.06 **

** Maria Theresa   724.27   330.18 **

** Use of narcotic toxin   724.37   81.12   492.04 **

** The endowment policy   725.15+   413.03 **

** Recovery of bad and doubtful debts   725.22   292.27 **

```
** Sandwichman                              725.25      154.30   **

** Distributor of throwaways               725.26      151.07   **

** Maimed sailor                           725.27      219.08   **

** Blind stripling                         725.27      180.31   **

** Eccentric public laughingstock. . . .   725.28     (159.15)  **

** Nadir of misery                         725.33      243.32   **

** Aged impotent . . . pauper              725.33      541.02   **

** Latration of . . . vagabond dogs        726.02       44.33   **

** Discharge of . . . vegetable missles    726.03      492.24   **

** Wilds of Connemara                      726.27      400.30   **

** Lough Neagh                             726.27      332.17   **

** The Giant's Causeway                    726.28      344.26   **

** Fort Camden and Fort Carlisle           726.29      624.18   **

** Brigid's elm in Kildare    726.30(G)    326.39      339.33   **

** The Salmon Leap                         726.31      332.22   **

** The Lakes of Killarney                  726.32      332.13   **

** Thomas Kernan                           726.34       71.24   **

** Pulbrook, Robertson and Co              726.35      239.14   **

** Jerusalem, the holy city                726.36      122.21   **

** Straits of Gibraltar                    727.02       56.29   **

** Statues, nude Grecian divinities        727.03       80.10   **
```

The PLAZA DE TOROS AT LA LINEA
      727.05   755.31

```
        ** The Camerons                    727.06      479.34   **

        ** The Dead Sea                    727.10       61.13   **

        ** A bispherical moon              727.17       59.04   **

        ** Imperfect varying phases of lunation  727.18  419.22 **

        ** A . . . perambulating female    727.19       59.04   **
```

** A pillar of the cloud by day	727.20	143.11	**
** Height 5 ft 9 1/2 inches	727.25	668.23	**
** Everyman	727.31+	386.05	**
** A nymph immortal	727.34	65.11	**
** Ever he would wander, selfcompelled	727.36	34.05	**
** Beyond the fixed stars	727.37	698.33	**
** Constellation of the Northern Crown	728.04	701.02	**
** The constellation of Cassiopeia	728.06	48.18	**
** A wreaker of justice on malefactors	728.08	122.29	**
** A sleeper awakened	728.08	377.23	**
** Of Rothschild or of the silver king	728.10	174.11	**
** The statue of Narcissus	728.23	543.07	**
** Preparation of breakfast	728.35	55.07	**
** Burnt offering	728.35	55.04	**
** Premeditative defecation	728.36	68.30	**
** Bath	728.37	85.06	**
** Funeral	728.37	57.11	**
** Advertisement of Alexander Keyes	728.38	107.35	**
** Unsubstantial lunch	728.38	171.20	**
** Bookhunt	729.02	227.27	**
** Visit to museum	729.01	80.10	**
** National library	729.02	15.35	**
** Torah	729.03	688.33	**
** Ormond Hotel	729.04	230.02	**
** Altercation with . . . troglodyte	729.05	293.25	**
** In Bernard Kiernan's premises	729.05	280.29	**
** Visit to a house of mourning	729.06	57.11	**
** Eroticism . . . exhibitionism	729.08	365.36	**

** Delivery of Mrs Mina Purefoy   729.09   158.36   **

** Visit to . . . Mrs Bella Cohen   729.10   475.18++ **

** Chance medley in Beaver street   729.12   450.08   **

** To and from the cabman's shelter   729.13   136.15   **

** Strainveined timber table   729.18   55.20   **

** Multicoloured multiform multitudinous 729.21   217.19   **

** Who was M'Intosh   729.23   109.29   **

** Where was Moses . . . ?   729.28   40.07   **

** Renewal of an advertisement   729.31   107.35   **

** Thomas Kernan   729.32   71.24   **

** Pulbrook, Robertson and Co   729.33   239.14   **

** To certify . . . female divinities   729.34   80.10   **

** Performance of Leah   729.37   76.23   **

** Mrs Bandman Palmer   729.37   76.23   **

** Gaiety Theatre   729.37   92.09   **

** The late Major Brian Cooper Tweedy   730.03   56.32   **

REHOBOTH (TERRACE)
    730.04   771.12

** Royal Dublin Fusiliers   730.04   47.18   **

** Gibraltar   730.04   56.29   **

** A pair of new violet garters   730.17   57.30   **

** Outsize ladies' drawers   730.17   63.40   **

** Redolent of opoponax   730.18   374.29   **

** Redolent of . . . jessamine   730.18   374.30   **

** Turkish cigarettes   730.19   108.13   **

** B.C.T. (Brian Cooper Tweedy)   730.25   56.32   **

** A commode   730.27   65.27   **

** Bought of Henry Price   730.29   (32.01) **

```
** Night article (on the floor, separate) 730.33      64.07  **

** Brass quoits                            731.06      56.27  **

** Some flakes of potted meat              731.15      75.02  **

** What preceding series?                  731.24+    655.36  **

** Mulvey                                  731.25     371.12  **

** Penrose                                 731.25     156.02  **

** Bartell d'Arcy                          731.26     156.06  **

** Professor Goodwin                       731.26      63.05  **

** Julius Mastiansky                       731.26      60.33  **

** John Henry Menton                       731.26     102.38  **
```

FATHER BERNARD CORRIGAN
      731.27   741.02++

```
** Farmer at the . . . Horse Show          731.27     374.16  **

** Maggot O'Reilly                         731.28     449.21  **

** Matthew Dillon                          731.28     106.19  **

** Valentine Blake Dillon                  731.29     155.22  **

** Christopher Callinan                    731.30     137.31  **

** Lenehan                                 731.30     125.10  **

** An Italian organgrinder                 731.30     171.06  **

** Unknown gentleman in the Gaiety         731.31     284.38  **

** Gaiety Theatre                          731.31      92.09  **

** Benjamin Dollard                        731.31      91.01  **

** Andrew (Pisser) Burke                   731.32     305.40  **

** Joseph Cuffe                            731.32      59.21  **

** Wisdom Hely                             731.32     106.26  **

** Alderman John Hooper                    731.33     113.29  **

** Dr Francis Brady                        731.33     587.01  **

** A billsticker                           732.02     618.20  **
```

** George Mesias	732.32	110.17 **
** Imminent provincial musical tour	733.01	75.23 **
** Corruption of minors	733.12	392.34 **
** The void incertitude 734.04	21.13	207.26 **
** Islands of the blessed	734.27	195.24 **
** Isles of Greece	734.28	124.01 **
** Land of promise	734.28	143.20 **
** Adipose posterior female hemispheres	734.28+	(59.04) **
** Milk and honey	734.29	393.37 **
** Curves of amplitude	734.31	173.36 **
** Kissed . . . her rump 734.38	123.23	530.22 **
** Martha Clifford	735.12	72.30 **
** Henry Flower	735.12	72.31 **
** Public altercation	735.13+	293.25 **
** Bernard Kiernan	735.14	280.29 **
** Exhibitionism of Gertrude 735.16	253.01	365.36 **
** Mrs Bandman Palmer . . . Leah	735.18	76.23 **
** Gaiety Theatre	735.18	92.09 **
** Invitation to supper at Wynn's	735.19	92.06 **
** Sweets of Sin	735.22	236.05 **
** Temporary concussion	735.23+	601.15 **
** No fixed occupation	735.26	(455.19) **
** Aeronautical feat	735.27	688.25 **
** 8 September 1870	736.05	168.26 **
** With female issue	736.06	21.42 **
** With ejaculation of semen. . . .	736.08+	223.31 **
** Second (and only male) issue	736.11	66.25 **

** Reflection of a lamp and shade   736.32   702.20   **

** Percy Apjohn   737.12   162.16   **

** Weary. . . . Weary?   737.13   3.41   **

** Sinbad the Sailor   737.17+   47.05   678.33   **

** A square round   737.24   515.01   **

** Auk's egg   737.25   196.16   **

** Roc's . . . rocs   737.25+   (64.22)   **

PENELOPE

** Yes   738.01#   61.31 **

BREAKFAST IN BED (BLOOM'S)
    738.02   764.07   772.43   778.11   780.15+

    ** <u>City Arms</u> hotel   738.02   35.27 **

    ** Pretending to be laid up   738.03   338.16 **

    ** That old faggot Mrs Riordan   738.05++   97.25 **

    ** End of the world   738.10   505.16 **

    ** Especially then   738.19   151.29 **

    ** Smutty photo . . . nun   738.26   721.28 **

    ** Sprained his foot   738.30   155.29 **

    ** The sugarloaf Mountain   738.31   155.30 **

    ** The day I wore that dress   738.31   155.27 **

    ** Father was the same   738.37   56.32 **

    ** The hotel story he made up   739.01   92.06 **

    ** Hynes kept me   739.02   90.04 **

    ** Menton . . . his boiled eyes   739.03+   102.38 **

ON THE SLY (Molly's term for Bloom's activities)
    739.12   743.37   746.17   766.28   (558.12)

** Scribbling something a letter   739.13   107.38   **

** Dignams death   739.15   57.11   **

** That slut that Mary   739.25++   409.26   **

** Ontario terrace   739.25   657.27   **

** Stealing . . . the oysters   739.33+   461.01   **

** The garters I found in her room   739.40   460.28   **

** Along by the Tolka   740.10   167.21   **

** The young May Moon   740.12   45.12   **

** He said Im dining out   740.13   92.06   **

** The Gaiety   740.14   92.09   **

** My garters the new ones   740.19   57.30   **

** Knitting that woollen thing   740.26   390.34   **

** Feel him trying to make a whore of me 740.31   369.41   **

** Father Corrigan   741.02++   731.27   **

I didnt like his SLAPPING ME BEHIND
    741.20   776.21

** His father   741.23   319.31   **

** That flower he said he bought   741.24   228.02+ **

** Smelt . . . of drink   741.24   265.10   **

** They stick their bills   741.26   618.20   **

** Talking stamps with father   741.30   56.34   **

** The port   741.31   227.12   **

** Potted meat   741.32   75.02   **

** That thunder woke me   741.34   394.33   **

** World was coming to an end   741.35   505.16   **

** Gibraltar   741.38#   56.29   **

** Act of contrition   741.40   221.23   **

** No soul inside only grey matter   742.01   633.29   **

```
** When I lit the lamp                    742.02    702.20  **

** I took off all my things . . .         742.06    368.32  **

** Perfuming                              742.07    374.29  **

** He must have eaten oysters             742.09    175.02  **

** He was in great singing voice          742.09    274.12  **

** Milly                                  742.22     21.42  **

** Mina Purefoys husband     742.23       158.36    161.06  **

** Meeting Josie Powell                   742.34++   156.32  **

** The funeral                            742.34     57.11  **

** Georgina Simpsons housewarming         742.38    444.23++  **

** To Floey                               743.10    115.19  **

** Lord Byrons poems                      743.11    124.01  **

** His sly eye                            743.37    739.12  **

** Trying to look like lord Byron         743.40    124.01  **

** My hairpins falling                    744.01     64.12  **

** That dotty husband of hers             744.07++   157.17  **

** Going about in his slippers            744.20    298.40  **

** A postcard up up                       744.21    158.11  **

** Hed say its from the Greek             744.36     64.20  **

** In the DBC (Dublin Bakery Company)     744.43++   164.03  **

** In the Irish Times                     745.09    160.07  **

** Goodwins . . . concert                 745.19     63.05  **

** In Lombard street                      745.23    110.15  **

** Katty Lanner                           745.26    575.30  **

** The stoppress edition                  745.28     35.22  **

** Bartell dArcy                          745.31    156.06  **
```

```
My BROWN PART
     745.35      780.37
```

He hadnt an idea about my mother till we were engaged (LUNITA LAREDO)
    745.43   761.37+   763.01   771.14   778.23

    ** Mad on the subject of drawers   746.03++   63.40 **

    ** Skirts blowing up to their navels   746.10   358.16 **

    ** Milly   746.11   21.42 **

    ** Looking slyboots   746.17   739.12 **

The way I used to GARDNER (STANLEY G.)
    746.37   747.17   749.01+   762.19+   762.41+

    ** Father waiting   746.41   56.32 **

    ** That other fool Henry Doyle   747.05   377.24 **

    ** Tearing something   747.06   377.23 **

    ** The charades   747.06   64.24 **

    ** Mine was the 8th   747.14   168.26 **

    ** At Dolphins barn   747.15   64.24 **

    ** Like Gardner   747.17   746.37 **

    ** Old frostyface Goodwin   747.22+   63.05 **

    ** In Lombard street   747.22   110.15 **

    ** Sending the port   747.28   227.12 **

    ** The 2 Dedalus girls   747.32   225.20 **

    ** When I threw the penny   747.34   225.10 **

    ** That lame sailor   747.35   219.08 **

    ** For England home and beauty   747.35   15.32 **

    ** There is a charming girl I love   747.36   92.06 **

    ** My clean shift   747.37   92.33 **

    ** This day week were to go   747.37+   75.23 **

    ** To Belfast   747.38   75.11 **

    ** His fathers anniversary the 27th   747.39   76.26 **

Hes so PIGHEADED sometimes (Molly's term for Bloom)
    748.12   752.41

** I love jaunting in a . . . car   748.15   253.42 **

** Idiots of men gaping at us   748.19   74.33 **

** That day going to Howth   748.22   (176.01) **

KATHLEEN KEARNEY and her like
    748.28   762.29

** On account of father   748.29   56.32 **

** The absentminded beggar   748.29   187.22 **

** A brooch for lord Roberts   748.30   421.14 **

** I had the map of it all   748.30   163.10 **

** The Stabat Mater   748.33   82.09 **

** He was a freemason   748.35   73.02 **

** Some of them Sinner Fein   748.37   163.38 **

** That little man . . . Griffith   748.40+   43.08 **

** After the war   748.43++   163.10 **

** Ladysmith   748.43   484.02 **

** Bloemfontein   748.43   458.01 **

** Gardner Lieut Stanley   747.01+   746.37 **

** First time I saw the Spanish cavalry   749.12   285.38 **

** The Dublins   749.17   47.18 **

** His father . . . selling the horses   749.18   319.31 **

** Up in Belfast   749.20   75.11 **

** Mrs Mastiansky   749.36   60.33 **

** From behind . . . like the dogs   749.36   89.08 **

** Stylish tie   749.40   254.04 **

** Socks with the skyblue silk things   749.40   254.01 **

** Tearing up the tickets and swearing   749.43+   265.35 **

** He lost 20 quid   750.01   325.35 **

** Over that outsider that won   750.02   325.31 **

** Lenehans tip	750.03+	125.10	**
** The Glencree dinner	750.04+	155.23	**
** The featherbed mountain	750.05	234.25	**
** Val Dillon	750.06	155.22	**
** What kind of drawers he likes	750.19	63.40	**
** What she hadnt	750.22	358.16	**
** Last . . . from ORourkes 750.33+	57.40	489.09	**
** Garters . . . the violet pair	750.41	57.30	**
** The face lotion I finished	750.43	84.03	**
** Made up in the same place	751.02	84.04	**
** Some of that opoponax	751.05	374.29	**
** The four paltry handkerchiefs	751.08	670.25	**
** Ill be 33 in September	751.20	168.26	**
** Look at that Mrs Galbraith	751.21+	586.42	**
** Like Kitty OShea	751.24	(35.02)	**

Mrs Langtry the JERSEY LILY
    751.27++   770.12

** The prince of Wales	751.28++	31.15	**
** A black mans Id like to try	751.30	443.17	**
** Her a--e	751.38	123.23	**
** That Ruby . . . he brought 751.41	64.25	235.37	**

FLAGELLATE
    752.01   765.04

** H. R. H.	752.08	31.15	**
** He ought to chuck that Freeman	752.12	57.36	**
** Like father	752.18	56.32	**
** In Mr Cuffes still	752.20	59.21	**

PINS AND NEEDLES
    752.36   770.35

** That place in Grafton street   752.37   168.10   **

** Pigheaded as usual   752.41   748.12   **

** Those statues in the museum   753.14   80.10   **

** In Holles street   753.20   268.40   **

** The job in Helys   753.21   106.26   **

** I was selling the clothes   753.21   268.39   **

** Strumming in the coffee palace   753.22   268.37   **

** That bath of the nymph   753.23+   65.11   **

** In that Spanish photo   753.24   467.13   **

** That disgusting Cameron highlander 753.26++   479.34   **

** After the Comerfords party   753.36   720.34   **

** Yes it was a few months after   753.39   66.25   **

** Met something with hoses in it   754.01   50.13   **

** Burns the bottom . . . for his Kidney 754.03   55.04   **

** Milly   754.07   21.42   **

** In No 28 with the Citrons   754.10   60.33   **

** Penrose   754.11+   156.02   **

** Doctor Brady   754.13   587.01   **

Frseeeeeeeefronnnng (TRAIN WHISTLE)
     754.38   762.24   (763.22)

** Loves old sweet sonnnng   754.40   63.31   **

** Those old Freemasons   754.43   57.36   **

** Photo bits   755.01   65.12   **

** Their 3 Rock mountain   755.10   343.14   **

** Faded all that lovely   755.14 (45.12)   (117.35)   **

That lovely FROCK . . . from the B MARCHE PARIS
     755.14   762.09

** Fathers friend   755.15   56.32   **

Fathers friend MRS STANHOPE (and MR STANHOPE)
    755.15++   756.35++   782.26

WOGGER she called him
    755.19++   756.37

      ** In old Madrid   755.21   275.27 **

      ** Waiting   755.21   275.23 **

Scrumptious currant SCONES
    755.25   756.02   See also 249.23

      ** Regards to your father   755.27   56.32 **

Also CAPTAIN GROVE [GROVES]
    755.28   756.11   757.20+   782.26

      ** The bullfight at La Linea   755.31   727.05 **

      ** Killiney hill   755.34   175.32 **

      ** At that picnic   755.34   155.30 **

      ** All staysed up   755.34   156.26 **

      ** I made the scones   756.02   755.25 **

      ** He was watching me   756.09+   371.12 **

      ** On the Alameda esplanade   756.10   319.39 **

      ** When I was with father   756.11   56.32 **

      ** Captain Grove   756.11   755.28 **

      ** Moonstone . . . of Wilkie Collins 756.18   229.10 **

      ** With Mulveys photo   756.21   371.12 **

      ** Lord Lytton Eugene Aram   756.22   135.16 **

      ** About the one from Flanders a whore 756.25+   109.36 **

      ** My shift . . . stuck in the cheeks 756.30   92.33 **

      ** She didnt put her address right on it 756.35++   755.15 **

      ** Wogger   756.37   755.19 **

      ** He didnt say anything. . . .   756.40+   371.12 **

      ** Waiting always waiting. . . .   757.06   275.23 **

      ** Ulysses Grant whoever he was   757.10   (195.14) **

** From before the flood   757.13   84.06   **

** Gunfire . . . to cross the lines   757.18   380.12   **

** Captain Groves   757.20+   755.28   **

** Father   757.20+   56.32   **

** Rorkes drift   757.20   457.15   **

** Plevna   757.21   56.32   **

** Medical in Holles street   757.37   97.29   268.40   **

** In the City Arms   758.02   35.27   **

** Broken bottles   758.06   378.16   **

** That wonderworker they sent him   758.08   289.16   **

** His letter   758.09++   61.37   **

** The card from Milly   758.10   21.42   **

** Floey Dillon   758.13+   115.19   **

** Her father   758.15+   106.19   **

** In old Madrid . . . love is sighing   758.32   275.27   **

** Atty Dillon   758.38   377.17   **

** Mulveys was the first   759.04++   371.12   **

MRS RUBIO
     759.05++   760.06   779.20   (762.07)

** A hairpin to open it   759.07   64.12   **

** The Union Jack flying   759.13   588.12   **

** An admirer he signed it   759.21   (313.12)   **

** Father   759.26   56.32   **

SHALL I WEAR A WHITE ROSE [Or shall I wear a red]
     759.28   781.32   783.08

** Under the Moorish Wall   759.30   371.13   **

** Don Miguel de la Flora   759.35   72.31   **

** Many a true word spoken in jest   759.36   338.15   **

** There is a flower that bloometh   759.37   86.32   **

On the BLACKWATER
    759.43   761.13

    ** Near OHaras tower   760.03   380.10   **

    ** The old Barbary apes   760.05   380.11   **

    ** Mrs Rubio   760.06   759.05   **

    ** That dog in the hotel   760.39   35.27   174.23   **

MOLLY DARLING he called me
    761.02   762.12

    ** Whatyoucallit   761.05   61.02   **

    ** On the black water   761.13   759.43   **

    ** Josie used to say   761.33   156.32   **

    ** My mother . . . Lunita Laredo   761.37+   745.43   **

    ** Europa point   761.40   629.36   **

    ** Going out to be drowned   762.05   4.28   **

    ** Captain Rubios   762.07   (759.05)   **

    ** That frock from the B Marche Paris   762.09   755.14   **

    ** Molly Darling   762.12   761.02   **

    ** That cheap peau despagne   762.17   85.04   **

    ** Gardner going to South Africa   762.19+   746.37   **

    ** Where those Boers killed him   762.20   163.10   **

    ** Frseeeeeeeeeeeeeeeeeeeeefrong   762.24   754.38   **

    ** In the dear deaead days   762.25   63.31   **

    ** Kathleen Kearney and . . . squealers 762.29   748.28   **

    ** Down the Alameda   762.37   319.39   **

    ** Gardner   762.41+   746.37   **

    ** All father left me   763.01   56.32   **

    ** In spite of his stamps   763.01   56.34   **

    ** Ive my mothers eyes   763.01   745.43   **

** Comes looooves old   763.09   63.31   **

** Too long for an encore   763.10+   75.23   **

** Winds that blow from the south   763.12   156.08   **

** He gave   763.12   156.06   **

** The choirstairs performance   763.13   745.32   **

** That big fan   763.15   (69.30)   **

** Sweeeee . . . eeeeeeee   763.22   63.31   (754.38)   **

** Queerlooking man in the porkbutchers 763.27   56.11   **

** The little bit of a short shift I had 763.37   92.33   **

** Those medicals   764.02   163.04   **

** Then he starts giving us his orders   764.07   738.02   **

** Him falling up the stairs   764.11   501.23   **

Those 2 lb pots of mixed PLUM AND APPLE
    764.20   781.10

** Forgetting   764.23   21.42   **

** Butchers meat from Buckleys   764.24   56.10   **

** Mrs Fleming   764.28   87.20   **

** Those ruck of Mary Ann coalboxes   764.34   (13.12)   **

WHIT MONDAY is a cursed day too
    764.34   770.16   See also 769.03

** No wonder that bee bit him   764.35   68.18   **

** At Bray   764.37   7.39   **

** The gold cup   764.38   85.40   **

** A mercy we werent all drowned   764.43   4.28   **

** That one calls flagellate   765.03+   235.37   752.01   **

** That longnosed chap   765.05   171.25   **

** Burke   765.06   305.40   **

** The City Arms hotel   765.06   35.27   **

```
** That book he brought me Sweets of Sin  765.10     236.05   **

** Some other Mr de Kock                   765.11+     64.39   **

** The way his father did                  765.27      76.27   **

** All the things he told father           765.28      56.32   **

** To send the girl down there. . . .      766.11      21.42   **

** His grandfather            766.12       378.36     155.39   **

** That little gimcrack statue             766.22     543.07   **

** Sly . . . from his side of the house    766.28     739.12   **

** Tom Devan                               766.34+    252.28   **

** At the Only Way            767.08        37.37     357.33   **

** In the Theatre royal                    767.09     272.25   **

** At the Gaiety                           767.13      92.09   **

** Beerbohm Tree in Trilby                 767.14+    526.09   **

** At the Broadstone                       767.20      74.13   **

** Martin Harvey                           767.29     357.33   **

** If a man gives up his life for her      767.31      37.37   **

** To go and poison himself                767.37      76.26   **

** Mrs Joe Gallaher                        768.02     449.15   **

** The trottingmatches                     768.03      79.16   **

** That old Mrs Fleming                    768.18      87.20   **

** All those prizes                        768.29     242.31   **

** Imagine climbing over the railings      768.30     668.20   **

** My old pair of drawers                  768.34      63.40   **

** The stupid old bundle                   768.36      87.20   **

** Yes that thing has come on me           769.03++   361.39   **

** Box that Michael Gunn gave 769.10       271.13     284.26   **

** At the Gaiety                           769.12      92.09   **

** Drimmies                                769.12     177.05   **
```

** Gentleman . . . staring down at me   769.14   284.38   **

** Talking about Spinoza   769.15   284.36   **

** Sweets of sin   769.32   236.05   **

** This damned old bed too jingling   769.34   56.27   **

** Wheres the chamber gone   769.41   64.07   **

** Holy horror of its breaking under me   769.41   662.29   **

** After that old commode   769.42   65.27   **

** Those kissing comfits   770.03   274.18   **

** O Lord how noisy   770.05+   282.27   **

** Like the jersey lily   770.12   751.27   **

** When was it last I   770.16+   361.39   **

** Whit Monday   770.16   766.34   **

** Floey   770.19   115.19   **

** Pins and needles   770.35   752.36   **

** I always used to know by Millys   770.36   21.42   **

Asking me had I frequent OMISSIONS
    770.39+   781.14

** I wouldnt trust him too far   770.41   7.16   **

** A thing of beauty and a joy forever   771.06   433.08   **

** The first night ever we met   771.11   64.24   **

** I was living in Rehoboth terrace   771.12   730.04   **

** Looking after my mother   771.14   745.43   **

** Home rule and the land league   771.18   496.21   **

** Song out of the Huguenots   771.19   168.20   **

** Rigmaroling about . . . persecution   771.22   36.10   **

** Chambers   771.29   64.07   **

** Like that Indian god   771.34   80.10   **

** The museum on Kildare street   771.35   80.10   **

** Great value for his money   772.01   113.25   **

** The lumpy old jingly bed   772.05   56.27   **

Reminds me of OLD COHEN
     772.06+   780.07

** He thinks father bought it . . .   772.07   56.28   **

** After 16 years   772.09   554.03   **

** Raymond Terrace   772.10   89.07   **

** Ontario terrace   772.10   657.27   **

** Lombard street   772.11   110.15   **

** Holles street   772.11   268.40   **

** Whistling . . . his huguenots   772.12   168.20   **

** The City Arms hotel   772.14   35.27   **

** Thoms   772.19   123.05   **

** Helys   772.19   106.26   **

** Mr Cuffes   772.19   59.21   **

** Drimmies   772.19   177.05   **

** His old lottery tickets   772.20   156.11   **

** The sack soon out of the Freemans 772.23   57.36   **

** On account of those Sinner Fein   772.23   163.38   **

** The Freemasons   772.24   73.05   **

** The little man he showed me   772.24   43.08   **

** Georges church bells   772.28   57.09   **

** Climbing down into the area   772.31   668.20   **

** That French letter   772.33   214.41   **

** The Aristocrats Masterpiece   772.37   235.19   **

** Then tea and toast for him. . . . 772.43   738.02   **

** Holles street   773.03   268.40   **

** Josie   773.12   156.32   **

** With my castoffs	773.12	(3.01)	**
** Her Denis	773.15	157.17	**
** Milly	773.17	21.42	**
** Hornblower . . . back way 773.19	67.24	86.23	**
** Throwing his sheeps eyes	773.19	511.14	**
** Mr Paddy Dignam	773.22	57.11	**
** The paper Boylan brought in	773.23	35.22	**
** Tom Kernan	773.26+	71.24	**
** Martin Cunningham	773.28	80.13	**
** Fanny MCoys husband	773.29	67.24	**
** Jack Power	773.35+	87.03	**
** Of course his wife is	773.36	93.34	**
** The Glencree dinner	774.08	155.23	**
** Ben Dollard base barreltone	774.08++	91.01	**
** Borrowed the swallowtail	774.09	268.22	**
** Holles street	774.09	268.40	**
** So sweetly sang the maiden. . . .	774.16	272.37	**
** When I sang Maritana with him. . . .	774.17+	86.32	**
** Goodbye sweetheart he always sang	774.19	256.13	**
** Bartell dArcy	774.20	156.06	**
** May Goulding	774.24++	5.16	**
** Im to take lessons	774.28	64.04	**
** Showing him my photo	774.29+	652.23	**
** At Mat Dillons	774.40	106.19	**
** He was on the cards this morning	774.41+	75.16	**
** A poet like Byron	775.11	124.01	**
** Milly	775.14	21.42	**

** At Dillons	775.14	106.19	**
** Taking Eppss cocoa	775.18	657.43	**
** Goodwin	775.21	63.05	**
** Professor of John Jameson	775.22	179.17	**
** Where softly sighs of love . . . star	775.23+	275.27	**
** Europa point	775.26	629.36	**
** Billy Prescotts	775.33	83.42	**
** Keyess ad	775.33	107.35	**
** That lovely little statue	775.41+	543.07	**
** Ill throw them the first thing	776.10	75.16	**
** Slapping us behind like that	776.21	741.20	**
** Julius Caesar	776.28	25.14	**
** The wife in Fair Tyrants	777.11	235.37	**
** I kiss the feet of you señorita	777.22	380.15	**
** Didnt he kiss our halldoor	777.23	378.36	**
** Winning over the boxing match	777.42	173.14	**
** The winds that waft my sighs to thee	778.05	86.32	**
** Don Poldo de la Flora	778.07	72.31	**
** How he came out on the cards	778.08	75.16	**
** To get his lordship his breakfast	778.11	738.02	**
** And losing it on horses	778.19	(265.35)	**
** A mother to look after them	778.23	27.38	**
** A mother . . . what I never had	778.23	745.43	**
** When I was watching the two dogs	778.29	89.08	**
** I ougtnt to have buried him	778.31	66.25	**
** That little woolly jacket I knitted	778.32	390.34	**
** His poor mother	778.39	5.16	**
** Heard me on the chamber	779.06	64.07	**

** The rosary	779.09	354.03 **
** Id go and drown myself	779.11	4.28 **
** Cantankerous Mrs Rubio	779.20	759.05 **
** He tell me the Italian	779.23	64.04 **
** A few olives in the kitchen	779.29	60.29 **
** Since I changed it the other way	779.31	705.23 **
** Not knowing me from Adam	779.33	38.06 **
** His writing and studies at the table	779.39	55.20 **
** Hes making the breakfast	779.41	55.07 **
** Red slippers like those Turks	780.03	381.12 **
** Cohens old bed 780.07	56.27	772.06 **
** Mamy Dillon	780.12	377.18 **
** Ill throw him up his eggs and tea	780.15+	738.02 **
** Moustachecup she gave him 780.15	21.42	62.37 **
** Hed like my nice cream too	780.17	63.13 **
** Mi fa pietà Masetto . . . forte	780.18	63.31 **
** My best shift and drawers 780.20++	63.40	92.33 **
** My brown part	780.37	745.35 **
** This bloody pest of a thing	781.08	361.39 **
** Mixture of plum and apple	781.10	764.20 **
** His omission	781.14	770.39+ **
** Wallpaper in Lombard street 781.23	110.15	155.36 **
** Better lower this lamp	781.25	702.20 **
** Findlaters	781.26	58.23 **
** Fridays an unlucky day	781.29	666.21 **
** Shall I wear a white rose	781.32	759.28 **
** Why dont they go and create	782.04	145.10 **

```
** The day we were lying . .   on Howth   782.13      176.01   **

** It was leapyear like now              782.16      171.21   **

** Yes 16 years ago                      782.16      554.03   **

He said I was a FLOWER OF THE MOUNTAIN
     782.18       783.06+     See also  49.33   72.31      73.11

** Only looked out over the sea          782.24      380.13   **

** Mulvey                                782.25++    371.12   **

** Mr Stanhope and Hester                782.26      755.15   **

** Father                                782.26       56.32   **

** Old captain Groves                    782.26      755.28   **

** Those handsome Moors                  782.38       28.14   **

** Glancing eyes a lattice hid           782.41      275.27   **

** For her lover to kiss the iron        782.41     (378.36)  **

** The sea the sea                       783.02        5.08   **

** The Alameda gardens                   783.03      319.39   **

** The jessamine                         783.05      374.30   **

** Flower of the mountain                783.06+     782.18   **

** Or shall I wear a red                 783.08      759.28   **

** Yes . . . yes . . . yes. . . .        783.08+      61.31   **

** Under the Moorish wall                783.09      371.13   **
```

ALPHABETICAL INDEX

coronal of vine leaves, 415.08
dream
   of his mother, 5.32
   of street of harlots, 47.05
fear
   of destruction, 242.17
   of thunder, 394.31
giver of life, 145.10
glasses broken at Clongowes, 560.03
Hamlet theory, 16.13, 18.10, 18.12
handkerchief, 4.37
hat, 17.08
injured hand, 648.41
Jesuit, 3.08
job at Deasy's school, 11.02
key to Martello, 11.35
"Kinch," 3.08
lapwing, 210.36
learner, 35.14
letter about lute, 518.14
lies about source of funds, 262.40
loneliness, 49.04
moving among Vikings, 45.18
no return to Tower, 23.20
pandied, 135.18
Parable of the Plums, 145.03, 149.25
Paris, 12.18
pay, 11.02
promise, 415.17
riddle, 26.33
school prizes, 242.31
tears coat, 584.07
telegram to Mulligan, 185.05
valise, 12.02
visit to dentist, 50.35
Deep summer fields, 168.42
Deepsounding, 256.42
Defoe, Daniel, 109.36
De Kock, Paul, 64.39
Demimondaine, 536.19
Deo volente, 220.39
Derwan's plasterers, 450.10
Desklamp, greencapped, 184.31
Destiny, 66.38
Destruction by fire, 398.04
Devan, Tom, 252.28
Devils, women as, 157.33
De Walden, Lord Howard, 174.02
De Wet, Christian, 163.11
Diamond panes, 202.08
Dickens, Charles, 37.37
Dicky meat, 98.04
Dignam, Freddy, 355.02
Dignam, Master Patrick, 101.22
Dignam, Paddy, 57.11

Dillon, Atty, 377.17
Dillon, Floey, 115.19
Dillon, Maimy, 377.18
Dillon, Mat, 106.19
Dillon, Tiny, 377.17
Dillon, Val, 155.22
Dillon's Auction Rooms, 128.30
   lacquey at, 226.31
Dineen, Father Patrick, 211.10
Dinner fit for a prince, 265.18
Dio boia, 213.23
Distant hills, 376.13
Distrait, Le, 187.17
Dixon, 97.28
Dlugacz's, 56.11
Do and do, 202.09
Do, Ben. Do, 256.42
Do you follow me? 89.27
Dodd, Reuben J., 94.41
   his son, 4.28
Dog, 44.33
   in Circe, 432.12
Dog-God, 507.30
Dogsbody, 6.02
Dogs, by the wall, 89.08
Dolan, Father, 135.18
Dolce far niente, 71.38
Dollard, Ben, 91.01
   belongings on show, 270.36
   gouty fingers, 257.13
   slops, 244.19
   tight pants, 268.22
   tympanum, 256.22
Dollymount, 297.15
Dolmetsch, Arnold, Stephen's letter
   to, 518.14
Dolphin's Barn Lane, 280.17
Dominant/return, 275.31
Domine-namine, 103.27
Done, 257.24
Don Giovanni, 63.31
Donizetti, Gaetano, 111.02
Donnybrook Fair, 86.30
Don't hesitate to shoot, 187.31
Don't, she cried, 257.17
Don't you know, 186.25
Doran, Bob, 74.01
Doran, Polly Mooney, 303.03
Doric, native, 126.01
Douce, 213.34
Dowden, Edward, 204.14
Dowie, Dr John Alexander, 151.07
Doyle, Henny, 377.24
Doyle, J.C., 63.31
Doyle, Luke, 64.24